United Nations Conference on Trade and Development

INVESTING IN

PRE-EMERGING MARKETS

**Opportunities for investment of
risk capital in the LDCs**

United Nations
New York and Geneva, 1998

Notes

Definition of country groupings:

The classification of countries in this Report generally follows that of the UNCTAD *Handbook of International Trade Development Statistics 1994. (United Nations publication, Sales No.E./F.95.II.D.15)* It has been adopted solely for the purposes of statistical or analytical convenience and does not necessarily imply any judgement concerning the stage of development of a particular country or area.

The United Nations has designated 48 countries as **least developed countries**: Afghanistan, Angola, Bangladesh, Benin, Bhutan, Burkina Faso, Burundi, Cambodia, Cape Verde, Central African Republic, Chad, Comoros, Democratic Republic of the Congo (formerly Zaire), Djibouti, Equatorial Guinea, Eritrea, Ethiopia, Gambia, Guinea, Guinea-Bissau, Haiti, Kiribati, Lao People's Democratic Republic, Lesotho, Liberia, Madagascar, Malawi, Maldives, Mali, Mauritania, Mozambique, Myanmar, Nepal, Niger, Rwanda, Samoa, Sao Tome and Principe, Sierra Leone, Solomon Islands, Somalia, Sudan, Togo, Tuvalu, Uganda, United Republic of Tanzania, Vanuatu, Yemen and Zambia. Except where otherwise indicated, the totals for least developed countries refer to these 48 countries.

Other Notes

The term "dollar"($) refers to United States dollars, unless otherwise stated.

The term "billion" signifies, 1,000 million.

The term "tons" refers to metric tons.

Annual rates of growth and change refer to compound rates.

Exports are valued f.o.b. and imports c.i.f., unless otherwise specified.

Use of a hyphen (-) between dates representing years, e.g. 1998-1990, signifies the full period involved, including the initial and final years.

An oblique stroke (/) between two years, e.g. 1990/91, signifies a fiscal or crop year.
Two dots (..) indicates that the data are not available, or are not separately reported.

A dash (-) or a zero (0) indicates that the amount is nil or negligible.

A dot (.) Indicates that the item is not applicable.

A plus sign (+) before a figure indicates an increase; a minus sign (-) before a figure indicates a decrease.

Details and percentages do not necessarily add to totals because of rounding.

UNCTAD/GDS/GFSB/3

UNITED NATIONS PUBLICATION
Sales No.E.98.II.D.2
ISBN 92-1-112423-9

Preface

At UNCTAD IX held in Midrand, South Africa, representatives of member countries requested UNCTAD to organize a Seminar for the promotion of private investment flows to the least developed countries (LDCs), as stated in paragraph 89 (g) of the Midrand text on "Partnership for growth and development" (TD/377). This Pilot Seminar was held in Geneva on 23-25 June 1997 and was co-sponsored by UNIDO. It was used by UNCTAD and UNIDO as a means of bringing together eminent persons from the private and public sectors in order to review salient features of the weakness of private investment flows into the LDCs and to identify solutions to reverse this situation. There is no doubt that the shortage of capital in these countries represents one of the most pressing problems facing the international community today and, unless solutions are found, the marginalization of the LDCs from world trade and global financial flows can only worsen.

To date the LDCs have attracted an insignificant share of foreign direct investment (FDI). In 1995, for example, together they only accounted for between 0.2 and 0.3 per cent of the total worldwide flows of FDI. Indeed, while over the past decade cross- border private investment in the form of equity investment funds has increased tremendously, and venture capital and portfolio investment funds have invested in emerging markets in ever-growing volume, the LDCs have largely missed out on this trend. Reversing this situation by showing that good investment opportunities do exist in these countries and discussing, with the participation of investors themselves, what LDC governments can do to improve the investment climate in their respective countries, were the main objectives of this Pilot Seminar.

The international community is now intensifying its efforts to support the LDCs in overcoming the challenge of modernizing their economies, and a more favourable investment environment has recently emerged in some of the LDCs. Many promising developments are now taking place in these countries and there is a need to take a more positive approach by not only focusing on the difficulties in LDCs, but also on the opportunities for investing in profitable projects available in some LDCs. In this light, this Report is designed to make a constructive contribution to publicize the investment opportunities existing in some LDCs, with special reference to the economic sectors of tourism, agro-related industries and infrastructure. The Report was prepared in cooperation with UNIDO.

Rubens Ricupero
Secretary-General of UNCTAD

Geneva, January 1997

CONTENTS

List of text tables

Abbreviations

ABEDA	Arab Bank for Economic Development
ACMF	African Capital Market Forum
ADB	Asian Development Bank
AIFMC	Asian Infrastructure Fund Management Company
ASEA	African Stock Exchange Association
BOO	Build-Own-Operate
BOT	Build-Operate-Transfer
CDC	Commonwealth Development Corporation
CIP	Centre for Investment Promotion (Mozambique)
CMSA	Capital Markets and Securities Act (Tanzania)
DBFO	Develop-Build-Finance-Operate
DEG	German Development and Investment Company
DFI	development finance institution
DSE	Dar es Salaam Stock Exchange
EBRD	European Bank for Reconstruction and Development
EIB	European Investment Bank
ESAF	Enhanced Structural Adjustment Facility
ESCAP	Economic and Social Commission for Asia and the Pacific
EPZ	Export Processing Zone
EU	European Union
FAO	Food and Agriculture Organization
FDI	foreign direct investment
FMO	Netherlands Development Finance Company
GATS	General Agreement on Trade in Services
GDP	gross domestic product
HMTTC	Hotel Management and Tourism Training Centre (Nepal)
IAS	International Accounting Standards
ICSID	International Council of Societies of Industrial Design
IDA	International Development Association
IDB	Inter-American Development Bank
IFC	International Finance Corporation
IFU	Industrialization Fund for Developing Countries (Denmark)
IIC	Inter-American Investment Corporation
IOSCO	International Organization of Securities Commissions
IPO	Initial Public Offering
ISIC	International Standard Industrial Classification
MC	management company
MIGA	Multilateral Investment Guarantee Agency
MVA	manufacturing value added
NIDC	Nepal Industrial Development Corporation
ODA	official development assistance
OGL	open general licence
OPIC	Overseas Private Investment Corporation
RAP	Rights accumulation programme
RMF	Ready-made garments
SAC	Structural Adjustment Credit

SADC	Southern African Development Community
SAEDF	Southern African Enterprise Development Fund
SEC	Securities Exchange Commission (Nepal)
TEPZA	Tanzania Export Processing Zone Authority
UNDP	United Nations Development Programme
USAID	United States Agency for International Development
VAT	value added tax
VC	venture capital
WAEMU	West African Economic and Monetary Union
WFP	World Food Programme
WTO	World Tourist Organization
ZPA	Zambia Privatization Agency
ZRA	Zambia Revenue Authority
ZSUG	Zambian Sugar

BACKGROUND

Increasing interest has been shown in recent years in the role of non-foreign direct investment (FDI) in emerging markets in the financing of the enterprise sector in the countries concerned. Such non-FDI flows are mainly equity investments in the capital stock of local companies in these markets, usually in the form of portfolio equity investment funds. Recent trends in foreign equity investment flows into developing countries suggest that these flows are becoming a significant source of external finance for investment. Over the years 1993 to 1995, total non-FDI flows were equivalent to almost a half of the FDI flows into the developing countries and countries in transition. This surge in equity investment in emerging markets took place against a background of structural changes in international capital markets and in the economies of the recipient countries.

Although there has been an explosion of investment in emerging markets through investment funds, the distribution of these equity funds is very strongly skewed towards those emerging markets with large stock market capitalization and/or with high growth prospects. Country equity funds are most of the time invested in countries with stock markets. Such investments are made in listed companies, and sometimes in unlisted companies with the expectation that capital gains will be reaped from the subsequent listing of such companies on stock markets when they become mature.

The LDCs have mostly been left on the sidelines of this surge in private non-FDI flows into developing countries, and one of the main problems related to the "investor neglect" of these countries is derived from the lack of adequate, reliable and up-to-date information of the investment potential in the LDCs. The present Report is designed to remedy this situation with respect to a number of LDCs in the regions of Africa and Asia and to specific economic sectors in these countries.

The Report is based on the results of studies undertaken by UNCTAD and UNIDO. It is focused on the identification of investment opportunities in the LDCs of interest to foreign private investors, with special reference to the sectors of tourism, agro-related industries and infrastructure. These investment opportunities are identified at the country level and, where possible, at the level of companies. Feasibility studies for investment in specific projects need to be discussed with companies at a later stage. A list of investment promotion agencies in LDCs is included for this purpose in Appendix II to this Report. Chapter I provides an introduction to the investment environment and capital market development currently prevailing in these countries. Chapter II outlines the scope and structure of equity funds and reviews investment policies. The focus in chapter III is on investment opportunities in the tourism sector of eight selected LDCs, while chapter IV examines investment prospects in the agro-related industries of six LDCs. Chapter V surveys the scope and status of some recent development projects in infrastructure in 23 LDCs and reviews the investment experience and opportunities in this sector in 15 countries. Appendix I reports the investment opportunities in the LDCs who have provided detailed replies to an UNCTAD questionnaire.

The Report was prepared by UNCTAD in cooperation with UNIDO and benefited from a financial contribution from the Government of Norway, which is gratefully acknowledged. The UNCTAD staff and consultants contributing to this Report under the direction of Anh-Nga Tran-Nguyen were Professor F. Vellas, Michael Jordan, Ana María Alvarez, Yuefen Li, and Dusan Zivkovic. The contribution of UNIDO was provided by Torben M. Roepstorff (chapter IV) with the assistance of Javed Ansari and Miguel Perez, and by Ricardo Seidl da Fonseca (chapter V) with the assistance of Bruno de Cazalet and Anna Joubin-Bret and specific research assistance given by Olmo Calvo Rodriguez and Antonia Treu. The Report was edited by Frederick Glover with the secretarial assistance of Ruby Addae and Sheila Addy.

CHAPTER I

INTRODUCTION

I.1. INVESTMENT ENVIRONMENT IN LDCS

Since the early 1980s, a large number of LDCs have embarked on a process of stabilization and structural adjustment. Although this has not been a very easy endeavour, as some of the programmes have not as yet yielded the expected results, the overall economic outlook for LDCs as a group has improved in the 1990s compared with the previous decade.

Over the period 1990-1995, 21 LDCs recorded average annual growth in GDP in real terms of over four per cent, with 11 countries having growth rates of more than five per cent.[1] In 1995-1996, LDC economies continued to display noticeable progress, with annual GDP growth rates estimated at 3.2 per cent, as compared with an average growth rate of·2.2 per cent over the period 1980-1990.[2] In 1996, the average GDP growth for LDCs for which data was available slowed to 4.7 per cent compared to 5.2 per cent in 1995.[3] These figures exclude a few LDCs afflicted by internal conflicts.

Inflation has also been reduced. In 1995, LDCs' average inflation rate was 23.9 per cent; and although still high, this compared well with the average rate of 35.7 per cent over the period

---

[1]   These countries are: Cambodia, Equatorial Guinea, Lao, PDR, Lesotho, the Maldives, Myanmar, Mozambique, Nepal, Solomon Islands, Sudan and Uganda.

[2]   UNCTAD, *The Least Developed Countries 1996 Report* (United Nations document, Sales No. E.96.II.D.3).

[3]   UNCTAD, *The Least Developed Countries 1997 Report* (United Nations document, Sales No. E.97.II.D.6), p.8.

1991-1994. The inflation rate was projected to decrease further to 19.2 per cent in 1996 and 13.2 per cent in 1997.[4] The central government fiscal deficit, as a percentage of GDP, was also reduced to 5.6 per cent in 1995, as compared with 9.5 per cent in 1988. The fiscal deficit, on average, is expected to remain at around 5 to 6 per cent in 1995/1996.

Important policy reforms have been implemented in the financial sectors of many LDCs in recent years.[5] Financial systems have been liberalized, with the reduction or removal of allocative controls over interest rates and lending; the introduction of market-based techniques of monetary control; and the easing of entry restrictions in domestic financial markets. Restructuring programmes have started to address the problem of financial fragility of parastatal banks, and banking laws and supervision have been strengthened.

Financial sector reforms seem to have borne fruit: the real rates of interest improved from -4.1 per cent in 1983-1989 to -2.4 per cent in 1990-1995.[6] Financial market reforms might have increased the volume of financial intermediation and financial savings and contributed to the increase in investment, which increased from 14.8 per cent of GDP in 1983-1989 to 16.0 per cent in 1990-1995.

In a number of LDCs, foreign exchange controls have been relaxed or completely abolished,[7] and in some others forex bureaux have been established in order to handle foreign exchange transactions which are no longer controlled by central banks.[8]

I.2. CAPITAL MARKET DEVELOPMENT

In general, official financial intermediation in the LDCs is not widespread, and an important amount of financial intermediation is still conducted via the informal financial sector. This is due to the limited development of the financial sector in most LDCs, although there is naturally substantial variation among different countries in the group. The institutional structure in LDCs is generally dominated by private and publicly-owned commercial banks, which provide the bulk of short-term formal-sector credit, and mainly concentrate on larger private and/or public sector enterprises. Longer-term formal-sector credit is often provided by development finance institutions (DFIs). Various other types of financial institution augment these two main formal-sector sources of credit, but they are mostly very small and unable to compete effectively. Capital markets exist in relatively few LDCs, and the markets for primary securities tend to be very thin, with the exception of the market for government securities. Formal-sector financial intermediation in LDCs has remained shallow for several reasons closely related to the structure outlined above.

---

[4]   IMF, *World Economic Outlook*, October 1996, table A.11, p. 181.

[5]   UNCTAD, *The Least Developed Countries 1996 Report*, Part Three: Financial Sector Reforms in LDCs, pp. 87-105.

[6]   IMF, *World Economic Outlook*, October 1996, table 17, p.74.

[7]   For example, in Djibouti, Gambia, Maldives, Uganda.

[8]   For example, in Guinea, Lao People's Democratic Republic, Sudan, Uganda, United Republic of Tanzania and Zambia.

One indicator of the level of formal-sector financial intermediation in LDCs is provided by the ratio of total banking sector claims on the private sector to GDP. This ratio illustrates the heterogenous experience among LDCs in this regard over the period 1990-1995. Although for most LDCs this ratio has registered either a declining or stable trend during the period (often with significant intra-period variation), a small number of countries have experienced a clear upward trend, including Ethiopia, Lao PDR, Lesotho and Nepal. The ratio of the monetary liabilities of the banking sector to GDP provides an additional indicator of the depth of the financial system in the economy. This ratio indicates a similar variation in experiences, but also highlights a deepening of the formal-sector's intermediation in the economy in the cases of Bangladesh, Bhutan, Equatorial Guinea, Nepal, Uganda, and the United Republic of Tanzania; in the cases of the Central African Republic and Rwanda the ratio trended upward as well, but suffered a decline in 1995; and in the cases of Chad and Zambia, the ratio staged a partial recovery over the period from previously higher levels.

With financial reform and liberalization, some of the elements which have impeded financial sector deepening are being addressed. In particular, reform of the mechanism by which interest rates are determined has taken place in many LDCs. The reform process has typically been carried out in phases, first by raising loan and deposit rates closer to the rate of inflation, then abolishing preferential lending rates to priority sectors, and finally removing administrative controls over interest rates. This process has helped to create positive real deposit rates in several LDCs, although in many cases real interest rates remain negative (this remains the case even for the majority of the group of LDCs which have recorded relatively high real growth rates). Only in five countries have deposit rates moved to positive real levels (Cambodia, the Gambia, Guinea, Lesotho and Samoa). In addition to interest rate reform, financial sector reforms have introduced market-based instruments of monetary control, removed restrictions on the types of activity that financial institutions can undertake, liberalized entry of new participants into the financial markets, and privatized government-owned financial institutions, especially government-owned banks, which have operated particularly inefficiently in many LDCs. Although these measures have been undertaken relatively recently and it is still difficult to clearly ascertain their impact, they appear to be having a positive impact on development of the financial systems in some LDCs. These measures certainly represent a start to addressing the need to deepen financial markets in these countries.

Although a large number of LDCs are now actively trying to promote the creation of domestic securities markets, it is nevertheless a difficult and delicate process. For securities markets to operate with some degree of efficiency, the conditions are a stable macroeconomic environment, a proper financial and capital market infrastructure, and an adequate regulatory, legal and supervisory framework, which should protect investors, promote public confidence and guarantee market discipline.

Organized stock exchanges already exist in Bangladesh, Bhutan, Malawi, Nepal and Zambia, although these exchanges are still relatively small in relation to overall economic size (in 1995, the ratio of market capitalization to GDP measured 4.5 per cent for Bangladesh, 1 per cent for Malawi, 5.5 per cent for Nepal and 14.7 per cent for Zambia) and the level of trading activity on the exchanges is relatively low. Five other LDCs have taken the preliminary steps to opening an exchange, including the establishment of the legal framework for capital market development. These include Angola, Madagascar, Mozambique, Uganda and United Republic of Tanzania.

With respect to African LDCs, it is worth noting the launching in June 1996 of the African Capital Market Forum (ACMF) to enhance capital market development in those countries. For many LDCs, it may not be realistic to expect the establishment of organized exchanges in the foreseeable future. In some cases, however, the promotion of capital market development on a regional or subregional basis may represent a realistic option.

To date, the West African Economic and Monetary Union (WAEMU), comprising Benin, Burkina Faso, Côte d'Ivoire, Mali, Niger, Senegal and Togo, offers a unique experience of a regional stock exchange. In December 1996, the member countries of WAEMU decided to establish a regional stock market to be located in the stock exchange of Abidjan, in Côte d'Ivoire.

In view of the improving economic situation in many LDCs, these countries can attract more risk capital investment. Very often the existence of rich natural resources, which are still underexploited or not exploited efficiently, gives investors an opportunity to realize potentially high returns. This dormant potential has been given additional attractiveness by a liberalization process that has eased foreign investors' access to these countries' markets. However, though investment opportunities exist in LDCs, most investors are still keeping their distance from these markets because of lack of information, misconceptions to varying degrees about LDC markets, and also due to the high costs associated with the search for the best opportunities in these often small markets.

Recently there seems to have been an increasing interest of foreign investors in some LDCs, as witnessed by the closed-end country funds that have been launched lately to invest in Bangladesh, Madagascar, Myanmar, and the United Republic of Tanzania. A number of regional funds have also been launched to invest in Africa.[9]

I.3. INVESTORS' MOTIVATION

Financial institutions and institutional investors with large amounts of capital often have difficulties in finding projects with good risk-adjusted returns. The phenomenon of large amounts of money saturating certain well-known emerging markets occurs relatively frequently. Though opportunities do exist in LDCs, most investors are still keeping their distance from these markets for the reasons already noted. Lately, there has been a change of attitude, both by investors who recognize the need to conquer the world's last investment frontiers and by LDC governments, which are starting to turn their attention to improving the investment environment.

Surveys of the market selection process of a few equity funds point to a number of factors that are taken into consideration by investors when they invest in emerging markets:

---

[9]   For example, Morgan Stanley's Africa Investment Fund, the Africa Emerging Markets Fund (an offshore fund managed in the United States), and the Regent Undervalued Assets Africa Fund. *The Economist* "African stock markets, No joke", 11 January 1997.

- *Macroeconomic and political stability*: this is invariably the essential precondition for foreign investment, as it provides a stable environment for the promotion of risk capital investment in high-risk ventures. In particular, stable exchange rates protect investors from exchange risk;

- *High growth potential*: experience has shown that most equity investment funds are concentrated in markets with high growth potential;

- *Ease of capital and income repatriation*: investors should be assured that the income and capital gains of their investments can be easily repatriated. In that respect, foreign exchange control is a major impediment to foreign investment;

- *Legal transparency and adequate investors' protection*;

- *Adequate financial information and reporting disclosure*;

- *Exit mechanisms*: portfolio equity investors are interested in the financial returns on their investments and, hence, prefer to invest in more liquid instruments. The usual exit mechanism for divestment is the stock exchange. Hence, the existence of liquid stock exchanges is an advantage. However, in the case of venture capital investment, other exit mechanisms can be used: secondary or "trade sale" of the investor's shares to another investor or company or repurchase of the investor's shares by the entrepreneur of the investee firm, as allowed by contractual agreements;

- In countries which have a stock market, investors also look at such factors as market liquidity (as measured by ratios of market capitalization to money supply) and the volatility of the stock market.

I.4. INVESTMENT OPPORTUNITIES

Not all LDCs present favourable prospects in all sectors. Being low-income countries, it is expected that the sectors more prone to rapid development would be those in which these countries have some comparative advantage, either because of their rich resource endowments (for example, in agriculture), or because their natural situation can be easily exploited to develop tourism.

The purpose of this Report is to identify countries with good potential for growth in the sectors of tourism, agro-industries and infrastructure. The type of investors that are targeted are those equity and venture capital fund managers who would take an equity stake in the projects presented in this Report.

The needs of LDCs in terms of infrastructure development are substantial. The need for external financing is obvious, and offers the private sector an access to these projects. Although there are a very few projects in LDCs which are envisaged as being financed only by the private sector, there is more and more evidence that these countries are moving towards co-financed projects between the public and private sectors.

In each of the sectors examined in this Report, a general assessment of the growth potential of the sector under consideration is undertaken, followed by the identification of specific countries which can offer good projects. Where possible, detailed projects are also presented. Appendix I reports on country investment opportunities presented to UNCTAD, and appendix II contains a list of investment promotion agencies in LDCs and the names of contact persons.

CHAPTER II

STRUCTURE OF EQUITY FUNDS

II.1. SCOPE OF EQUITY FUNDS INVESTING IN EMERGING AND PRE-EMERGING MARKETS

As indicated in the Introduction, the type of investors to whom this Report is addressed are mainly equity and venture capital fund managers with an interest in developing countries. This chapter analyses the possible structure of equity funds that are active in emerging and pre-emerging markets.

General classification

In recent years, a wide variety of equity investment funds have been established, They can be broadly classified as follows:

- *Portfolio Funds*: are invested in securities quoted on established stock exchanges, either in the investee country or in international money centres. While these funds are not the subject of this Report, they comprise the vast majority of emerging market funds and most major international fund managers are only interested in investment in countries with established stock markets or countries where such markets are likely to grow rapidly, e.g. in eastern Europe.

- *Private Equity Funds*: are invested in minority stakes in larger unlisted enterprises and often have a strong industry specialization. The size and specialization of private equity funds leads them to focus very heavily on economies with large markets or on those countries hosting large natural resource or infrastructure projects.

- *Venture Capital Funds*: are invested in significant minority (sometimes majority) holdings in smaller companies not listed on stock exchanges. This type of fund is the main potential model for equity funds for the LDCs.

Each of these types of funds have distinct characteristics.

Target market

Equity and other investment funds raise capital from investors on the basis of a plan to invest in "eligible enterprises" in a specific target market expected to offer attractive investment opportunities. This target market may be defined in terms of:

- *Geographic coverage*: equity and other type of funds may have (i) global (ii) regional or (iii) country scope.

- *Sectoral focus*: funds may be focused on one or more industrial sectors, e.g. natural resources, high-tech industries, etc..

- *Transactional focus*: funds may be set up to specialize in specific types of transactions, e.g. privatizations, joint ventures, franchising etc..

The way in which a particular fund is structured depends on the priority that the sponsoring investment managers and the funds' potential investors attach to the following key factors.

- *Potential returns* : for private institutional investors, funds should have identified a target market (geographically and/or sectorally) which offers the prospect of above average returns on their capital. This factor alone virtually eliminates their interest in country funds targeted at individual LDCs whose underlying economic performance and prospects are poor.

- *Diversification*: the target market should be sufficiently broad to allow the fund to diversify its risks by investing in a portfolio of varied investments. Indeed, the investment policies of most funds require that the fund will not commit more than, at most, 15 per cent of available capital in a single portfolio company, nor more than 33 per cent in any single business sector, The need for diversification usually means that country funds are only appropriate in countries with relatively diversified economies, and regional funds with sector specialization need to cover a broad enough geographic focus to minimize the potential impact of negative industry or cyclical trends.

- *Size*: the capitalization of investment funds reflects a balance between the investors' interest in committing funds to the target market and the minimum amount needed to sustain a competent and motivated fund manager. Since managers' fees are typically related to the amount of funds committed (around 2.5 per cent for smaller VC funds), the level of staff and administrative costs of establishing and operating a fund effectively determines the minimum financially viable size of fund, although this may be mitigated if donor funding is available to subsidize management costs.

- *Focus*: funds can more easily attract capital and are more likely to be successful if the fund vehicle is focused on a specifically defined target market (whether geographic, sectoral or transactional) with demonstrably attractive prospects in which the managers have a proven track record. Efficient management of unquoted equity investments (whether private equity or venture capital) is also only practicable within a reasonably compact and coherent geographic area.

The interaction of these, often conflicting, requirements is illustrated by the structure of the investment funds supported by four major international development finance institutions (DFI), although the approaches taken by each of them differs as a result of their distinct objectives and operational policies.

- The United States Overseas Private Investment Corporation (OPIC) supports the creation and capitalization of investment funds that make direct equity and equity-related investments in new, expanding or privatizing companies in emerging market economies, by providing long-term, secured loans and loan guarantees that supplement the funds' private capital. These funds are managed by experienced professional private investment fund managers. OPIC has committed funds to 24 such funds (mainly in the past three years), 20 of which are operational.

- International Finance Corporation (IFC) has been actively involved in promoting and investing in over 100 emerging market funds, about a half of which (in terms of number) are venture capital funds. IFC participates as equity investor and also often acts as a sponsor of funds, assisting in structuring and mobilizing capital and in identifying professional fund managers.

- Commonwealth Development Corporation (CDC) has invested in 25 investment capital funds (as at the end of 1996) in the emerging economies in which it is authorized to operate. In about a half of these funds, CDC provides management for the fund, generally through wholly owned, dedicated and locally registered fund management companies.

- US Agency for International Development (USAID) has provided funding (mainly through grants and technical assistance) to a range of venture capital projects in developing countries and, since 1990, in 10 Enterprise Funds which have made both equity and loan investments in the countries of Eastern Europe and the former Soviet Union.

Together, these agencies have commited funds to around 130 private equity and venture capital funds in emerging markets. The most salient conclusions from this analysis are:

- A majority of the emerging market equity funds (88 out of 130) have a country specific focus. However, most of these country funds are targeted at large economies, relative to the group of LDCs.

- The average size (committed capital) of country funds has varied substantially between those supported by OPIC and IFC, most of which are more oriented to private investor criteria and return expectations, and those supported by CDC and USAID. However, there is a consensus among these institutions as well as private fund managers that the minimum economic size for a professionally managed private equity/venture capital fund is around $20-25 million;

- Largely as a result of this consideration, as well as of the need to diversify portfolio risks, recently formed emerging market funds targeted at the lower income LDC's have generally had a regional focus, including subregional groupings in Africa and Asia and for the Pacific islands.

- Based on similar factors, few regional or country funds have a specific sectoral focus.

- Infrastructure funds, which are all global or regionally focused are substantially larger (exceeding $100 million).

In addition, these agencies are working on a number of new initiatives:

- The United States Administration has recently introduced legislation in the US Congress to support development in Africa, which includes provision for OPIC to support (through OPIC-guaranteed loans) an equity investment fund and an infrastructure fund targeted at the region.

- CDC is currently raising capital for a South Asia Fund for equity investment in Bangledash, Bhutan, India, the Maldives. Nepal, Pakistan and Sri Lanka.

Many of the UN's designated LDCs are eligible for equity investment from these DFI supported, or other existing, funds. For example,

- Enterprises in 16 of the African LDCs are eligible for equity funding from the Commonwealth Afnca Fund, the West Africa Growth Fund, Zambesi Fund or from various country funds;

- Several Asian LDCs are eligible for Asian private equity or infrastructure funds;

- CDC is in the process of establishing the Kula Fund to make equity or quasi-equity investments in private sector companies in the Pacific region, including five designated LDCs, initially targeted at $15 million.

The potential for setting up additional equity investment funds for the LDCs is limited. First, these countries are diverse and geographically dispersed. Second, most of them have unfavourable economic characteristics and weak financial infrastructure. Thus, of the 23 LDCs not covered by existing funds:

- Thirteen countries are small (with populations of 1 million or less, and with proportionately small GDPs);

- Six others (Afghanistan, Angola, Haiti, Sudan, Yemen, Zaire) presently suffer from severe security problems;

10

• Fifteen are classified as "highly indebted" by the World Bank and the International Monetary Fund (IMF).

II.2. FUND STRUCTURES

Equity and other investment funds are generally structured to achieve tax efficiency and accountability by the institution's management for the financial performance of its investments. These objectives are usually the driving forces determining (a) the legal structure of the investment vehicle and (b) the contractual relationships between investors and investment managers.

Two-tier structure

Private equity and venture capital funds have increasingly adopted a two-tier organizational structure, where the funds pooled in the investment vehicle are managed by a separate fund management company, with contractually defined functions of investing, supervising and divesting investors' capital. The rationale for separating the legal and operational structure of the fund from that of the management company derives from several factors:

• *Transparency*: a two-tier structure clearly distinguishes between the roles, and financial interests of the investors from those of the managers;

• *Fiscal efficiency*: allows the Fund vehicle to be legally structured and domiciled in a tax efficient location regardless of whether that legal form and location would be operationally appropriate for the management company;

• *Clarity of Responsibility*:   focuses operational responsibility on the management company.

• *Flexibility*: allows for changes to be made to the status of each component. e.g. by flotation of the fund, without necessarily requiring changes in the other components.

Fund vehicle

It is proposed to establish the Fund as a dedicated investment vehicle in a well-regulated and tax efficient location. The main options are as follows:

Legal form

The purpose of the investment vehicle or Fund is to allow common investment of pooled amounts of capital from different sources. The choice of legal structure (and often of the geographic location or domicile) of the fund is made so as to provide a clear legal status and to delimit the liabilities of investors; to minimize tax charges (particularly by avoiding double taxation of income or capital gains from investee companies both when received by the fund and when distributed to investors); to allow management charges and remuneration to be flexibly related to the profits of the Fund; and to be simple and cost-effective to administer. The most commonly used legal forms for venture capital (VC) institutions are:

- *Corporations.* Setting up a VC institution as a stock corporation, which was general during the early years of VC in both the United States and Europe, had the advantages of being legally well defined, and recognized by regulatory authorities. However, stock corporations incur additional tax burdens where corporate taxes apply. They are also generally intended to have an indefinite life and can be difficult to dissolve.

- *Partnerships.* This structure, under which investors become limited partners in an entity whose interests are managed by a general partner under defined contractual terms, has become increasingly favoured. Partnerships have the advantage that in most tax jurisdictions only the partners and not the entity are taxed. They are easy to form, to change and to dissolve. On the other hand. partnerships require detailed legal definition of the rights and obligations of the partners, and in many developing countries are not recognized as a legal entity.

- *Trusts.* In countries where corporations are subject to high taxes and partnerships are not legally recognized, a trust instrument may be used. Trusts can provide many of the benefits of a partnership but do not of themselves ensure tax-free through passage of income. In addition, they require appointment of an independent trustee, whose custodial duties are often incompatible with the risk-seeking objectives of equity investors, and whose services impose an additional expense and restrictions on management action.

Term

Most private equity funds are structured as closed-end funds, i.e. the investor group is closed after a defined (minimum) amount of capital has been raised and the life of the fund is of a fixed duration.

- Equity funds typically have an eight to ten-year term, at the end of which the assets are distributed to investors and the fund vehicle is wound up, unless an agreed proportion of the investors (e.g. 75 per cent) agree to an extension, for example, in order to allow an orderly liquidation of the fund's investments.

- Infrastructure funds usually have a longer (e.g. 12-year) life, reflecting the time needed to implement and recover the substantial investments needed in transportation, power and telecommunication projects from user charges over an extended period.

Drawdowns and Distribution

VC funds generally create a pool of capital available for investment by the managers, but the investors' commitments to pay in their capital (and their claim on the proceeds of the funds' investments) are subject to defined investment criteria and a number of financial conditions, including:

- capital is drawn down from investors in tranches "as needed" to fund investments in investee companies;

- drawdowns may only be permitted during a limited commitment period, for example, in the first five years of the life of the fund;

- funds are obliged to distribute income and capital received from investee companies as soon as possible after receipt (e.g. at the end of the next six monthly period).

Location

The increasing interest of international institutional investors in cross-border investment has stimulated and been assisted by the development of offshore financial centres, providing favourable legal and tax regimes for investment fund vehicles.

- *Fiscal efficiency*. Investors look to establish or invest in investment vehicles in tax jurisdictions which offer the following advantages:

  - Exemption from income tax on dividends received;
  - Exemption from tax on capital gains
  - Dividends paid by the fund would not be subject to a withholding tax
  - Treaties with the investor's country of origin for avoidance of double taxation.

- Liberal *Foreign Exchange* regime to ensure the free and prompt repatriation of funds to investors.

- *Adequate Professional and Regulatory Infrastructure*. The regulatory framework and level of legal and accounting services must be adequate.

Clearly, favourable fiscal and legal environments in the target countries are also critical conditions to induce a fund to invest.

Corporate Governance

Equity funds generally have a board of directors responsible for overseeing the affairs of the fund, monitoring its performance and exercising the rights of the fund under the management contract with the management company. The board is usually composed of directors appointed by the investors, in proportion to their participation in the capital of the fund, and some independent directors who contribute special and impartial advice.

Management company

Emerging market funds are generally managed by professional managers, who constitute a Management Company (MC) as a special purpose, limited liability company to provide their services and advice to the fund, under an investment advisory agreement.

Location. The operational base of the MC is generally selected on grounds of efficiency (communications, services) and proximity to the companies that will be the major source of deal flow for the Fund. Thus, most emerging market funds are based in their country of operations, or regional financial centres, for example Abidjan or Singapore.

Capitalization and Shareholding. Management companies require modest amounts of funding to cover the projected shortfall of income over operating expenses until the fund's investments begin to generate returns. The average capitalization of over 30 fund management companies in which IFC has participated was less than $1 million, and for equity funds in smaller markets less than $500,000. The distribution of shareholding should reflect the distribution of commitments and responsibilities for the operation of the fund. If an international fund manager is involved in the management of the fund, he/she will take a significant stake in the shareholding.

Remuneration

The MC is remunerated for its services through a specifically defined fee formula which generally combines:

- A fixed annual payment related to the volume of the funds invested. Private sector institutional investors generally limit the level of this fixed fee to around two to three per cent of the net asset value, which effectively sets a minimum economic size of the fund. The relatively high costs associated with professionally managed equity investments (arising from the extensive evaluation, negotiation. legal documentation and supervision) apply to even very small transactions and lead most funds to set a minimum acceptable size of investment: generally above $200,000 even for small country funds;

- a variable incentive fee or "carried interest" based on the profits earned (usuafly defined as a percentage of the distributed profits (e.g. 20 per cent) above a specified hurdle rate of return on the investors' capital (12-15 per cent).

The mix of these elements varies with the size and nature of the equity fund involved. and is also subject to intense negotiation between the investors and managers. Many private institutional investors require that a substantial proportion of the carried interest (50 per cent or more) should be payable to individual members of the management team.

Staffing

The MCs typically have a light overhead structure. Smaller equity funds generally, have two or three full-time professional staff, although they may draw on the information and advice of parent management companies or of financial institutions that invest in the fund vehicle. In view of this, the quality of the managers is critical and ideally should include:

- Professional experience (business and financial skills) ;
- Good negotiating skills;
- A track record (reputation among investors), international fund management is a major advantage in raising large amounts of capital;
- Local knowledge and contacts.

Professional services (for legal, auditing and custodial services) would be outsourced and charged directly to the fund company.

II.3. INVESTMENT POLICIES

Objectives

In general terms, the objective ef equity funds is to secure attractive returns for investors (derived from dividend income and capital appreciation on underlying holdings in investee companies) through investment in enterprises (or transactions) with good prospects for growth and profitability. A clear statement of investment objectives forms a critical element of the prospectus or offering memorandum used to solicit investors to participate in a fund.

Guidelines

A fund operates within the framework of policies that authorize and limit the type of investments it may make. These policies will indicate:

- the type of company in which the fund may invest (e.g. size, industrial sector, stage of development);

- limits to the fund's participation in investee enterprises, i.e. in financial terms (between $250,000 and $5 million) and the percentage of the company's total capitalization: it is of the essence of private equity investment that a fund investor takes a "significant minority" stake that is sufficient to allow it to exercise strategic direction on other shareholders and the management;

- limits to the fund's exposure to individual companies (generally not more than 10-15 per cent of total available capital), sectors or countries (generally not more than 30-35 per cent) designed to ensure that the portfolio of the funds investments are diversified;

- the type of financing instruments in which the fund may invest, which may include:
  - common stock
  - preference shares
  - income notes
  - convertible loans

- the level of investment returns which the fund intends to seek: investors in equity funds are generally looking for projected discounted (post-tax) returns of over 20 per cent or more to compensate for the relatively high risks of this type of investment (e.g. as compared to debt instruments).

Supervision

Fund managers generally expect to follow the affairs of investee companies closely in order to provide advice and direction, and to protect the fund's investments. They do this through appointment of auditors acceptable to the fund, monitoring financial and other information, by site visits and often through membership of company boards of directors: the fund will secure the contractual rights to take these actions as conditions of its investment.

Divestment

Since realizing substantial capital gains on equity investments is essential to achieving high financial returns, the timing and conditions of the sale of investments are key elements of fund management. Depending on their investment objectives and the stage of institutional development of the countries where they operate, equity funds generally aim to divest their investments through a mix of three basic exit routes:

- *Flotation* of the investee company through an Initial Public Offering (IPO) of shares to the public through a stock exchange. This method usually offers enhanced marketability and higher exit valuation for the investment through the higher price-earnings multiples of quoted shares.

- *Secondary or "trade sale"* of the fund's shares to another investor or company. This is probably the most commonly used route, although in larger developed economies the transaction is often initiated by the acquirer, which has identified the investee company as having a good strategic fit with its own operations.

- *Repurchase* of the fund's shares by the entrepreneur or the investee firm. The original investment agreements often give the fund the option to sell (put) its shares to the original or other investors on specified conditions, e.g. at a price determined as a multiple (say six times) of the company's post-tax earnings in a year (or the average of several years) during the period for which the option is open.

It is too early to assess the actual experience of emerging private equity funds (whose investments typically take around five years to mature) of using these exit routes. However, in general terms;

- Most early emerging market equity funds had difficulty in liquidating their investments: this is cited by the International Finance Corporation (IFC) as a major reason for the poor financial performance of several of its initial funds. These funds generally divested by trade sales to an existing shareholder in the investee company, or to a new strategic investor.

- There have so far been very few cases of divestment of shareholdings of LDC equity funds through flotation on local stock exchanges. In most emerging economies, even long-established stock markets are dominated in terms of capitalization and turnover by large, established enterprises, which may provide opportunities for portfolio funds but have played little role in the flotation of new, smaller companies in which equity funds typically invest. In addition, the owners of smaller investee companies may be unwilling to incur the transaction costs and disclosure requirements of listing a company.

- The prospects for stock market divestments are better in the case of funds which invest in privatizations, as has recently occurred in Zambia.

- Repurchase agreements may be particularly relevant for funds which seek to focus on joint venture enterprises involving substantial foreign shareholding.

Distribution

Investment funds are generally required by their policies to distribute the proceeds from their investments in investee companies (dividend income and sales of securities) to the fund's investors as soon as possible after they are received (or on fixed payment dates during each financial year. Fund managers are also required to liquidate a fund's residual investments within its contractually defined duration.

II.4. FUNDING

Funding Cycle

Equity and other investment funds, designed to attract private sector financing, follow a formalized cycle of design, fund raising and closing as follows:

- *Design.* New funds are generally initiated by prospective founder investors or managers who identify a potential demand for financing, define a suitable fund and management structure, and prepare financial plans and information memoranda that will be required by other investors.

- *Fund raising.* Soliciting funds from investors is a formal and officially regulated process which involves the establishment of the fund vehicle and the offering of shares (or participations in partnerships) to target groups of investors. This involves setting a target amount of financing that is compatible with both the identified investment demand (within the target market for the fund) and the potential supply of investible capital from prospective investors. This target amount varies widely depending on the investment scope of the proposed fund.

- *Closing* .The offering usually specifies that the fund will be closed after funding commitments have been received for the specified target amount of funds or the offer will lapse if a sufficient minimum amount has not been obtained within an agreed offering period. A fund can only begin to operate after a satisfactory closing.

Potential Investors

In global terms, capital for equity funds comes from four main sources:

- *International institutional investors.* The largest group of investors in emerging market funds are the institutional investors (insurance companies, pension funds, portfolio managers) in the major world financial markets of Europe, North America and, increasingly, in Asia. They are unlikely to invest in LDC markets, except as part of a diversified portfolio of a broader-based regional fund for Asia and perhaps Africa.

- *Professional fund managers.* Increasingly emerging market funds are managed by professional management companies, many of whom originate with or have affiliations with venture capital investors in developed countries.

- *Development finance institutions.* As already noted, most of the multilateral and bilateral development finance institutions with the resources and authorization to make equity investments in local enterprises in emerging markets have become active in promoting and investing in investment funds. They are a major source of funding for any new funds, although DFIs have varying geographic areas of operation, and differing investment policies and criteria. In addition, most of them are charged to supplement rather than replace private investment and therefore will only invest in combination with private investors.

- *Domestic institutional investors.* Local insurance companies and pension funds have substantial assets in relation to their economies. In the past, these have been mainly held in the form of government securities and real property.

The availability of finance for new funds depends critically on how private investors assess the actual and perceived returns and risks in the target markets.

- Substantial amounts have been raised from private institutional investors for what are regarded as attractive investments; for example, more than US$ 500 million in the case of the Asian Infrastructure Fund. However, these investors generally take a selective approach to asset allocation and country risk, and rarely participate in funds targeted at the LDC economies.

- Fund management firms (or their parents) frequently invest in the LDC some of funds they manage, though generally in token amounts of around 5 per cent of fund capitalization.

- DFIs have been major investors in equity funds targeted at emerging markets. In the CDC-managed funds referred to earlier, about one-third of the capital has been subscribed by other development institutions with similar objectives (including DEG, EIB. IFU, FMO, Proparco and Swedcorp).

- In recent years, emerging market funds have begun to attract capital from domestic institutional investors, for example, 25 per cent of the newly formed West African Growth Fund has been committed by local insurance companies.

Investment Incentives and Guarantees

A range of measures has been developed to promote equity investment in emerging markets: some measures apply to investment fund vehicles directly, others to the direct equity investments made by a fund (or other private investor) in investee companies. They include:

- MIGA and OPIC (for US investors) provide guarantees against political risks (expropriation, currency inconvertibility, war and civil strife). Premia for such cover are related to market insurance rates and to country risk.

- Some countries offer tax credits and rebates for investments in eligible venture funds.

Although these incentives may be influential in attracting investment in certain marginal locations, the general experience of emerging market equity funds is that the development of a freer, more transparent and well-regulated environment for equity investment, including favourable tax treatment for capital gains is generally more effective than specific and preferential advantages for designated classes of investors or investments.

Technical Support

Development or donor agencies have also provide indirect support to equity funds:

- British, French and US economic cooperation agencies have given grant funding to pay the salaries of professional foreign managers for the initial years of the operation of funds, when they generate little income in a number of African countries;

- Other donors, including the European Union, finance technical assistance to investee companies, for example. major programmes of post-privatization support have been provided to enterprises in which new venture funds in Eastern Europe have participated.

CHAPTER III

INVESTMENT OPPORTUNITIES IN THE TOURISM SECTOR

III.1. GLOBAL ASSESSMENT OF THE TOURISM SECTOR

The profitability of tourism investments in LDCs cannot be based on historical data as flows of international tourists to these countries have always been weak, even if they have somewhat increased in recent years in countries that have enjoyed civil and military peace. Nevertheless, three main aspects of tourism development in LDCs can be analysed:

- the growth rate of tourism in LDCs compared to the rest of the world;
- the main factors favourable to tourism investment in the LDCs;
- the risk factors that can undermine tourism investment in LDCs.

A stronger growth rate of tourism in LDCs than the world average

Together, the LDCs have recorded a higher growth rate of international tourism than the world average in recent years. This expansion of tourism development relates to the period between 1992 and 1996 (table III.1).

**Table III.1. Trends in tourist arrivals in LDCs and in the world
1988-1996**

Regions	1988-1992 *Percentage*	1992-1996 *Percentage*
LDCs[a]	**+16.8**	**+32.0**
Europe	+26.0	+15.1
Africa	+42.2	+15.1
East Asia and the Pacific	+37.7	+38.7
South Asia	+28.5	+22.2
The Americas	+24.1	+11.7
The Middle East	+24.1	+44.7
World	+27.3	+18.1

Source: World Tourism Organization (WTO), *Yearbook of Tourism Statistics 1997* (Madrid, 1997).
   a The figures for LDCs do not include Equatorial Guinea, Eritrea, Guinea, Guinea Bissau, Liberia, Mauritania and Mozambique.

However, it should be noted that tourism flows to the LDCs as a whole are weak. They only represented 2.3 million arrivals in 1988, 0.58 per cent of the total of world international arrivals, which then stood at 395 million. In 1996, the LDCs' share of 594 million world tourism arrivals increased to 0.61 per cent and accounted for 3.6 million arrivals.

The trend in international tourism receipts in LDCs during the period 1988 to 1992 progressed at a faster rate than the world average (table III.2), but the LDCs share of world international tourism receipts remains very small accounting for 0.32 per cent in 1988 and 0.36 per cent in 1996. Indeed, total receipts were $0.63 billion dollars in 1988 compared with $202.56 billion total world receipts. In 1996, the figures were, respectively, $1.53 billion and $425.41 billion. It should be observed that the LDCs share of international tourism *receipts* is smaller than their share of international tourism *arrivals*.

**Table III.2. Trends in international tourist receipts in LDCs and in the world
1988-1996**

Regions	1988-1992 *Percentage*	1992-1996 *Percentage*
LDCs	**+55.1**	**+55.3**
Europe	+49.5	+32.5
Africa	+33.3	+33.3
East Asia and the Pacific	+56.6	+74.4
South Asia	+47.3	+39.2
The Americas	+66.6	+24.7
The Middle East	+5.8	+48.1
World	+53.4	+37.1

Source: WTO, *Yearbook of Tourism Statistics 1997* (Madrid, 1997).
   a The figures for LDCs do not include Equatorial Guinea, Eritrea, Guinea, Guinea Bissau, Liberia, Mauritania and Mozambique.

Main factors favourable to tourism investment in LDCs

Tourism investments can be considered as offering good financial opportunities in LDCs for three main reasons:

Tourism is a service activity requiring large manpower

It is a highly competitive sector and labour costs play an essential role. From this point of view, most LDCs enjoy an especially important comparative advantage because of the low labour costs prevailing in these countries. This advantage is particularly important, not only *vis-à-vis* industrial countries, but also *vis-à-vis* the newly industrializing countries and countries specialized in international tourism, which are experiencing a rapid growth in labour costs. In these conditions it is increasingly difficult to maintain high service standards in hospitality and catering while remaining competitive. For this reason, large hotel and tourism groups seeking opportunities for maintaining both their profitability and their competitiveness can be attracted to invest in those LDCs with buoyant tourism sectors.

The World Trade Organization's General Agreement on Trade in Services (GATS) will benefit tourism and travel in LDCs

Much of the international trade in services at the present time is clouded by discriminatory practices and protectionism. In tourism, these restrictions affect companies in many ways, such as their ability:

- to move staff to a foreign country;
- to create and operate branch offices abroad;
- to effect currency payments and transfers;
- to use trademarks, etc.

LDCs that adhere to the GATS are required to allow foreign suppliers of services full access to their domestic markets and to be treated as equally as domestic suppliers.[10] For tourism and travel-related businesses this will mean:

- Tour operators, hotel enterprises and other tourism and travel-related companies from a foreign country will be able to set up operations in these LDCs;

- In the hotel sector, GATS will facilitate franchising management contracts, technical service agreements, licensing and patents;

- If national treatment is fully granted, foreign companies will be able to sell their services under the same terms and conditions as domestic companies and suppliers.

---

[10]   See World Trade Organization, *GATS* (agreement on trade and tourism), (Geneva, 1995).

Tourism is a sector where the choice of destinations and products is constantly expanding

Most LDCs are new tourism destinations and this novelty is a factor that attracts those international tourists who are seeking new experiences. LDCs are often located near large international tourist generating centres. For example, African LDCs are located within the same time zone and just a few hours travel time from European countries, Asian LDCs in the Pacific are near to the tourist generating countries of Australia and New Zealand, and LDCs in the Americas are close to the United States. Consequently, these LDCs are able to expand their tourism supply in their respective regions by diversifying their range of products and their tourism destinations.

International tourism is increasingly oriented towards the demand for new products focused on culture and the environment. These current trends in tourism demand can also favour tourism investments in LDCs by developing their historical and natural heritage. The characteristics of novelty which these destinations display attracts several segments of international tourism clientele, in particular, those seeking discovery, adventure and eco-tourism, which now constitute the fastest growing areas of international tourism. However investment opportunities in LDCs not only depend on international tourism demand trends, but also on the specific situations and conditions that exist in each of these countries.

Risk factors that can undermine tourism investment in LDCs

There are specific risks associated with investing in the tourism sector, which stem from the unstable demand character of international tourism to which tourism enterprises are extremely vulnerable. Risk factors exist in several LDCs. They include:

- political and economic instability risks;
- risks associated with insufficient transport facilities;
- health and security risks.

Political and economic instability risks are particularly important in the tourism sector, because tourism is not only a service activity, it is also primarily a sector that needs heavy investment, notably in real estate and equipment. These types of investments require stable political and economic environments, which is not the case in certain LDCs today. Economic instability affects the profitability of tourism investments by provoking fluctuations in exchange rates, prices and, especially in cases of unforeseen worsening of the situation, changes in the taxation system.

Risks associated with problems of transport are a major factor for the slow development of tourism potential in many LDCs. Access may be restricted, not just to reach the country but also to reach tourism destinations within the country. Only a few LDCs own international airline companies with networks of international stopovers operating in the large tourist generating markets of Europe, North America and Asia. As a result, the quota of seats available on aircraft is not sufficient to allow increases in tourism supply. In addition to these insufficient international air transport facilities, there are also often internal transport difficulties.

The main health risk to tourists is associated with food, particularly in countries where the local food industry does not, or is unable to, provide the necessary sanitary guarantees. Security risks to tourists can give a destination a negative image which deters investors from committing funds to tourism projects.

This general analysis shows that there are indeed tourism investment opportunities in LDCs, which explains the recent strong growth rate of tourism in these countries compared to the rest of the world. However, when the specific risks associated with tourism activity are taken into account, it appears that certain LDCs have particularly favourable conditions for important tourism investment projects and these must be identified.

Most LDCs are new tourism destinations, which are particularly well endowed with natural tourism assets and resources. While many of them have experienced strong growth in their tourism sector since the beginning of the 1990s, others have seen this sector decline because of political or military instability. However, the overall positive results remain fragile. There are constraints in the hotel and transport facilities and the tourism sector in these countries lacks structure and is very concentrated on a small number of tourism sites that are exploited by too few operators.

Trends in international tourism arrivals in the LDCs

Between 1992 and 1996, tourism flows to LDCs countries have increased strongly from 2.7 million arrivals to more than 3.6 million - an increase of over a third in four years. This is a higher growth rate than the world average for tourism arrivals during the same period, 32 per cent compared with 17 per cent (table III.3).

The breakdown of tourism arrival flows by country reveals that these are particularly strong into certain countries, in some cases doubling in four years. These are Cambodia, the Central African Republic, Lao People's Democratic Republic, Myanmar, Samoa and Uganda. Together, these six countries accounted for 734,000 tourist arrivals in 1996 compared with 282,000 in 1992.

The trends indicate that international tourism is not only growing in LDCs with developed tourism sectors, such as the Maldives. Nepal and Tanzania, but also in many countries where tourism has recently developed. However, between 1992 and 1996, there have been large trend variations in the international tourist arrivals in different LDCs. The trends fall into three categories: those that are increasing at a very rapid rate, those that are increasing at a slower rate or stagnating and those that are declining. For example, in Africa from 1992 to 1996:[11]

---

[11]   Information on Equatorial Guinea, Eritrea, Guinea, Guinea Bissau, Liberia, Mauritania and Mozambique is not available.

- Certain countries such as Burkina Faso (+80 per cent), Cape Verde (+79 per cent), Tanzania (+62 per cent), Madagascar (+42 per cent) have all recorded high growth in tourist arrivals.

- The increase in tourist arrivals has been at a slower rate in Niger (+38 per cent), the Comoros (+31 per cent), Ethiopia (+27 per cent), Mali (+15 per cent), Togo (+14 per cent), Benin (+13 per cent) and Zambia (+8 per cent).

- In Angola, Burundi, Chad, Djibouti, Gambia, Lesotho, Rwanda, Sierra Leone, Somalia and Sudan tourist arrivals have shown a sizeable decline.

- In the other regions of the world, with the exception of Afghanistan, the arrivals growth rate in LDCs has risen. Thus, despite strong overall growth, international tourism arrivals in the different LDCs are not progressing at a uniform rate.

Trends in international tourism receipts in the LDCs

The growth rate of tourism *receipts* in LDCs has risen strongly from $1 billion in 1992 to more than $1.5 billion in 1996. In fact, the increase of 55 per cent in four years was substantially higher than that of *arrivals* which was 32 per cent. The breakdown by country shows that Tanzania, the Maldives and Nepal had the largest international tourism receipts that together accounted for 43 per cent of total receipts in LDC countries (table III.4).

The highest growth rates between 1992 and 1996 were registered by Myanmar (+275 per cent), Bangladesh (+187 per cent), Tanzania (+129 per cent), Samoa (+129 per cent), Uganda (+116 per cent) and Haïti (+113 per cent). Receipts in Nepal increased at a slower rate than the LDC average, recording a 38 per cent rise. Over the same period, receipts in Burundi, Djibouti, Gambia, Guinea, Malawi, Niger, Rwanda, Sierra Leone, Togo, Zaïre and Zambia all fell.

Therefore, receipts in LDCs vary considerably between the different countries, not only in terms of their individual share of total international tourism receipts for the sector, but also in terms of their growth rate.

Table III.3. Tourist arrivals in the LDCs, 1988-1996 (in thousands)

Countries	Arrivals		
	1988	1992	1996
Afghanistan	9	6	4
Angola	39	40	8
Bangladesh	121	110	164
Benin	75	130	147
Bhutan	2	3	5
Burkina Faso	83	92	166
Burundi	99	86	31
Cambodia	20	88	195
Cape Verde	18	19	34
Central African Rep.	5	7	29
Chad	21	17	7
Comoros	8	19	25
Djibouti	29	28	20
Equatorial Guinea			
Eriteria			
Ethiopia	76	83	105
Gambia	102	64	46
Guinea		33	97
Guinea-Bissau			
Haiti	133	90	150
Kiribati	3	4	4
Lao People's Dem. Rep.	25	30	63
Lesotho	110	155	108
Liberia			
Madagascar			
Malawi	35	54	77
Maldives	99	150	156
Mali	156	236	339
Mauritania	36	38	44
Mozambique			
Myanmar	26	27	157
Nepal	266	334	407
Niger	33	13	18
Rwanda	36	5	1
Samoa	49	38	76
Sao Tome and Principe	1	3	2
Sierra Leone	75	89	39
Solomon Islands	11	12	14
Somalia	40	20	10
Sudan	37	17	10
Togo	104	49	56
Tuvalu	1	1	1
Uganda	40	92	214
United Rep. of Tanzania	130	202	326
Vanuatu	16	43	45
Yemen	60	72	75
Zaire	39	22	37
Zambia	108	159	172
Total	2376	2780	3684

Source: WTO, *Yearbook of Tourism Statistics 1997* (Madrid, 1997).

III.2. IDENTIFICATION OF LDCS WHERE THE TOURISM SECTOR OFFERS THE MOST DEVELOPMENT POTENTIAL

The criteria for identifying countries with the greatest potential for developing tourism are based on the analysis of recent trends in tourism arrivals and receipt flows. Ten LDCs with more than 150,000 tourist arrivals in 1996 and with receipts of $50 million or more should be considered. Countries receiving more than 150 000 tourists in 1996 are mainly African (Burkina Faso, Malawi, Uganda, Tanzania and Zambia). Other LDCs with high numbers of arrivals in that year were Nepal, the Maldives, Cambodia and Myanmar (table III.5).

In this first group of ten countries, the growth rate of international tourist arrivals is weaker in Malawi and Zambia than the average growth rate in LDCs. Between 1992 and 1996, arrivals in Malawi increased only by 1 per cent and in Zambia by 8 per cent compared with the LDCs average of 32 per cent. LDCs with annual receipts of $50 million or more are Haïti, Cambodia, Lao, Madagascar, the Maldives, Myanmar, Nepal, Uganda, Tanzania and Vanuatu (table III.6). However, the trend of international tourism receipts in Cambodia has been sluggish and has not risen between 1992 and 1996, and despite featuring in the list of the top ten countries in terms of arrivals, Burkina Faso only recorded a 1 per cent growth over this period compared with the 55 per cent average growth for all LDCs.

The rankings show that growth trends differ from country to country, both in terms of tourism arrivals and in terms of tourism receipts. In the first instance, five countries featured in both rankings have been selected because of their high growth rates of tourism arrivals and tourism receipts. These are the Maldives, Myanmar, Nepal, Uganda and Tanzania. Those that are progressing less rapidly than the LDC average in terms of *arrivals* (Zambia and Malawi) and in terms of *receipts* (Cambodia, and Burkina Faso) have been eliminated. Five other countries with above average growth have also been selected. These are Haiti, Lao People's Democratic Republic, Madagascar, Bangladesh and Vanuatu.

Table III.4. Tourist Receipts in the LDCs, 1988-1996
($ million)

Countries	Receipts		
	1988	1992	1996
Afghanistan	1	1	1
Angola			9
Bangladesh	13	8	23
Benin	40	32	29
Bhutan	1	3	5
Burkina Faso	11	24	25
Burundi	2	3	1
Cambodia		50	50
Cape Verde	3	7	10
Central African Rep.	5	3	5
Chad	7	21	35
Comoros	3	8	9
Djibouti	5	6	4
Equatorial Guinea			
Eriteria			
Ethiopia	19	23	38
Gambia	18	27	22
Guinea		11	1
Guinea-Bissau			
Haiti	19	38	81
Kiribati	1	1	1
Lao People's Dem. Rep.	1	18	50
Lesotho		19	19
Liberia			
Madagascar	20	39	61
Malawi	11	8	5
Maldives	55	113	212
Mali	38	11	17
Mauritania	12	8	11
Mozambique			
Myanmar	8	16	60
Nepal	94	110	146
Niger	11	17	15
Rwanda	7	4	1
Samoa	18	17	39
Sao Tome and Principe	1	2	2
Sierra Leone	15	17	6
Solomon Islands	5	6	6
Somalia			
Sudan	29	5	7
Togo	36	39	8
Tuvalu			
Uganda	8	38	82
United Rep. of Tanzania	40	120	322
Vanuatu	18	56	60
Yemen	21	47	39
Zaire	7	7	5
Zambia	5	51	60
Total	639	1043	1582

Source: WTO, *Yearbook of Tourism Statistics 1997* (Madrid, 1997).

Table III.5.   LDCs receiving more than 150,000 tourists in 1996

Countries	Arrivals 1992	Arrivals 1996
Nepal	334	407
Maldives	236	339
United Republic of Tanzania	202	326
Uganda	93	214
Cambodia	88	195
Zambia	159	172
Burkina Faso	92	166
Bangladesh	110	164
Myanmar	27	157
Malawi	150	156

Source: WTO, *Yearbook of Tourism Statistics 1997* (Madrid, 1997).

Table III.6.   LDCs receiving $500,000 or more in income from tourism in 1996

Countries	Receipts 1996
United Republic of Tanzania	322
Maldives	212
Nepal	146
Uganda	82
Haiti	81
Madagascar	61
Myanmar	60
Vanuatu	60
Cambodia	50
Lao People's Democratic Republic	50

Source: WTO, *Yearbook of Tourism Statistics 1997* (Madrid 1997).

The 10 countries thus identified as displaying a high potential for future tourism development are:

Africa	Uganda
	United Republic of Tanzania
The Americas	Haiti
East Asia	Lao People's Democratic Republic
South Asia	Bangladesh
	Myanmar
	Nepal
Indian Ocean Region	Madagascar
	Maldives
Pacific Regions	Vanuatu

Despite very strong potential, tourism development in LDCs today is fragile and vulnerable to the vagaries of the changing regional and international economic situation. Therefore, it is particularly important to analyse the potential of tourism investment and to identify opportunities.

III.3. ASSESSMENT OF POTENTIAL FOR EXPANSION OF THE TOURISM SECTOR IN IDENTIFIED COUNTRIES

The potential for expansion of the tourism sector in LDCs can be appraised by examining the development of the tourism sector in neighbouring countries and by identifying the opportunities and types of investments needed in each LDC. Studies identifying specific tourism development projects have been carried out in the 10 selected LDCs indicated above. However, these projects must be reviewed with the authorities in charge of tourism in each country so as to draw up an accurate catalogue of tourism investment possibilities for the private sector.

To assess the potential for expansion of the tourism sector in the identified countries the following aspects must be taken into account:

- the situation and stage of development in each country;
- regional tourism development conditions;
- the returns-on-investment which can be achieved.

The specific situation in each country

The tourism sector is characterized by the fact that international tourism demand can switch very quickly from one country to another as a reaction to changes in the political and economic situation in the receiving countries. As a result, the profitability of tourism investments in LDCs depends on a number of essential factors that must exist if a real development of international tourism is to be encouraged.

Three main conditions will favour tourism investment opportunities:

The first concerns specialization by LDCs on one or several segments of the tourism market

This condition is particularly important as trends show that international tourism demand is increasingly concentrating on niche products. It also corresponds to the economic characteristics of LDCs, which need to focus their strategies of tourism development on niche products so that they can enter into direct competition with more advanced countries. Eco-tourism is a niche area that LDC's could exploit successfully by protecting and developing their natural resources.

The second condition concerns the choice of natural comparative advantages, which should be exploited

Each country has specific natural advantages that cannot all be exploited at the same time. Thus, tourism investment must be concentrated on the advantages that are selected after taking account of the development priorities that have been set by the government authorities in the country. For example, trends in the number of available hotel rooms in LDC's show that there are many opportunities for investment in the hotel sector, particularly in Nepal, Uganda and Bangladesh (table III.7).

31

Table III.7. Hotel Room Capacity in 10 LDCs, 1992

Country	Number of Rooms 1992	Number of Rooms 1996
Bangladesh	3,063	4,085
Myanmar	1,653	7,615
Nepal	5,992	11,124
Haiti	1,050	1,400
Madagascar	3,040	3,040
Maldives	4,323	5,500
Lao People's Democratic Rep.	1,989	3,345
United Republic of Tanzania	6,150	6,935
Uganda	2,941	3,673
Vanuatu	516	666

Source: WTO, *Yearbook of Tourism Statistics 1997* (Madrid, 1997).

The third condition relates to the access facilities for tourists that exist in each of the LDCs

The situation is often quite different in each LDC. Certain LDCs own international airline companies with networks of international stopovers which yield a great advantage to these countries. On the other hand, for many LDCs, the first tourism development problem is that of transporting tourists to the country because they lack the necessary air transport facilities. For example BIMAN, the Bangladesh airline company, links Dhaka with the main Asian and European capitals as well as with New York and Tokyo.

The development of international tourism represents a major economic development stake for most LDCs. Indeed, in terms of international tourism arrivals and receipts, the success recorded since the beginning of the 1990s will not be sustained if solutions are not found to the problems of adaptation of accommodation infrastructure and of the distribution of international tourism flows around the country. From this point of view, LDCs have essential advantages : their tourism wealth, which is both diversified and complementary, and the possibility of using the major entry routes into international tourism.

For development to succeed, the level of required investment largely depends on the ability of LDCs in establishing a range of quality investments in the following tourism subsectors: Air Transport; Airport Facilities; Incoming Operation Services; Road Transport; Hospitality and Catering; Tourism and Leisure Facilities.

The required level of investment depends on each country's situation. The main task being to identify niches where private investments should be concentrated as it is not possible for LDCs to satisfy all segments of international tourism demand at the same time. The analysis of a number of tourism development master plans in those LDCs with strong tourism potential identifies the appropriate types of tourism investments in the following country examples: Bangladesh, Lao People's Democratic Republic, Madagascar, the Maldives, Nepal, Uganda and Vanuatu.[12]

---

[12] In all of these examples, the information must be checked and updated with the tourism authorities in each country.

BANGLADESH

Tourism Demand:	166,000 arrivals in 1996
Tourism Receipts not including transport):	$38 million in 1996
Accommodation Capacity (rooms):	4,085 in 1995
(beds):	8,224 in 1995

Tourism Potential:

1. Business tourism	Dhaka
2. Eco-tourism	Sunderbans
3. Seaside tourism	Cox's Bazar
4. Cultural tourism	Rajshashi, Dhaka
5. Tourism discovery and adventure	Sylet/Moulvi Bazar
	Chittagong Hill Tracks

Investments:

According to the Bangladesh Strategic Master Plan for Tourism, most of the product development programme is intended to be financed and implemented by private sector interests, and a significant proportion of the investments will require foreign exchange funding.

The following institutions and organizations may be expected to provide direct investment in private sector enterprises:

- Regional development finance institutions;
- International development finance institutions;
- International commercial banks;
- Airlines, hotel chains and tour operators.

Potential foreign investments can be identified as follows:

- Investments in four-or five-star hotels - Dhaka

  The indicative costings for a 300-room hotel in Dhaka can be based on an anticipated investment cost of $85,000 per room. The total number of employees would be 350 or more and the total payroll expenses could be expected to range between 15 and 20 per cent of total revenue. The potential rate of return on total investment could be between 6.9 per cent and 9.4 per cent.

- New chalets bungalows - Parhapur

The indicative costings for a 50-room unit in Parharpur or other similar locations can be based on an anticipated investment cost of $20,000 per cottage unit. The potential rate of return on total investment could be between 9.8 per cent and 11.9 per cent.

LAO, PDR

Tourism Demand:	63,000 arrivals
Tourism Receipts (not including transport):	$50 million
Accommodation Capacity (rooms):	3,345
(beds):	6,690
Occupation Rate:	Approximately 30 per cent

Tourism Potential:

1.	Cultural tourism	Luang-Prabang
2.	Business tourism	Ventiane
3.	Eco-tourism	Plaine des Jarres

Projects under way:

Cooperation

Development of protected natural zones (UNDP, World Bank, Governments of Australia, the Netherlands, Sweden, and the United States);

Hospitality and tourism training (Asian Development Bank, Government of Thailand).

Investments:

Tourism complexes - private sector projects financed by Thailand and Malaysia.

Note: The financial profitability of tourism investments in Lao largely depends on future trends in tourism demand and the adaptation of supply to this demand, particularly demand from the Asian market. See Government of Lao PDR, *Strategie de Developpement Touristique et Renforcement Institutionnel National* (Vientiane, 1996).

MADAGASCAR

Tourism Demand:	77,000 arrivals in 1996
Tourism Receipts (not including transport):	$61 million in 1996
Accommodation Capacity (rooms):	3,040 in 1995
(beds):	6,904 in 1995

Tourism Potential:

1. Seaside tourism   Nosy Be, Sainte-Marie
2. Business tourism   Anatanarivo
3. Nature and forests   Villes moyennes

Investments:

A market study of the Malagasy tourism sector concluded that there is the possibility of attracting two categories of tourism clientele:

High spending tourists. The target is for 72,000 arrivals by the year 2000 with 80 per cent staying in resorts and 20 per cent combining stays in seaside resorts with tours around the country.

Tourists on a medium budget. The strategy is to attract 134,000 arrivals by the year 2000 including more than 16,000 business tourists.

To respond to this expected growth rate of tourism demand, four categories of accommodation should be considered as offering investment opportunities:

-       High category seaside hotels (up to 400 rooms);
-       Medium category seaside hotels equivalent to the international three-star category with a capacity of 80 rooms;
-       High category business and tourism hotels with a capacity of 150 rooms;
-       Medium category touring hotels with between 15 and 60 rooms.

The tourism development master plan for Madagascar indicates that the profitability of the investment in these hotel projects should produce a rate of return of between 16 and 19 per cent.[13]

---

[13]   See Government of Madagascar, *Tourisme à Madagascar, Contribution a l'elaboration d'une politique de developpement touristique à moyen et long termes* (Antananarivo, 1991).

THE MALDIVES

Tourism Demand:	339,000 arrivals in 1996
Tourism Receipts:	$212 million in 1996
Accommodation Capacity (beds):	10,524 in 1995
Tourism Potential:	

    1. Seaside and Resort tourism   Mahé and Ari, North and South atolls to the central region Vilingi Island

    2. Eco-tourism and Marine tourism   Remote atolls

Investments:

The 1996-2005 Tourism Master Plan for the Maldives estimates that by the year 2005, there will be 650,000 tourist arrivals and 20,500 resort beds in the country. To cope with this expansion, it recommends substantial private sector investment to develop the tourism industry. It is estimated that the required investment capital over the next 10 years (corresponding to the life of the Master Plan) will be $600 million a year, then $70 million a year for the next five years (table III.8). Both domestic and foreign capital would be required for this purpose. Foreign capital would make up three-quarters of the investment and domestic capital would be sought for the rest.

Private sector mobilization of capital is preferred, not only because this sector can recognize the market opportunities, but also because the ability to finance the substantial amounts of capital to develop the industry should come from the private sector, which can operate efficiently and cost effectively. The role of the Government is to provide a business environment conducive to stimulating a positive response from the private sector.

Most of the capital will be required for the construction of new resorts and for the refurbishment of existing resorts. But there is also a significant need for capital for airport expansion and other infrastructure, such as a service centre at Raa airport.

Resort Development

In the existing central region atolls of Mahé and Ari, committed projects already account for 1,000+ new bed-space additions. The take-up of development rights on existing island resorts is considered to be capable of adding a further 1,000 beds (table III.9). In the nearby atolls (north and south expansion areas to the central region), the allocation of 3,500 beds suggests that 20 to 30 new resorts should be developed by 2005.

For the Southern region, it is foreseen that the majority of the 3,000-bed development should be focused on Vilingili Island. Development of the more remote atolls through the regional airport growth pole strategy should be responsive to market forces, and in accord with the guidelines for the maintenance of sustainable environmental conditions.

Table III.8. The Maldives: Tourism Investment Programme
($ millions)

Investment	1996-2000	2001-2005
Private Resort Development	200-250	250-300
Infrastructure Development		
Private	28	-
Gan Airport (international)	-	20
Raa Airport	20	20
Others (e.g. service centre)		
Public	10	36
Hulule Airport		
Total	**Say, 60**	**Say, 100**
Overall	**250-300**	**350-400**

Source: European Commission, *Tourism Master Plan for the Maldives, 1996-2005* (Brussels).

Construction Industry

Tourism can encourage the local construction industry, which has shown that it is capable of building capacity of around 1,000 beds per year that would meet the needs of the tourism industry.

Facilitation by the Government to attract Private Sector Investment

The Master Plan recommends that the Government of the Maldives should:

- mobilize domestic capital by enabling private sector companies to issue securities to investors, but with full safeguards for such investors;

- mobilize foreign capital by creating a transparent framework for foreign investors, but ensuring a 'level playing field' for local investors;

- monitor and fine tune the conditions for resort leases, based upon a transparent framework for the operation of resorts and involving regular statistical reporting by the resorts;

- ease the burden of direct taxation on the tourism industry.

Table III.9. The Maldives Resort Development
(bed-space)

Location	Existing	Total (%)	New additions	Year 2005 Total	Total (%)
Central Region (Malé and Ari Atolls)	9,655	92	2,500	12,155	59
Nearby Atolls (Accretion Growth)	769	7	3,500	4,269	21
Southern Region (Seenu and Gaafu Dhaalu)	100	1	3,000	3,100	15
Other Regions (Airport Growth Poles)	0	0	10,000	20,524	5
Total	**10,524**	**100**	**10,000**	**20,524**	**100**

Source: European Commission, *Tourism Master Plan for the Maldives, Plan 1996-2005.*

N E P A L

Tourism Demand: 404,000 arrivals in 1996
Tourism Receipts (not including transport): $130 million in 1996
Accommodation Capacity (rooms):   11,124 in 1995
                              (beds):   21,807 in 1995

Tourism Potential:

1. Environment, Trekking and Mountaineering   Gorkha
2. National Parks and Wildlife   Pokhara
3. Business Tourism   Kathmandu

38

The context of Investment:

A WTO Case Study in 1993 shows that tourism in Nepal has a short history,[14] as the country was only opened to investors in 1951. Tourism, together with carpets, is now one of the two principal sources of foreign exchange. Tourism is less important than carpet manufacture as a source of employment, but it plays a strong role in particular localities, especially in mountain communities. The majority of tourists are holidaymakers; business tourism is very modest, and there is only limited conference and incentive travel to Nepal. Adventure tourism is important, but is highly seasonal. Future prospects are for continued growth, pursuing the objective of increasing the average tourist spend per day by attracting more higher-spending visitors and by persuading those tourists that come to stay longer.

The current tourism focus is heavily concentrated on Kathmandu, while even trekking is concentrated on only three areas of the country, the Annapurna region, the Mount Everest area (Khumbu), and Langtang. Developing facilities outside the Kathmandu Valley is highly dependent on an improvement in transport facilities, especially air transportation.

Tourism Industry

The tourism industry in Nepal is characterized by family and other privately-owned businesses. There are very few publicly-owned companies. There is no vehicle for mobilizing domestic capital for equity investment in larger projects. At the same time, foreign investment has been extremely limited. The small number of relatively large hotels have for the most part been favoured by royal patronage; the principal exception being a hotel that was initially financed by the IFC. The largest travel agency, the only one with a modern coach fleet, has also been supported by well-placed individuals.

State-owned enterprises within the tourism sector are few in number. There is a small hotel company which does not function well. Royal Nepal Airlines has played a role in developing Nepali tourism through expanding international services aimed, in recent years, at reducing the dependence on tourism that comes to Nepal via India. It has a monopoly on domestic routes, and weaknesses in these domestic services have constrained the development of tourism outside Kathmandu.

Regulation

A relatively large number of government departments are involved in different aspects of tourism investment. To establish a new business requires separate dealings with these agencies. There is no "one-stop shop" as is found in Indonesia, and obtaining relevant permission has in the past been a time-consuming business, especially for organizations not favoured by appropriate patronage. The present Government aims to streamline these procedures.

All existing travel business is licensed by the Department of Tourism, and establishing new businesses is also licensed by this Department. Although there is a Foreign Investment

---

[14]   WTO: *Case Study: Tourism Financing in Nepal* (Madrid, 1993).

Promotion Division within the Ministry of Industry, prominent figures in the private sector have argued that the Government is more concerned with negative control, and not in the pro-active promotion of new investment.

The foreign exchange control regime is strict, and requires businesses to convert foreign currency into local currency immediately it is received. Obtaining permission to spend foreign currency can take three months. Against a background of a depreciating currency, this has encouraged travel businesses to circumvent the rules. It also acts as a disincentive to foreign investment, although in theory it is possible to repatriate dividends in full and to repatriate capital.

Weaknesses in public administration, including poor management of state enterprises, are widely recognized, including by the present Government.

Investment

Nepal is heavily dependent on donor finance for public sector investment. Until now there have been no specific projects for the tourist sector, although there have been supporting investments in areas such as roads and airports. The Department of Tourism has had no implementation capacity of its own, nor any defined projects available for submission to prospective funding agencies. Hotel investment has been heavily dependent on the Nepal Industrial Development Corporation (NIDC), which acts as a development bank. Other Nepalese banks have been reluctant to lend for time periods adequate for a hotel project to be able to repay its loan. State-owned and private sector commercial banks do not generally lend for more than five to seven years, which is often inadequate for hotel development.

Nepal is to be the first recipient of an Asian Development Bank (ADB) tourism sector loan, linked with UNDP and also possibly, European Commission funding. This will give the Government the opportunity to improve its implementation capacity in tourism, and to become more professional in its approach. In order to encourage the private sector to take advantage of the opportunities, and for Nepal to achieve its objectives of spreading tourism more widely, and of increasing the average tourist spend through the provision of better facilities, the Government should consider the following measures:

- To improve the efficiency of state enterprises, particularly the national airline and the state banks, including the NIDC. The banks should be required to improve debt recovery.

- To simplify the regulatory regime for foreign investment, and to move towards a "one-stop shop". This would best be accompanied by improved promotion of investment opportunities as well as by better marketing in general for tourism in Nepal.

- To promote the mobilization of domestic capital through the development of the nascent stock exchange, and through measures to promote the growth of publicly-owned companies.

- To carry out a review of incentives for the tourism industry, which should consider the extension of incentives to areas other than hotels (notably the import of tourism coaches), and by encouraging specific types of investment, such as hotel projects outside Kathmandu, and existing hotel refurbishment.

- To liberalize the foreign exchange regime in step with changes already made by India.

Foreign investment

Foreign investment has been actively encouraged in Nepal only in recent times. Such investment is seen as supplanting domestic capital resources, providing access to foreign technology and know-how, giving an improved approach to international markets.

A separate division, the Foreign Investment Promotion Division, has been created in the Ministry of Industry to deal with all matters concerning foreign investment. Although this includes investment in tourism, the Department of Tourism also aims to play a role in promoting investment in the tourism sector. It is thus concerned with the scale of investments permitted, criteria to determine the approval of projects, repatriation of capital, remittance of profits and dividends and employment of foreign technical personnel. Remittance of dividends of foreign investors is permitted in full in convertible currency in the case of investments that have been made in convertible currency or in the form of machinery or other capital goods, which have been paid for in convertible foreign exchange.

In the case of repatriation of capital, permission is granted to sell shares of investments made only after the company has commenced operations. In such cases the repatriation of capital in convertible foreign exchange is permitted where convertible foreign exchange has been invested in equity shares of any industrial enterprise as follows:

- 20 per cent per annum of the amount realized on the sale of equity shareholding;

- 25 per cent per annum of the amount realized from the sale of equity shareholding, where the shares are sold through agencies that sell shares in Nepal.

Security of investment

Businesses established under the Foreign Investment and Technology Act are assured of security of the investments made in Nepal. The Act states that no industrial enterprise will be nationalized. However, in the very rare event when the Government is forced to take over an industrial enterprise in the national interest, or for security reasons, compensation would be paid within six months on the basis of an equitable evaluation.

The Government has also signed Investment Protection Agreements with two industrialized countries, France and the Federal Republic of Germany. Under these Agreements French and German investments in Nepal enjoy full protection and security. The Foreign

Investment and Technology Act also provides for arbitration in the event of a dispute arising out of the enforcement of the Act of application of the rules made thereunder.

Incentives

The Government provides incentives for investment in hotels, but not for other forms of tourism investment. These incentives include a five-year tax holiday, rebates on customs duty, and exemption from sales tax on specified imported commodities. These incentives are more limited than for manufacturing businesses. A high level of import duty is applied to tourist coaches, and as a result a considerable number of existing coaches are of advanced age, often 20 years old.

Companies indexed in the Securities Exchange Centre Ltd (SEC) and government-owned corporations are subject to 40 per cent corporate income tax. Fifteen per cent of the dividends distributed by companies and corporations subject to corporate income tax are liable to tax in the hands of the shareholders. Other dividends are tax exempt. Investors in hotels, resorts and other de luxe type, accommodation facilities are entitled to a five-year income tax holiday from the date of commencement of operations.

Tourism industries are granted special concessions such as rebates on customs duty and exemption from sales tax on imported commodities. However, these concessions are mainly for hotel construction, and do not apply to other components of the tourism sector, such as travel agents and trekking. Like the hotels, travel companies also enjoy 5 to 10 years of tax holiday.

An exemption of 50 per cent of the applicable registration fee on the land purchased to build a new hotel or to expand capacity is allowed to hotels registered as public limited companies.

Fund Providers - Nepal Industrial Development Corporation (NIDC)

The NIDC is a wholly owned government development bank. A large portion of its funds come from the World Bank at a concessional rate of interest. The NIDC is by far the largest provider of long-term funds to the hotel industry. The hotels that the NIDC has funded to date include the Yak and Yeti whose very first loan was repaid and now the NIDC also participates as a member of a consortium in financing this hotel's extension. The other hotels drawing on NIDC funds include the Soaltee, Annapurna, Everest, Shangri-la and Kathmandu, all located in Kathmandu.

The interest rate charged by NIDC varies, but it can be as low as four per cent, which makes it very attractive to borrow from NIDC. The debt-equity ratio agreeable to the bank is normally 60:40 but in some cases 50:50. The collateral is normally established by a first mortgage.

Tourism Project

The improvements in tourism-related infrastructure are designed to augment Nepal's foreign exchange earnings by increasing higher segment tourist stays and spending. Activities under the project will be principally in Pokhara, which is planned to be developed as the second major hub of tourist activities after the Kathmandu Valley. The project provides for a package of modest but strategic components of a catalytic nature to facilitate private sector activity, concurrently strengthening public-private sector linkages, providing for institutional development and integrating environmental improvements and poverty alleviation.

Areas of Improvement:

The tourism project covers the following components:

Conservation Area Improvement (Ram Krishna Tole and Ganesh Tole)

- The Conservation Area in Pokhara is an outstanding collection of historic buildings. This project component will comprise about 1 km of infrastructure and environmental improvement within the Conservation Area, together with about 4.5 km of associated footpath, drainage, sewerage and lighting improvements. It will provide basic infrastructure services for the buildings to be restored for tourist and other uses.

- Lakeside Footpath and Garden

  This component will provide a 2 km lakeside footpath and small footbridge. The garden, which will be adjacent to a proposed tourism service centre will display the wide variety of indigenous plants and colourful flowers of the region.

- Sarangkot Access Road

  This component provides for the repair and surfacing of about 5 km of existing unpaved road. There will also be a short length of path from the end of the road to the beginning of existing steps to the summit of Sarangkot, which at 1,700 m, offers spectacular views of the Annapurna range.

- Pokhara Airport Upgrading

  This component provides for essential interim upgrading of the existing airport, which is in poor condition. It covers runway improvement and a new control tower and terminal building.

- Eco-tourism Development and Trekking Circuit

  This component will provide a model for new trekking areas and for the improvement of existing routes. It combines the concept of short or "soft" treks

43

to "sightseeing" tourists with controlled management of trekking numbers. It will provide two 20-30 bed local style model tourist lodges, located, fully serviced campsites, alternative energy sources including two mini-hydro schemes, community development projects and training for local private entrepreneurs in conjunction with HMTTC (Hotel Management and Tourism Training Centre).

Gorkha

- Conservation Area Environmental Improvements

This component provides for environmental improvements in the core area of the historic town of Gorkha adjoining the Lower Palace. It will comprise the provision of 1 km of new or improved road and footpath, water supply, drainage and sanitation facilities, street lights and litter bins. It will include part of the steps leading to the Upper Palace with views of the Manaslu range and the fertile valley below. This component will also provide for the landscaping/site developments of the Lower Palace grounds.

Kathmandu

- Development of the Hotel Management and Tourism Training Centre (HMTTC)

HMTTC was established in 1972 in the 75 year-old Rana Palace which is now in a poor condition. The physical facilities are inadequate and inappropriate for a national hotel training/tourism institution. The works will include the provision of about 2,300 sq m of improved training and teaching facilities, together with a new water supply source, refurbishment of the existing Palace and other buildings and improved access and landscaping. Improvement of the physical facilities. HMTTC is expected to encourage greater involvement of the private sector, the continuation and development of UNDP/ILO support and the development of more advanced training courses.

Finance

For hotel investment, the cost of construction per room is estimated at between $35,000 to $80,000 - excluding land. The payback period according to hoteliers could be about 15 years (WTO Case Study 1993).

U G A N D A

Tourism Demand: 240,000 arrivals in 1996
Tourism Receipts (not including transport): $100 million in 1996
Accommodation Capacity (rooms):   3,673 in 1995
                                (beds):   6,244 in 1995
Tourism Potential:

1. Nature and Wildlife   Rift Valley
2. Nature and Water Falls   Murchison Falls
3. Nature and Forests   Kidepo Valley

Selection of Projects:

Seven projects have been selected and approved by the Project Steering Committee
(Ministry of Tourism, Wildlife & Antiquities, Integrated Tourism Master Plan) using four criteria:

- Importance in plans for priority areas;
- Priority in the development programme;
- Prototypical character;
- Demonstration of new types of project appealing to private investors or aid donors.

The projects are thus a comprehensive and integrated part of the development strategy of
the National Structure Plan:[15]

1. *Safari camp of high standard (Class A)*

This project is designed for Ishasha. At the same time the camp is a general model,
demonstrating a project type new to Uganda.

2. *Adventure Tourist Service Centre*

This Service Centre is a model for development of a new tourism product. The Centre is
designated for Nyakalengija and is also a prototype for similar developments elsewhere.

---

[15] See Government of Uganda, *Integrated Tourism Master Plan* (Kampala, 1993); and Uganda
Investment Authority, *The New Uganda: Trade and Investment Opportunities, Tourism Sector
Profile* (Kampala, 1997).

3. *Safari camp of minimum standard (Class B)*

The camp is planned for Nyakalengija and is complementary to the Adventure Tourist Service Centre. At the same time the project is a prototype for a minimum standard safari camp.

4. *Model Safari lodge (56 beds/28 rooms)*

The project is for a high standard lodge designed for the international travel market. The model could be used for Lake Mburo or Bwindi and also provide useful designed guidelines for similar developments elsewhere (New Paraa lodge/lodge on Victoria Nile).

5. *Nature interpretation and reception centre*

This centre is designed for Mweya as a part of the Plan and can be also regarded as an important prototype for this type of project.

6. *Model block of sanitary facilities*

This project highlights the basic facilities which should be provided wherever large numbers of visitors congregate.

7. *Model border tourist reception and information centre*

The border tourist reception and information centre will meet the need for facilitation, information and a number of services for an important proportion of tourists arriving by land from Kenya.

Investments:

The projections of holiday visitors (Tourism Master Plan) to 2002 are based on an annual growth rate of 15 per cent. The average rate of growth of holiday arrivals from 1991 to 1997 is estimated at 23 per cent. The growth rate for holiday visitors beyond 1997 may be regarded as unduly pessimistic. In this situation, a sudden large influx of tourists faced with little accommodation warrants the expectation of good opportunities in accommodation investments:

Safari Lodges: are basically hotels of a rather special character, which are compatible with a location in a natural environment and are used by visitors embarking on game drives or other open air pursuits. Such lodges are built in tourism zones on the fringes of (or just outside) national parks or other protected areas. Three-star standards or better are to be preferred in particularly choice locations. The optimum size for their purpose is considered to be about 60 beds with a maximum of 100.

The buildings will normally not exceed one storey in height. The safari character is expressed by the use of local and traditional materials. Roofs will be pitched, and thatched, singled or tiled. These design criteria should apply to all new buildings in national parks and protected areas and also to any rebuilding.

Safari Camps: are essentially tented accommodation units using minimum structures built of durable materials. They can be regarded as semi-permanent and can therefore be located in a protected area in places that will not unduly disturb game. The two-bed sleeping units consist of tents similar in size and furnishings to a lodge bedroom protected by a canvas flysheet. Restaurants, bars and dining shelters can be accommodated in marquees or a larger version of the tent shelter. The maximum size for Safari Camps is 40 beds.

Two standards of Safari Camps can be proposed:

Safari Camps (Class A) are equivalent in facilities and services to a good two-three-star lodge with each tent having its own shower, wash-basin and flushing WC. This type of accommodation has proved very popular and these Camps can charge higher tariffs and enjoy better occupancy rates than Safari Lodges.

Safari Camps (Class B) have similar tented sleeping arrangements but are served by separate, communal sanitary facilities at a standard of one shower, wash-basin and flushing WC for men and women for every ten beds. Guests prepare their own food in a communal, fully-equipped, self-catering kitchen adjacent to a dining shelter.

Project Analysis: Types of Project

The preliminary sketch designs of each type of project are costed and their revenues, operational costs, benefits and impacts assessed.

Safari camp (Class A), type of project: Ishasha

A site for this Safari Camp (40 beds) is identified in the Local Development Plan : Ishasha. It would be highly profitable as a private sector investment as indicated by the following measures of feasibility:

-	Net present value:	$1.4 million
-	Internal rate of return:	57.7 per cent
-	Pay back period:	2 years

Safari camp (Class B), Nyakalengija

This project of 40 beds forms part of the complex of tourist facilities shown in the plan for a Tourist Reception and Accommodation Centre located just inside the boundaries of the Rwenzori Mountains National Park beyond Nyakalengija. It would also be very profitable as shown by the following data:

- Net present value: $519,000
- Internal rate of return: 44.6 per cent
- Pay back period: 2.5 years

Model Safari lodge

This lodge of 56 beds could be taken as a model for use in or on the fringes of protected areas and for rebuilding of vandalized lodges such as Mweya and Paraa. The profitability of the project is demonstrated by the following data:

- Net present value: $610,000
- Internal rate of return: 20.1 per cent
- Pay back period: 4.2 years

V A N U A T U

Tourism Demand: 45,000 arrivals in 1996
Tourism Receipts (not including transport): $60 million in 1996
Accommodation Capacity (rooms):   666 in 1995
                          (beds):   1,641 in 1995

Tourism Potential:

1. Seaside tourism   Efate, Espiritu Santo
2. Environment and Volcano   Tanna
3. Marina and Yacht Club   Port Villa

Investments:

The high levels of occupancy that currently prevail and the fact that there are, in reality, only 500 or so hotel rooms in Vanuatu shows that there is an urgent requirement for additional hotel rooms in Vanuatu. The 1995-2000 Tourism Master Plan for the Republic of Vanuatu estimates that by the year 2000, there will be a strong need for more accommodation capacity. With targets projecting an extra 40,000 tourist arrivals per annum by 2000 as against 1994, industry and government will be able to encourage investors to add around 500 rooms of good standard (international three-stars or higher) in resort hotels on stream for business before 2000.

As well as the main need for more rooms in the larger hotel properties, additional rooms in small-scale properties are also required in the five to twenty unit range. At least 100 extra rooms in this category established over the next six years are feasible. Most should be international three-stars or higher, which means a higher standard than most of Vanuatu's existing small-scale properties for tourists. There is also scope for additional rooms at the cheaper end of the tourism sector, such as backpacker hostels. Many tourist destinations around the world are discovering that backpackers might not spend much per night on accommodation, but they usually spend more on all items per visit than other tourists because they tend to stay longer. This tourist segment is too valuable to be ignored.

The three main hotels in Port Villa experienced an annual average room occupancy exceeding 75 per cent during 1993. These levels indicate that the hotels are mostly full during the peak holiday season. However, currently no hotels or resorts in Vanuatu would be classified internationally above four-star standard overall. There are reiterated recommendations from Vanuatu's principal overseas markets that a five-star or deluxe resort in Vanuatu would fill a gap in the present range of accommodation. Precise concepts for a such a five-star or de luxe resort have been investigated in the Master Plan, but a small-size to medium-size property seems appropriate. The best investment opportunities in Vanuatu exist in developing integrated resorts and bungalow resorts.

Investment procedures

The Government of Vanuatu encourages the expansion of the tourist sector. However, the domestic savings base is small, so foreign investment is welcomed but hindered by the lack of access to clearly defined guidelines together with protracted bureaucratic procedures for permits and licences. Specific legislation does not exist for tourism development in Vanuatu. Such incentives as do exist are generally administered through the Government's basic policy on investment.

The major attraction for investment in Vanuatu is its status as a "tax haven", which excludes the imposition of corporate tax, income tax, estate duties and capital gains tax. In addition, the country is free of withholding tax and does not have any treaties or double taxation agreements with other countries. The Minister of Finance may, at his discretion, grant exemption or reduction of customs duty on all or part of any goods imported for tourism development projects. This applies also to extensions of existing developments and is evaluated on a case by case basis for up to three years from the start of the project.[16]

Land lease

There is currently no freehold land system in Vanuatu and, as a result, land can be obtained only on a lease basis. Other than in exceptional circumstances, currently no lease can be granted for a period exceeding 75 Years. It is understood that the Government is considering certain provisions for making freehold land available in urban areas.

---

[16]   See Government of Vanuatu, *Tourism Development Master Plan and Institutional Strengthening of Government Tourism Agencies* (Port Villa, 1995).

Finance

A notable example of an investment vehicle to finance development projects is the Commonwealth Development Corporation's (CDC) investment fund in the South Pacific. The CDC is introducing a system to finance development projects in the South Pacific islands. The objective of the system is to demonstrate that profitable equity investments can be made in companies in the developing world. A $15 million fund will be managed by CDC from Papua New Guinea and Fiji and will be made available for a 10-year period for investments in all economic sectors. This will not be a portfolio fund, but will facilitate direct equity investments in companies. The investment range for each company is between $200,000 and $2 million, but the sum invested must represent a minority stake.

A return-on-investment of 25 per cent is required and funds will be mostly available for company expansion, but also for company start-ups. The initial investors are CDC, the Asian Development Bank (ADB), the European Investment Bank (EIB) and Proparker (France) as well as some regional institutional investors. The success of the venture will encourage private sector investors to contribute to a second round of investment.

Regional tourism development conditions

An analysis of the tourism situation prevailing in countries neighbouring LDCs can reveal opportunities for large tourism demand growth. A review of tourism arrival flows shows that there is a strong growth in tourism arrivals in the selected LDCs indicated in Section III.3 compared with other countries in the same region - for instance, Uganda and Tanzania are progressing at a more rapid rate than Kenya. Tourism receipts flows are also progressing faster in Uganda and Tanzania than in Kenya.

However, when the international tourism receipts of LDCs are compared with those of the other countries in their region, it is clear that all LDCs, with the exception of the Maldives, have an insufficient share of regional receipts. *In contrast to the arrivals and receipts trends, the accommodation capacity trend is not growing at a fast rate in most LDCs.* This confirms that there are potentially important investment opportunities in these countries.

Accommodation capacity is distinctly lower in most of the selected LDCs compared with other countries in their respective regions. Because international tourism demand in these countries is increasing, investment opportunities can be particularly important. However, it should be noted that the average annual occupation rate in hotels and other tourism establishments is often less than 50 per cent and in certain countries just 40 per cent.

Despite great potential, the development of tourism in LDCs today is particularly vulnerable to the vagaries of the international and regional economic situation. For this reason, an active policy designed to strengthen tourism structures by attracting investment in the sector should be pursued.

The returns-on-investment which can be achieved

To attract private investment into tourism development, the following conditions are particularly important:

- **Availability of national and international funding to finance tourism infrastructure and superstructure development**

The tourism sector is a service activity needing investments, particularly hotels. It is not possible to realize sustainable tourism development in LDCs without such investments.

- **Availability of a trained and qualified workforce**

Although labour costs are low, training/skills development should not be neglected. LDCs can increase competitiveness and expand tourism by developing a well-trained workforce, as quality in the sector plays an essential role in the development and positioning of products.

- **Support of public authorities in facilitation, promotion and taxation**

This support plays an essential role in the success of tourism development in LDCs.

III. 4. CONCLUSION

This first analysis of investment opportunities in LDCs suggests that there are good possibilities of attractive returns on investment in many countries. The rate-of-return on tourism investments can be more than 15 per cent, as in the case of Madagascar and Uganda in the examples described earlier in this report. However, these opportunities lie in developing niche tourism products for which a more detailed country-by-country analysis is required. Indeed, it should be noted that, with the exception of the Maldives, the tourism sector accounts for only a small proportion of the GNP in LDCs. Tourism is just emerging in these countries, which can be seen as an advantage. For example, Bangladesh's slogan is: "Come to Bangladesh before the tourists". One could equally say "Come to the LDCs before the tourists". However, developing the tourism sector needs financial and human resources as well as the support of national policies, notably in the areas of taxation and customs treatment.

This report concludes that there are three types of tourism investments that would offer real investment opportunities in most LDCs :

1. International three-star, four-star hotels

These are modern hotels with the technological facilities and the comfort of large, international five-star hotels, but charging tourist lower prices than these luxury hotels. In many LDCs, the choice ranges from a few luxury establishments with very high prices (daily room rates frequently over US$200) to small local hotels, often operating with insufficient services and facilities. Consequently, there is a gap in the market for the international standard hotel charging medium prices that would satisfy both the business and the tourist traveller.

2. Integrated tourism resorts

Tourism development needs the development of accommodation structures that will cater for the needs of tourists while being profitable. Therefore, using local materials as much as possible in conjunction with the imported equipment needed for construction will reduce the cost of investing and favour local firms. Safari Camps in Uganda and Tanzania, for instance, can enjoy profit margins of more than 25 per cent because of the low level of investment needed compared with the construction of a hotel.

3. Small tourism enterprises

The tourism sector is a service sector, and there is room for many small specialized enterprises to complete the range of services offered by the larger firms, and there are opportunities of launching the following businesses in LDCs:

- incoming operations with tour guides;
- internal transport operations with cars and drivers;
- handicrafts with housekeeping services;
- bungalows with housekeeping services.

These small enterprises constitute a network of partners that diversify tourism supply and encourage client loyalty. Selecting the most appropriate tourism investments for each country is essential, but must be based on understanding the stage of development reached in the country, so that any new economic activity that is introduced meets the requirement of sustainable development.

CHAPTER IV

INVESTMENT OPPORTUNITIES IN AGRO-RELATED INDUSTRIES

IV.I. GLOBAL ASSESSMENT OF AGRO-RELATED INDUSTRIES

Ago-related industries broadly comprise industries which use agricultural raw materials as inputs and industries which provide equipment, materials and inputs for agricultural production. The Activities covered are shown in Table 1V.1

**Table IV.1 Share of agro-related branches in
total manufacture value added 1980-1993,**
(Percentage)

	Industrialized countries		Developing countries	
	1980	1993	1980	1993
Food products	10.1	9.9	15.5	14.8
Beverages	2.3	2.0	3.3	3.3
Tobacco	0.7	0.6	2.2	2.1
Textiles	5.0	3.7	9.8	8.1
Wearing apparel	3.0	2.1	3.6	2.9
Leather	0.5	0.3	0.7	0.6
Footwear	0.8	0.5	1.2	0.7
Wood products	2.2	2.1	2.6	2.2
Non metallic minerals	3.0	2.4	4.4	4.1

Source: UNIDO

The share of agro-related industries in the total manufacturing value added (MVA) of industrialized countries and of developing countries as a whole was respectively equivalent to 24 percent and 39 per cent. These numbers show that agro-related industries are declining activities in both groups, while in LDCs, agro-related industries represented in 1995 about 68 per cent of their total MVA. Thus, there seems to be a reallocation of agro related industries in the poorer countries, which have abundance of natural resources and large availability of cheap labour.

There is good potential for the growth of agro-industrial activities in African and Asian LCDs. In the Asian region these industries are likely to be export-oriented, particularly in textiles, clothing, leather and footwear. However, in Africa the growth potential of agro-related industries oriented towards exporting is much more limited, but investment opportunities do exist in respect of domestic demand-oriented food processing and associated labour-intensive activities.

Table IV.1 provides estimates of value added of the agro-industrial activities in 1990 and 1995 of 20 African and 3 Asian LDCs for which data are available. In 1995, the total value added of agro-industries amounted to about $2.5 billion in the African LDCs and to $2.2 billion in the three South Asian LDCs, while the total manufacturing value added (MVA) of the 23 African and Asian LDCs in 1995 was about S7 billion. Thus, the value added by agro-industrial activities in these 23 LDCs accounted for 68 per cent of the total MVA in 1995.

In 1995, gross fixed capital formation in agro-industries amounted to $1.1 billion dollars in eight African LDCs and to nearly a half of that total in Bangladesh and Nepal (table IV.2). Investment levels typically fluctuate wildly in the various LDCs, as illustrated by the extraordinary high shares of Zambia and Nepal in the total gross fixed investment of these ten LDCs in 1995. Major project are few and far between in the eight African LDCs, with the exception of Zambia, and large-scale privatization seems unlikely to develop quickly, except perhaps for breweries in southern and eastern Africa, but the positive growth prospects for agro-industrial activities in these and other African and Asian LDCs should provide a strong stimulus to investors. The industrial activities of 48 LDCs are summarized in table A.1V.1 of the annex to this chapter and indices of manufacturing output in African LDCs for 1990 and 1995 are indicated in table A-2 of this annex.

IV.2. AGRO-INDUSTRIAL DEVELOPMENT PROSPECTS IN SELECTED LDCs

This section presents selected country profiles, indicating investment prospects across agro-related industries, and succinctly highlights the regulatory regime operative in some LDCs focusing specifically on the attractiveness of investing in agro-related industries. In this section, countries are selected on the basis of availability of detailed information on their agro-industry sectors, but also because of good growth potential of these sectors. Particular emphasis is placed on an assessment of the policy environment and macroeconomic policy stance in important countries. Risk assessments are also presented. An attempt is made to identify investment levels and structures of viable projects in agro-industrial branches. Assessing expected rates of return has not been feasible on a systematic basis, although some anecdotal and eclectic evidence is presented. Investment partners with which such projects may be undertaken are identified for some LDCs.

Table IV.2 Total value added and value added
of agro-industrial activities, 1990 and 1995
($ million)

Country	Agro-industries		Total value added
	1990	1995	1995
Sudan	278.0	330.0	405.6
Benin	56.8	66.7	83.0
Burkina Faso	170.5	185.7	216.7
Cape Verde	-	-	26.2
Gambia	8.2	9.0	20.9
Mali	97.4	105.3	131.4
Niger	20.4	21.7	32.4
Togo	63.6	62.0	72.9
Ethiopia (including Eritrea)	385.3	403.8	557.7
Somalia	15.6	15.4	20.0
Uganda	96.9	148.7	185.8
Burundi	98.5	91.4	98.1
Central African Republic	52.0	36.7	43.8
Rwanda	185.8	203.5	278.8
Zaire	24.6	17.4	27.4
Lesotho	58.8	97.2	109.0
Madagascar	106.2	96.0	136.7
Malawi	80.1	73.3	125.4
Tanzania	53.6	57.4	105.2
Zambia	619.6	526.9	780.4
Total African LDCs	2,472.0	2,548.2	3,457.4
Bangladesh	1,125.9	1,683.3	2,606.1
Myanmar	298.9	193.3	522.4
Nepal	220.6	346.1	438.6
Total Asian LDCs	1,645.4	2,222.7	3,567.1
Total LDCs	4,117.4	4,770.8	7,024.4

Source: UNIDO

**Table. IV.3. Gross fixed capital formation in
Agro-industries, selected LDCs, 1990 and 1995
($ million in constant 1990 prices)**

Country	Agro-industries		Total Fixed Capital Formation
	1990	1995	1995
Gambia	0.4[a]	0.6[a]	0.8
Niger	1.0[b]	1.2[b]	12.3
Togo	3.8[c]	3.9[c]	7.5
Ethiopia (including Eritrea)	11.4	11.6	19.4
Central African Republic	7.9[d]	5.8[d]	6.8
Malawi	26.0	26.9	37.4
Tanzania	25.4	32.0	55.8
Zambia	168.6	886.6	1,112.7
Bangladesh	92.9	140.9	282.2
Nepal	190.7	335.9	420.1

Source: UNIDO
Notes a.   International Standard Industrial Classification (ISIC) codes 311, 313, 321, 323, 332 and 369 only.
      b.   ISIC codes 311, 313, 323, 332 and 369 only.
      c.   ISIC codes 311, 313, 322, 324, 331, 332 and 369 only.
      d.   ISIC codes 311, 313, 314, 321, 332 and 369 only.

BANGLADESH

Macroeconomic prospects

Bangladesh has been successful in sustaining macroeconomic stability. Population growth is lower. The country's rice output has increased dramatically. During 1990-1995, GDP growth averaged 4 per cent per year and ESCAP expects it to accelerate to 7 per cent during 1996-2000. GDP growth during 1996 was about 5.5 per cent. Inflation has been kept at a single digit level, averaging 5% in 1990-95, while the current account deficit was roughly equivalent to 3.5 per cent of GDP during the same period.

Structural reform programmes have been in place since the late 1980s. Policy liberalization has brought about a gradual deregulation of the investment and financing regime. A small capital market has been buoyant during most of 1994 and since 1995, with about 200 listings and capitalization approaching $4 billion. Agro-related companies, especially textile firms, are a large segment of the capital market and have generally returned average performances.

FDI inflows have totalled $765 million in 1995 and $865 million in 1996. Portfolio flows are small. There is only one national country fund and investment in it is about $30 million. Bangladesh is also a major recipient of ODA from OECD sources but there are indications that both FDI and ODA flows are levelling off. This could have serious consequences as Bangladesh's domestic investment rate is only about 14 per cent and national savings are even lower. Terms of trade have declined in 1995 and 1996, the trade balance has deteriorated and the takka is expected to fall in value by about 8 per cent this year. ODA inflows amount to some $1.7 billion per year and total external debt now reaches approximately $20 billion. Most long-term publicly guaranteed debt is of a concessional nature and the debt service to export ratio is below 15 per cent. External debt as a proportion of GNP is less than 60 per cent.

The political system remains rather unstable. The two major parties tend to use extra-parliamentary means resulting in potential instability. Bangladesh remains a fragmented and fragile society with more than 50 per cent of the population bordering on the poverty line.

Privatization has slowed. There is major trade union opposition to privatization, especially within the infrastructure, energy and telecommunication sectors. The Government's response has been to invite foreign and domestic private investment into these sectors while maintaining state enterprises that are large employers.

Bangladesh has a stock market located in the capital Dhaka. The Dhaka Securities Exchange experienced high volatility. The Government is reinforcing the prudential and supervisory rules and regulation of the market.

Investments in agro-industries

Agro-industries are among Bangladesh's main manufacturing producers (tables IV.4 and IV.5). In value terms, ready-made garments, jute products, leather, fertilizers, sugar, paper, tea and cement are Bangladesh's main products. Agro-based industries have generally grown at a faster rate than basic metal or metal and machinery industries. The performance of the textile sector, particularly garments and leather has been outstanding. Paper, fisheries and flour milling have also done well as well as fertilizers. There has been a general decline in jute, cotton and vegetable oils.

The garments industry has grown due to Bangladesh's low labour costs. Production comprises mainly cutting, sewing and trimming of general and retail label garments for international subcontractors through about 300 buying houses, located mainly in Bangladesh. They arrange supply of inputs and monitor output quality. They also provide designs and specifications of the technology which is relatively simple. Investment requirements are modest and working capital is largely financed offshore. Investment costs are modest, ranging between $175,000 for small firms to $500,000 for medium firms. A venture capital fund of $100 million for example, could finance between 200 and 500 firms. Finding this number of firms with high growth prospects within the Bangladesh garments industry is realistic.

for example, could finance between 200 and 500 firms. Finding this number of firms with high growth prospects within the Bangladesh garments industry is realistic.

Foreign financing arranged by buyers has played an important role in development of the ready-made garment (RMG) industry. The specially bonded warehouse (SBW) scheme is available to RMG manufacturers to gain access to international capital markets for what would otherwise have been working capital requirements that domestic banks might have found difficult to meet. The industry has also benefited from lower corporate and import taxes. Quota allocations among producers have been efficient, and the industry has enjoyed strong political support.

Even without changing the subcontracting nature of the industry, there is scope for entering more profitable international garment markets. Bangladesh currently has the lowest unit value among the top ten exporters to the United States. Bangladesh exports could play a greater role in the fashion end of the cotton, synthetic and other fabric-based apparel industry. This move has commenced, with the growth in export value at constant prices exceeding the growth in volume. It has been encouraged by importing countries' using import volume rather than value to define quotas and the absence of quotas on higher value apparel.

Policy regime and incentive structure

The Bangladesh policy regime is moderately liberal. Agricultural inputs, especially irrigation equipment and agricultural machinery, are subsidized. Privatization has stalled and, despite the World Banks's explicit linkages of aid to privatization of 15 state enterprises, the present Government may not pursue what is seen as a deeply unpopular policy.

Generous incentives are offered for foreign investment. Under the export processing zones scheme (EPZ), tax havens as well as guarantees and infrastructural facilities are provided to both domestic and foreign investors. Major incentives offered include:

(a)   foreign investment welcomed in all industries except arms, nuclear energy, forestry, security, printing and railways;
(b)   tax holidays granted to new companies for five to seven years;
(c)   generous accelerated depreciation allowances in lieu of tax holidays;
(d)   concessionary duty on imported capital machinery, the highest being for export-oriented industries;
(e)   VAT exemption on capital machinery inputs.

Table IV.4. Bangladesh: Production and value of selected manufactured items, 1990/91-1994/95.

	1990/91	1991/92	1992/93	1993/94	1994/95
Jute manufactures					
Thousand tonnes	434	416	446	421	425
Tk billion	12.9	11.2	11.4	10.3	10.5
Cotton cloth					
Million metres	60	59	45	32	17
Tk billion	1.1	1.3	1.0	0.8	0.4
Cotton yarn					
Million kilogrammes	56	60	61	58	49
Tk billion	6.7	9.5	8.0	6.9	6.3
Ready-made garments					
Million items for export	169	212	259	286	345
Tk billion	21.3	26.2	29.7	34.1	46.1
Leather for export					
Million square metres	10	11	13	15	15
Tk billion	-	5.5	5.7	6.6	7.8
Cement					
Thousand tonnes	275	272	207	324	316
Tk billion	1.0	1.0	0.8	1.2	1.3
Steel ingots					
Thousand tonnes	58	37	7	6	25
Tk billion	710	522	101	75	36
Paper					
Thousand tonnes	90	88	90	90	83
Tk billion	2.6	2.4	2.7	2.8	2.7
Chemical fertilizers					
Thousand tonnes	1,533	1,736	2,051	2,366	2,145
Tk billion	6.4	7.5	9.1	9.7	8.3
Sugar					
Thousand tonnes	246	195	187	221	270
Tk billion	6.8	4.9	4.7	5.7	7.3
Tea					
Thousand tonnes	44	46	49	51	47
Tk billion	2.2	2.2	2.2	2.6	2.0
Shrimps and frog legs					
Thousand tonnes	6.2	6.3	6.2	7.2	8.3
Tk billion	1.3	1.6	1.7	15.	1.7
Cycles					
Number	34,373	16,657	12,965	12,784	13,223
Tk billion	53	31	25	23	23
Motorcycles					
Number	9,918	8,537	8,610	6,136	7,625
Tk billion	400	395	450	338	429
Motor vehicles					
Number	1,481	1,083	807	610	610
Tk billion	474	400	366	338	388
Diesel engines					
Number	2,235	343	103	491	520
Tk billion	124	12	3	32	33
Televisions					
Thousands	57	44	61	77	79
Tk billion	497	407	555	641	748
Dry-cell batteries					
Millions	62	58	58	65	62
Tk billion	562	585	583	647	620

Source: Bangladesh Bureau of Statistics, *Monthly Statistical Bulletin Bangladesh*, published by The Economist Intelligence United Limited 1996, *EIU Country Profile 1996-97*.

Table IV.5. Bangladesh: Indices of manufacturing production
by sector, 1990/1991-1994/1995.
(1980/81 = 100)

	1990/91	1991/92	1992/93	1993/94	1994/95
Food, beverages and tobacco	147	140	135	153	171
Fisheries products	480	513	480	564	645
Flour milling	145	153	189	191	218
Sugar	112	154	93	110	134
Tea	114	97	126	132	121
Vegetable oil and soybeans	113	117	39	58	50
Cigarettes	86	115	73	80	110
Jute, cotton textiles and					
Leather industry	206	2236	273	288	327
Cotton	120	128	124	115	96
Jute	74	71	76	72	72
Garments	6,894	8,646	10,579	11,702	14,079
Leather tanning	166	194	215	244	251
Paper and paper products	200	250	262	297	341
Chemicals, fertilizers, petroleum					
and rubber products	174	200	240	275	282
Pharmaceuticals	98	128	164	188	233
Soap and detergents	110	113	128	144	173
Matches	92	103	115	127	100
Fertilizers	369	417	493	569	516
Paints and varnishes	152	159	174	189	270
Petroleum products	96	90	116	105	121
Non-metallic products	217	189	210	225	215
Glass	88	200	218	211	278
Cement	84	84	63	99	97
Basic metal products	51	39	42	74	127
Re-roll mill products	51	40	45	80	132
Fabricated metal and machinery	134	144	146	150	156
Engines and turbines	89	23	20	25	21
Electrical machinery	128	149	202	202	122
Cable wires	224	255	293	310	459
Motor vehicles	94	65	30	38	69
Motor cycles	169	145	146	104	130
Radio, televisions and telephones	120	92	125	144	145
Total manufacturing	171	189	214	235	262

Source: Bangladesh Bureau of Statistics, *Monthly Statistical Bulletin Bangladesh*, published by The Economist Intelligence Unit Limited 1996, *EIU Country Profile 1996-97*.

Note: International financing may be used as a means for increasing value added and enhancing industry control of marketing channels. Two other industries which could follow in the footsteps of RMG and experience strong growth in Bangladesh are leather and silk.

There are no restrictions on the remittance of profits and dividends. However, expatriate staff can remit only 50 per cent of their salaries. Provisions are made for repatriation of their savings, retirement benefits and personal assets at the time of their return.

Foreign investors are also likely to gain from lowering of corporate tax rates, which are being reduced, as are import controls. Import permits have been abolished but import of textiles is still restricted. The highest rate of import duty is now only 45 per cent. The takka is fully convertible on the current account. Investments in EPZ are especially attractive. Here, import of capital and raw materials is duty free, foreign currency earnings can be retained, and income tax exemptions are extended for a ten-year period.

Major players and institutions related to agro-business

Government and semi-public

- Board of Investment: one-stop agency for obtaining all necessary registrations and approvals for foreign investment including private loans; also coordinates provision of infrastructural and other facilities to foreign investors;

Transnationals in agro-industries:

Reckitt and Coleman, Glaxo Bangladesh Limited, Lever Brothers, Bata Shoe Company, Bangladesh Tobacco Company, Ciba Geigy (insecticides and pesticides), Azmet Bangladesh, As Salam Fabrics, Denudi Tea Company, International Oil Mills, James Finchley, Karnaphuli Fertilizers, Nestle, Noyapara Tea Company, Total Tread, New Zealand Milk Products;

Selected chambers of commerce and industry:

- Federation of Bangladesh Chambers of Commerce and Industry (FBCCI), Federation Bhaban, 60, Motijheel Commercial Area, Dhaka (Telephone: [02] 864680, 864760, 240102-3);
- Metropolitan Chamber of Commerce and Industry (MCCI), Chamber Building, 122-124, Motijheel Commercial Area, Dhaka (Telephone: [02] 230714, 861487-89;)
- Dhaka Chamber of Commerce and Industry (CDDI), Dhaka Chamber Bhaban, 65-66, Motijheel Commercial Area, Dhaka (Telephone: [02] 232693, 232562, 255106);
- Foreign Investors Chambers of Commerce and Industry (FICCI), 4, Motijheel Commercial Area, Dhaka (Telephone: [02] 881240-45);
- Chittagong Chamber of Commerce and Industry (CCCI), Chamber Building, Agrabad Commercial Area, Chittagong (Telephone: [031] 502325, 504117).

Domestic businesses

- Beximco Textiles Limited: textile weaving and finishing;
- Industrial Promotion and Development Company of Bangladesh Limited: development finance;
- Karnaphuli Fertilizer Company Limited: urea and ammonia production;
- Padma Textile Mills Limited: yarn spinning mill;
- United Leasing Company Limited: leasing finance.

MADAGASCAR

Macroeconomic prospects

Madagascar, with a GNP per capital of $ 230 in 1995, is among the poorest countries in the world. The Malagasy economy was in severe crisis throughout the 1980s and early 1990s. Despite faster growth in 1988 and 1989, the annual rate of GDP growth in the 1980s was only 1.1 per cent, less than the population growth. In 1991, strikes and political disturbances led to a sharp fall in GDP and, since then, recovery has been slow, at 1.8 per cent in 1995 and an estimated 2 per cent in 1996. Inflation has decreased considerably, from more than 40 per cent in 1995 to 19 per cent in 1996. The Malagasy franc was allowed to float in 1994, declining in value from Mgfr 1924:$1 to more than Mgfr 4000:$1 but has since stabilized around that level.

After the years of socialism, by 1980, the economy had run into trouble, and the Government signed the first stand-by arrangement with IMF. Several liberalization measures were taken during the following decade with the support of IMF and World Bank, but were interrupted by social unrest in 1991.

In 1994, a range of policies was agreed with IMF and World Bank, including maintenance of a floating exchange rate, reduction of the budget deficit, higher interest rates, introduction of value-added tax, removal of all import prohibitions and liberalization of the vanilla marketing, telecommunications, air transport and petroleum sectors. In August 1996, the IMF and World Bank approved the Government's economic policy framework document for 1997-1999, which aims to build upon the structural adjustment steps that have already been taken during the last three years. The Government aims to diversify from its traditional exports of coffee, vanilla and cloves into textiles, shellfish and tourism. Another objective is the restoration of self-sufficiency in its staple food, rice, which was achieved in 1996 through price incentives and investments in irrigation.

Industrial output has been contracting since 1980. In 1995, the secondary sector contributed only 13.6 per cent of GDP. Agro-industries account for more than 70 per cent of MVA, especially concentrated in food and beverages (25 per cent) and textiles (35 per cent).

Madagascar has had a trade deficit for many years. Its export earnings are very sensitive to fluctuations in the price of coffee and vanilla. Traditionally, current account deficits were financed by borrowing, resulting in a heavy debt burden. After 1981, borrowing was no longer possible and only rescheduling of debt and ODA has maintained the balance of payments, since flows of private investment are negligible.

Investments in agro-industries

Agricultural production has been declining in per capita terms for the last 20 years, mainly due to lack of adequate infrastructure and investment. The World Bank has estimated that diversification and improved productivity could raise output by 40 per cent per year in the short term. With the Government's commitment to expand and diversify agricultural production, there seems to be good scope for development of agro-industries providing inputs to agricultural productivity, such as building materials for irrigation. The staple food is rice, and main crops for export are coffee, vanilla, cloves and cotton.

Livestock resources are important, but Madagascar (due to poor management) exports only a fraction of its EU beef quota under the Lomé Convention. Fish processing offers considerable potential. Currently, half of the catches are made by foreign fleets. Production of prawns has expanded greatly in recent years, due to investments by Japanese firms and the European Investment Bank, and prawns are now one of the country's main exports with excellent prospects for future growth.

Textiles make up the single largest manufacturing sector, an important element being the presence of Mauritian investors who are benefiting from low labour costs. Following the privatization of state-owned firms already started in other sectors, the Government is likely to withdraw from the cotton company HASYMA and the sugar corporation Siramany Malagasy (SIRAMA).

The following are some agro-industrial projects recently identified by UNIDO:

- GROUPE AGRICO is a firm that collects and distributes apples. With 198 employees, it has an annual turnover of $1.1 million and has grown substantially during the last four years. Currently it exports 10 per cent of its production and is interested in raising $700,000 for investment in refrigeration equipment to export to the European market. For this, it will also need a partner with a commercial network already established. The firm is considering expansion of its activities to other fruits, including pears, apricots, pineapple and pok-pok, and to start making juices and marmalades.

- MATRACEM ($250,000 turnover, 100 employees) makes high quality furniture for offices and houses. With a well-trained workforce and equipment in good condition, it is seeking $1.5 million to expand its business in Zone Franche Industrial, for exporting which would create 100 new jobs.

- STEDIC represents several important foreign firms and manufactures matches in Madagascar. It employs 750 people and has an annual turnover of $4.6 million, an excellent knowledge of the Malagasy business and the will to grow and develop. STEDIC is currently interested in the fisheries sector and is looking for a partner to invest $6.15 million in a plant in Morondave, which will produce 900 tonnes of prawns. The national production was 7,567 tonnes in 1994 but is expected to reach 75,000 tonnes annually over the next decade.

- COROI, in joint venture with the French group BIOLANDES, will produce scented plants and essential oils in the Diego-Suares region with a total investment of FFr70 million.

- The Malagasy State, together with the German textile group Engineering Beratungsgesellschaft für die Textilindustrie GmbH (SEDITEX), has relaunched the Majunga Textile Company (SOTEMA) after a year of paralysis due to non-payment of electricity bills. The Government will fund its debts of FFr53 million and has reached an agreement with the electricity company.

- CODAL ($1 million turnover, 65 employees) is a firm that preserves fruits and vegetables, especially green pepper. It is well organized and financially solid and intends to introduce high quality green beans into the French market.

- COJUM ($760,000 turnover, 270 employees) produces lime, fruit juices and mineral water. It does not export at the moment and would like to start selling in Mauritius and Réunion. The company is interested in buying second-hand equipment for manufacturing juice containers.

- LECOFRUIT ($256,000 turnover, 250 employees) already exports green beans to Europe but would like to expand its activities.

- RAMANANDRAIBE ($10 million turnover, 4,000 employees) is an important group exporting coffee, cocoa and vanilla but would like to find a partner in order to expand into the preservation and export of fruit.

- Société d'Expansion d'Appui et de Développement (SEAD) ($1 million turnover, 100 employees) produces seeds, livestock feed and flowers, exporting 75 per cent of its output. It is looking for partners to diversify.

- CHOCOLATERIE ROBERT ($770,000 turnover, 150 employees) produces quality chocolate and would like to produce for another brand, offering participation in its capital.

- BONGOU ($180,000 turnover, 45 employees) produces vinegar, condiments and foie gras, with a good brand name. It wants to start manufacturing ready-prepared meals for export.

- SEVIMA (100 employees) cuts and processes meat. It is state-owned and is awaiting privatization.

- LA HUTTE CANADIENNE ($500,000 turnover, 250 employees) produces foie gras, dairy products and sausages, with a quality image for its products and would like to expand activities to Réunion and Mauritius;

- REFRIGEPECHE-OEST ($4 million turnover, 150 employees) deep freezes prawns and would now like to raise them as well.

A recent study by UNIDO concluded that industrial firms in Madagascar were undercapitalized in 1996. Credit is expensive and difficult to obtain; firms only seek this in extreme circumstances. Lack of legal instruments for protecting investors against exchange rate fluctuations is also significant. Expansion of leasing and joint venture financing is possible and has been recommended to the Malagasy authorities.

Policy regime and incentive structure

The exchange rate regime was drastically reformed in May 1994, allowing the Malagasy franc to fluctuate freely. The value of the currency against the dollar dropped immediately from Mgfr 3000:$1 to stabilize at around Mgfr 4000:$1. At the same time exporters were allowed to hold foreign exchange accounts in Madagascar.

After 1975, foreign investment was not encouraged when several foreign-owned firms were nationalized, but in 1985 a new investment code changed attitudes. Firms investing in Madagascar can deduct 50 per cent of the amount of the investment from the corporate tax. There are no restrictions for the repatriation of profits, wages and pensions, rents, licences or royalties. With the objective of encouraging exports, in 1991, the EPZ (Zone Franche Industrielle) was created. Firms that are exporting are given several fiscal benefits if they locate in the Zone.

Although there have been important improvements in the regulations regarding business relations and investments, the legal framework is still very old and not well adapted to current circumstances, resulting in inefficiencies, delays and lack of rigour in the imposition of sentences.

The main advantages that Madagascar has to offer to an investor are:
- good human resources;
- an international language spoken by the entire population;
- insignificant time difference with Europe, allowing better contacts;
- abundant and cheap labour supply;
- existence of Zone Franche status for export businesses;
- recent liberalization process;
- determination of the Malagasy industry to develop.

Major players and institutions related to agro-business

Public: Ministère des Privatisations.
Private: ARO, the most important insurance company.
Joint-venture firms: - FIARO dependent of ARO;
                       - SITEM, which has participation in small firms;
                       - Groupe Joseph Ramanandraibe;
                       - SOMAPAR, currently in the process of privatization.

MOZAMBIQUE

Macroeconomic prospects

Since the restoration of peace in 1992 and elections in 1994, the political situation in Mozambique has improved markedly, and the role of government in the economy has been steadily reduced. With considerable help from donor countries, the massive task of rehabilitating the country's infrastructure is beginning to show results. Mozambique is, meanwhile, forging new bilateral relationships with South Africa, Zimbabwe and other countries in the region, which serve to expand market opportunities for businesses located in Mozambique.

During 1994-1996, total concessional credit amounted to roughly $1.2 billion as part of an economic rehabilitation loan in response to wide ranging reforms introduced since the end of the civil war in 1992. The reforms seem to have started producing results as GDP is estimated to have grown by 6 per cent in 1996. During 1996, commodity exports rose by 24 per cent and the rate of inflation fell from 54 per cent in 1995 to slightly more than 20 per cent.

The Food and Agriculture Organization (FAO) and World Food Programme (WFP) have predicted a 1.3 million tonne grain harvest for 1996. This estimate, which is 25 per cent higher than 1995 output, is based on a survey conducted by the two organizations. WFP has, however, warned of the difficulties in moving crops from food-surplus to food-deficit areas due to the bad state of the country's roads and ports. The largest surpluses are in the far north, whereas the south remains in deficit. Moving large quantities of grain is a logistical and financial problem.

In response to improving economic conditions, IDA has approved a $100 million credit to support the Government's economic recovery programme, which aims at sustaining growth and reducing poverty. This credit, the fifth to the country, will support reforms to stabilize the economy. The most critical reforms supported by the credit include the privatization of the two state-owned banks and the private contracting of the operations and management of Maputo port and connecting railway. In addition, household surveys will be carried out to assess how the liberalization of the cashew industry will affect small-scale farmers and women.

Private sector development is central to the economic recovery strategy, so the Government plans to improve and simplify legal and regulatory frameworks as well as the tax system, to support private sector growth. These reforms are aimed at boosting exports, strengthening the competitive edge of domestic products and services and the Government's revenue base.

A central problem in assessing Mozambique's economic performance is the wide variation in official statistics. Nevertheless, progress made in 1995 and 1996 is not in doubt. GDP fluctuates with agricultural performance, and both 1995 and 1996 were relatively drought-free. The recovery is, therefore, fragile. The diversification of the structure of production, especially the growth of industry and transport, are crucially important to ensure long-term recovery.

Total external debt exceeded $5.5 billion, representing more than 440 per cent of GNP, although, following the new ESAF, reschedulings and cancellations will lighten this burden. The budget deficit to GDP ratio has been reduced to under 5 per cent in 1995.

Exports are dominated by primary commodities, although even these have performed badly since the late 1970s, due to poor supply conditions generated by the effects of the war, unsuitable government policies and world market conditions. Fish accounts for the largest percentage of total exports as the long coastline escaped the worst of the fighting. Export earnings from shrimp and lobster comprised 45 per cent of total earnings in 1995, while cotton made up nearly 12 per cent and cashews 5.6 per cent. Mozambican exports face two key challenges: to expand primary commodity exports and related processed products, such as cotton and cashews, and to diversify into manufacturing and mineral exports. Cashew exports were on the rise in 1996, based on a strong crop, improved prices paid to growers and better performance by privatized processing firms.

In the long term, it is possible that Mozambique could begin to export food to South Africa, where shortfalls in domestic supply are anticipated within the next decade. Increasing food exports to the Southern African region must involve a higher degree of processing. Southern African countries already account for over 30 per cent of Mozambican exports.

A significant improvement in economic performance is expected and GDP growth in 1997 would be around 6 per cent. This was, of course, conditional on Mozambique's receiving concessional debt forgiveness treatment from the bilateral donors and multilateral institutions. Mozambique was classified among the unsustainable highly indebted poor countries.

The political situation remains unsettled with the main opposition party expressing dissatisfaction with the results of the 1994 elections and not co-opted into a national government. There is a serious law-and-order problem.

Economic instability arises due to the prevalence of extreme poverty exacerbated by the breakdown of the road and transport infrastructure, which makes moving food from grain-surplus areas in the North to the grain-deficit regions extremely difficult. The liberalization programme has had no visible impact on poverty and has contributed to an upsurge in unemployment. The national trade union movement has strongly opposed the structural adjustment reforms. The union movement is, however, politically weak. The local business community has expressed resentment with regard to the tight monetary policy pursued since 1994. Criticism of the Government's divestiture and privatization programmes has also been growing.

Investment in agro-industries

Agriculture is the most important economic sector. Although agricultural production has been rising since 1994, with much of the country's farming areas sparsely irrigated and dependent on rainfall, frequent fluctuations cannot be ruled out. Nevertheless, Mozambique was self-sufficient in maize in both 1995 and 1996. Rice production has fallen but the most important cash crops - cotton and cashews - have done well, as have sugar cane and copra.

The annex tables A.IV.3 to A.IV.8 illustrate the importance of agro-related industries to the Mozambican economy. Adding value by processing cotton, copra, cashew nuts, sugar, sisal and horticultural products is an immediately attractive option compared with development of the country's ample mineral resources. The latter requires much higher levels of investment while the gestation period for development of agro-related industries is also likely to be significantly shorter than for minerals.

The industrial sector suffered a significant loss of capacity during the civil war. Major factories are now concentrated on cotton ginning, textiles, clothing and cashew processing but need considerable new capital investment. Investment growth can be spurred as can the development of the transport sector. Since the early 1990s, ports and transport routes have undergone something of a renaissance. The main focus of the transport sector is the vital link between Maputo and the industrial core of South Africa, known as the Maputo Trade and Development Corridor.

There are good prospects of Mozambique becoming an important exporter of food (including food manufactures) to Southern Africa, particularly South Africa. This would require increased processing, not just of existing cash crops but also of maize, horticultural products and beans. Processing of maize is particularly important since rice production is declining and Mozambique cannot afford to spend scarce foreign exchange on grain imports. Moreover, there has been something of a maize revolution in southern Africa, with many drought-resistant maize varieties having been developed. Processing maize increases its acceptability as a substitute for rice and wheat in urban markets. Mozambique has the potential to develop into a major maize producing and processing centre serving much of southern Africa.

Mozambique's industrial potential is illustrated by the fact that, before the civil war, the country had one of the most diversified industrial sectors in sub-Saharan Africa. Since 1996 there has been a dramatic increase in production of food manufacturing, beverages, wood products and cement.

Currently, it is estimated that more than half of MVA is generated in agro-industrial branches. The market output of both cash and food crops has been growing rapidly since 1992, auguring well for agro-industries. Fishing has become an important source of foreign exchange earnings, and fish processing can and should be developed rapidly. Shrimp production rose by 14 per cent in 1995 and an estimated 20 per cent in 1996. Shrimp are now the leading export commodity, having accounted for 44 per cent of export earnings in dollar terms in 1995. The sustainable annual fish catch is estimated at around 500,000 tonnes, mostly made up of anchovy or mackerel although shrimp and prawns account for 14,000 tonnes. Mozambique's fishing fleet is limited, but there are a number of joint ventures and direct licensing schemes with Japanese, Spanish, Portuguese and South African fishing firms. The European Union (EU) has an agreement with Mozambique to catch 20,000 tonnes of fish and shellfish per year in return for a grant of $35.2 million. Japan has granted Mozambique $5 million to survey unexplored areas in the 200 nautical-mile zone off the Mozambican coast. EU is committed to providing assistance for increasing domestic fish processing from catch landed by foreign vessels. This represents yet another area in which ODA and private financing can be profitably linked.

Between 1985 and 1996 some $600 million were invested in Mozambique, over a half of this during the last three years. Of this total, $360 million was foreign direct investment, almost a half during 1993-1996. The United Kingdom and Portugal are the biggest foreign investors, accounting for a half of all foreign investment, South Africa invests about 20 per cent and the United States 5 per cent. Total foreign accumulated direct investment since 1985 is $363 million, of which $267 million are still active. The United States' interest has been growing. For example, according to African Economic Digest (AED), a major United States agro-business firm is currently negotiating to buy a state-owned flour mill in Beira under the privatization programme.

Policy regime and incentives

The signing of an agreement between South Africa and Mozambique to develop the Maputo Development Corridor, linking Maputo with Witbank has generated widespread investor interest. The environment for foreign investment is favourable.

Generally, the legislation does not make distinctions based on investor origin. However, some general restrictions on profit repatriation do exist, and an investment in export processing zones requires at least 26 per cent local participation. Access to foreign exchange has been significantly liberalized over the past few years, but availability of foreign exchange is not always assured. Foreign exchange retention accounts are permitted for as much as 65 per cent of foreign exchange earnings without formal justification. Under new exchange regulations being formulated, this should become 100 per cent during 1997. Although nationalization is a theoretical possibility, when deemed absolutely necessary for reasons of national interest or public health and order, there has been no significant case of nationalization since the new constitution was adopted in 1990.

The judicial system is generally weak and ineffective in resolving commercial disputes. For this reason, most disputes go unresolved or are settled by the parties concerned. The size of the business community is small enough so that a damaged reputation from a commercial dispute or illegal activity can also damage business. Specific performance requirements are built into management contracts and, sometimes into sale contracts of privatized entities. Although these contracts have not generally been monitored for compliance, the situation is changing. Various tax incentives are available according to the region of the country and the nature of the investment concerned, usually between a 50 and 80 per cent reduction in industrial contribution tax and supplementary tax. Customs exemptions are possible for the importation of capital equipment and raw materials. To qualify, a minimum investment of $50,000 is required. In addition, legislation supports the creation of duty-free manufacturing zones.

Private ownership is protected under law, but outright land ownership is disallowed. Instead, land-use concessions are granted by the Government for periods of 50 years with an option to renew. Concessions serve as proxies for land titles. The lack of a title, however, makes it extremely difficult for local businesses to obtain financing secured by collateral. Confusion among concessioning authorities - ministries, provincial governorates and local districts - exacerbates the situation. New land tenure legislation is being formulated, but outright ownership does not appear to be imminent. Key areas to watch are whether the new legislation provides for the clear determination of a concessioning authority, a mechanism for third party transfer and effective dispute resolution. Apart from land, the law guarantees the security and legal protection of property, including industrial property rights.

New regulations governing the Centre for Investment Promotion (CIP) have made the investment approval process automatic within ten days if no objections are voiced by the relevant ministries, provincial governorates, in the case of investments less than $100,000, or the Minister of Planning and Finance, in the case of investments less than $100 million. The Council of Ministers must review investments of more than $100 million and investments involving large tracts of land, defined as 5,000 hectares for agriculture and 10,000 hectares for livestock or forestry activities. The Council has 17 working days to voice an objection before automatic approval but, in practice, the automatic nature of the process has yet to make itself felt.

Most investment in industry is in agro-related branches (annex table A.IV.8), being particularly strong since 1992. From June 1995 to June 1996, CIP approved 260 new investment projects worth $270 million, most of them in agro-related branches. An Industrial Free Zone and a capital market are in process of establishment. Financial services are offered by both domestic and foreign banks. There are two domestic commercial banks, Banco Comercial de Mozambique (BPD) and Banco Polular de Desenvolumento (BCM). Foreign banks were allowed to invest in Mozambican financial institutions in 1994 when interest rates were deregulated, and in 1995 commercial activities of the central bank were assumed by BCM.

In 1996, the Government privatized BCM and plans were afoot for the divestiture of the BPD, scheduled for early 1997. Portuguese interest in BPD and other Mozambican banks has been strong. In July 1996, 51 per cent of the joint stock of the BCM was sold to a group of foreign investors, including Banco Mello, Uniao do Bancos Portugueses (UBP), National Merchant Bank of Zimbabwe and the Mozambican insurance company Impar. A total of 51 per cent of the shares of BCM are held by foreign investors. The Government intends to retain 51 per cent of the BPD's shares.

Before 1992, Banco Standard Totta de Mozambique (BSTM) was the only private bank operating in the country. It has since been joined by Banco Português do Atlántico (BPA), Banco de Fomento e Exterior (BFE) and Banco International de Mozambique (BIM), the main shareholder of which is the Banco Comercial Português (BCP).

TANZANIA

Macroeconomic prospects

The economy has been growing at an annual average rate of about 3.5 per cent per year during 1994-1996. In early 1997 the IMF extended a new ESAF loan worth $234 million, amounting to an international official approval of the macroeconomic stance of the current Government. The last IMF programme in Tanzania came to a grinding halt in 1992, and negotiations for its extension were curtailed in late 1994 following a massive tax and corruption scandal.

While the resource base is extensive - Tanzania being one of Africa's largest countries in terms of population and natural resource endowment - the current account deficit is a continuing problem for the government authorities, amounting to 17.5 per cent of GDP 1995. Despite a reduction of the budget deficit to around 3 per cent of GDP in 1995, inflation rate remained high, exceeding 30 per cent in 1995.

The Dar es Salaam Stock Exchange (DSE) is being established and is expected to open its doors in 1997. This opening has been postponed several times since July 1996. If the DSE is to be a success, the availability of securities is crucial. So far, attention has been devoted to shares in parastatals, currently being privatized, as well as some companies in the private sector. The Government is considering a proposal made by the Capital Market Security Authority (CMSA) to float some 25 per cent of its shares, in the companies being divested to Tanzanian nationals. However, many state companies that are being divested do not qualify for listing. To qualify for listing, a firm must have a good five-year track record and allow for wide ownership and the ability to transfer shares.

According to the CMSA, Tanzania Cigarettes Company and Tanzania Breweries Company, both recently privatized firms, qualify for a DSE listing. Shares offerings will be made out of equity held by the Government. Equities held by the CDC and IFC might also be considered with CMSA permission. Other agro-industrial companies that may be listed include East Urambara Tea, Kilombero Valley Tea, Mushi Leather Industries, Mafundi Tea Company, Tanzania Sisal Spinning and Tanzania Breeder and Seed Mills.

DSE is to be modelled on the Nairobi Stock Exchange (NSE). Exploratory talks have been initiated with NSE officials with the ultimate objective to integrate share trading throughout the region. Such integration was recommended at the conference of the African Stock Exchange Association (ASEA) in Mauritius in 1996.

According to a USAID study conducted in 1996, the lag between lodging of investment applications and business take-off in Tanzania was between 545 and 1,095 days. The Government has taken steps to reduce this, privatized some 130 of the approximately 380 state enterprises, and improved efficiency within the public sector.

Initiated in the 1980s, financial restructuring picked up pace in 1991 with the enactment of the Financial Institutions and Banking Act by the Tanzanian Parliament. This was followed by the Foreign Exchange Act which allowed for the relaxation of most foreign currency regulations. It was during this period that the creation of private banks and bureaux de change came into effect. To date the country has seen the establishment of more than 20 bureaux de change and several foreign banks, Standard Chartered, Meridian BIAO, CitiBank, First Adili Bank, Euro African Bank and Trust Bank.

Other reforms include auctioning of foreign currency, issuance of treasury bills and sale of shares of the national bank. Six financial institutions are in a process of restructuring. They include the National Bank of Commerce (NBC), Cooperative and Rural Development Bank, Tanzania Investment Bank and Tanzania Postal Office Savings Bank. Others are Tanganyika Development Finance Company and the People's Bank of Zanzibar.

Investment in agro-industries

The manufacturing sector's share of GDP is only about 8 per cent, making the Tanzanian manufacturing sector among the smallest in Southern Africa, measured in terms of current dollars. There was a long and sustained economic downturn from 1986 to 1994. Manufacturing, however, accounts for more than 15 per cent of export earnings. If semi-manufactures are included, the export share of the manufacturing sector increases to 27 per cent in 1995. In 1980 this share had been as high as 50 per cent. Food manufacturing, textiles, leather, wood and paper products account for about 55 per cent of MVA in a typical year. Textiles and paper products are export-oriented branches with export to output ratio exceeding 30 per cent. During the period 1990-1997, industrial policy favoured the agro-processing branches (table IV.6).

During 1995-1997, foreign investments were made in the following agro-industrial projects:

- In November 1995, Tanzania Breweries - supported by South African Breweries - began production at a new $27 million plant in Mwanza, supplementing existing operations in Dar es Salaam and Arusha in a bid to double 1994 output to 8.25 million cases a year.

- Capital Breweries, a subsidiary of JV Group, is converting an old Pepsi bottling plant in Dodoma to produce bottled beer and, in 1996, went into brewing at an adjacent plant. It is also relying on imports from Kenya Breweries, having obtained a $2 million line of finance from PTA Bank.

Table IV.6. Tanzania: Production of selected products, 1994-96

Product	Unit of measure	Attainable capacity	Production 1994	Production 1995	Projected production 1996
Beer	Million crates	16.80	4.60	7.10	10.43
Chibuku	Million litres	22.20	18.60	11.50	14.09
Cigarettes	Billions	5.90	3.60	3.80	4.44
Konyagi	Cartons	2,500,000.00	200,823.00	224,007.00	250,000.00
Soft drinks	Million crates	38.28	10.10	11.10	11.96
Cooking oil	Tonnes	52,000.00	22,622.00	28,190.00	31,820.00
Textiles	Million metres	198.00	41.70	37.70	67.00
Blankets	Millions	2.50	0.55	0.59	0.75
Yams	Tonnes	11,200.00	1,870.00	1,900.00	5,200.00
Bags (gunny)	Millions	37.50	3.70	4.40	21.50
Canvas	Million metres	6.00	3.30	2.80	4.50
Fishnets	Tonnes	534.00	214.00	207.00	330.00
Leather	Million square feet	30.00	0.10	2.30	9.50
Paper	Tonnes	79,000.00	16,763.00	17,200.00	11,200.00
Printing ink	Tonnes	220.00	1,050.00	1,860.00	15.00
Paper packages	Tonnes	37,200.00	8,257.00	8,180.00	11,200.00
Hand hoes	Number	-	268,868.00	91,632.00	55,000.00
Matchets	Number	-	43,000.00	21,194.00	10,000.00
Ploughs	Number	40,000.00	6,000.00	7,214.00	15,000.00

Source: UNIDO.

- Zanzibar's edible oils plant, at the Amaan Free Trade Zone industrial complex, is to start production after completion of rehabilitation. Production was planned to start in November 1996. Work on rehabilitating the plant, which remained idle for nearly 15 years after installation of machinery, was under way for more than two years after it came under joint ownership of the Government and Al-Ghurair enterprises of the United Arab Emirates. The Dubai company took 80 per cent of the shares while the Zanzibar Government settled for the remaining 20 per cent. The plant is to operate 24 hours daily and import most of its raw materials. Initial daily production will be 50 tonnes, and by-products will be sold to local soap manufacturers.

- A special programme to raise food production was launched in low-income food deficit districts in the 1995-1996 season. Pilot projects are operating in Morogoro and Dodoma regions to grow maize and rice intensively, which have traditionally been imported. The projects aim to raise maize production per hectare from the present one tonne to five tonnes and for rice from two tonnes to six tonnes.

- A prawn fishing project was launched in the Rufiji delta in 1997 on a 600 hectare farm. The project is intended to fish prawns for export. Prawn fisheries have developed into a profitable trade in Tanzania, and the main centres are at Bagamoyo and Rufiji, where wild prawns exclusively are exploited. Exports of prawns are estimated at between 1,000 and 1,500 tonnes per year. Economically important species are prawns, smaller shrimp, catfish, sharks, octopus, sea-cucumber, sanje and chewa. Prawns are either sold fresh to collectors and traders in ice boxes or smoked. Current major world markets are Japan and the United States, with a much smaller share consumed in Europe. Countries in the European Union imported 1,039 tonnes of prawns from Tanzania in 1994.

- The Capital Brewery Limited (CBL) started bottling Kenyan-made beer under licence in a bid to stem the tide of South African imports to the region and take advantage of high demand in Tanzania, raising Tanzania's overall annual beer production capacity to 10.1 million crates. The Executive Chairman of the JV Group, which owns Capital Breweries, said in 1996 that the $35 million CBS plant, which is expected to employ 500 people, will produce 1.6 million crates of Kenyan beer brands per year. Recent market surveys indicate that annual demand for beer in Tanzania stands at 20 million crates. The prices of CBL bottled Kenyan beer "won't be much different from those of Tanzania Breweries Limited". The second phase, to last 12 months, will consist of construction and equipping of the brewing section for an initial capacity of another 1.6 million crates per year, thus doubling production to 3.2 million crates. The third phase will cover the construction of another bottling plant in Mbeya, in southern Tanzania, which is expected to realize the company's production target of 6.4 million crates per year by late 1998. Currently, CBL is one among more than 12 agents licensed to distribute Kenyan beer. Some 5 million crates of Kenyan beer are imported into the country annually and CBL's share is some 1 million crates.

Tanzania's first international investors forum organized by the Tanzanian Ministry of Industry and Trade, UNDP and UNIDO, was held in November 1996. The Dar es Salaam Forum attracted some 464 participants, including 264 foreign investors from 44 countries. International mobilization work was done through the UNIDO network. The highest number of delegates came from India (34) followed by the United Kingdom (20), Sweden (29), Canada (21), Kenya (18), Lebanon (16), South Africa (15) and the United States (13). Some 168 investment projects in agro-allied, manufacturing, mining and tourism industries, worth more than $1 billion, were on offer and a total of 71 transfer of technology requirements were presented by local entrepreneurs.

By the conclusion of the four-day Forum, four contracts and 75 letters of intent had been signed covering investment projects worth $786 million. A list of project proposals is presented in table IV.6 showing the sectoral distribution of letters of intent signed at the Forum.

CDC manages a small venture capital fund, the Tanzania Venture Capital Fund. CDC has an equity stake of 33 per cent, its own investments amounting to some £1.7 million. The Fund finances small and medium sized companies and has also provided a loan of £2 million to the Tanzanian Development Finance Corporation, in which it has a 26 per cent stake. Other agro-businesses financed by CDC include:

- Chrismill Farms: Pineapple processing (20 per cent equity stake, £142,000 loan);
- East Usamdara Tea Factories: 60 per cent stake, loan worth £7.1 million;
- Tanganyika Wattle: Tanning, timber, tea factory (84 per cent stake, loan of £14.9 million;
- Tanzania Seed Company: 38 per cent equity stake.

With the exception of Chrismill Farms, all others are CDC managed companies. CDC also has a 33 per cent stake in an equity management company.

IFC has commitments in a small number of agro-businesses amounting to less than $10 million. IFC is expected to play a major role in the development of DSE. There is also scope for identifying large-scale grain milling and fertilizer projects that could be financed by ODA and IFC funds with the objective of promoting food security. These could provide opportunities for attracting portfolio investment.

Policy regime and incentives

Tanzania now has one of the most liberal investment regimes in Africa. Foreign investment is guaranteed by domestic legislation, bilateral agreements and international agencies such as MIGA. There are no controls on remittances, and the shilling is fully convertible on the current account. A summary of new investment-related policies is presented in table IV. 8.

The Tanzanian Government has created an EPZ and has developed an attractive investment package, including full foreign ownership of businesses, no duty on goods destined for export and exemption from import or sales tax on machinery, equipment, spare parts, raw materials and supplies for investment within the EPZ. Other incentives include a ten-year tax holiday on dividends and, thereafter, a 10 per cent withholding tax as well as exemption from income taxes for a ten-year initial period on dividends, interest
on shares, loans and any other type of income received by the investor. There are no exchange control restrictions on export proceeds, business expenses and foreign capital transactions. Zanzibar, under World Trade Organization regulations, is quota-free for export of garments to the United States and Europe.

Major players and institutions related to agro-business

- Investment Promotion Centre: one-stop agency of business coordination and investment facilitation;
- Ministry of Industry and Trade;
- Tanzania Bureau of Standards;
- Dar es Salaam Stock Exchange;
- Centre for Agricultural Mechanization;
- Small Industries Development Organization;
- Bank of Tanzania;
- National Bank of Commerce;
- Cooperative and Rural Development Bank (partly privatized);

- Meridian BIAC (taken over by Stanbic in 1995);
- Standard Chartered;
- First Adili Bank (Tanzanian private sector);
- Trust Bank;
- Euro African Bank;
- Tanzania Investment Bank;
- Tanganyika Development Finance Limited;
- The People's Bank of Zanzibar.

In 1997 there were 23 parastatals on offer in Tanzania for privatization (table (IV.9).

Table IV.7. Tanzanian Investors' Forum 1996:
Sectoral distribution of letters of intent

Sector	Number of letters of intent	Value ($ million)
Agro-industries	16	15.83
Manufacturing (including textiles, wearing apparel, leather, wood products and paper)	41	36.58
Tourism	6	76.30
Mining	25	198.38
Infrastructure	2	458.00
Total	90	785.09

Source: UNIDO.

Table IV.8.
Tanzania: Summary of new investment-related policies

Policy	Modality
Public-private sector coordination mechanism	Establishment of the National Business Council
Industrial policy	New industrial policy to guide investment outlays over the next 25 years
Investment policy	Revised and transparent investment policy simplifying approvals and award of investment incentives into the National Insestment Promotion Protection Act 1990 to be revised accordingly
Tanzania Investment Faciliatator	Establishment of an autonomous investment authority to operate as an one-stop agency for promotion, appraisal, approvaland effective implementation of investment projects, facilitation of land conveyance and provision of permits and utilities
Tax policy	Establishment of the Tanzania Revenue Authority, simplification and rationalization of tax regime including customs tariff and tax collection
Financial policy	Establishment of a capital market and security authority including a stock exchange
Land policy	New land policy which guarantees legal provisions, draws the guidelines for granting long-term leasehold to investors and ensures land property rights as basis for collateral
Immigration law	Rationalization and facilitation of immigration formalities, prompt provision of long-term work permits, and removal of visa requirements for citizens of countries of strategic investment and trade importance
Labour law	Under review in consonance with market economy
Export processing zones	Establishment of export processing zones (EPZs) and Tanzania Export Processing Zone Authority (TEPZA)
Privatization policy	Creation of the Privatization Trust Fund
Import-export policy	Improvement of export shipping procedures and overhauling and streamlining of import procedures

Source: Economist Intelligence Unit.

Table IV.9.
Tanzania: List of industrial parastatals on offer for privatization in 1997

Name of parastatal or enterprise	Final products	Status
Tanzania Breweries Limited (TBL)	Beer	Share sale majority Shareholding by M/S Indol of South Africa
Mwanza Breweries	Beer	See TBL
Southern Paper Mill (SPM)	Ground wood, bleached kraft, pulp, newsprint, writing paper, sack wrapping, liner, fluting	Share sale, awaiting investors
Ubungo Farm Implements	Ploughs, wheelbarrows, hand hoes, machetes, shears, garden tools	Negotiations in progress
Mbeya Farm Implements (ZZK	See Ubungo Farm Implements	Share sale, awaiting investors
Trailers and Lowloaders Manufacturing Company	Tractors, low loaders investors	Share sale, awaiting
Tanzania Tractor Manufacturing Company	Tractors	Asset sale, most current assets sold, interest in leasing (TRAMA) factory
Moshi Hand Tools - SIDO	Hand tools	Share sale, MEBO
Mbey Textile Mills	Textiles	Share sale advertised, TEXPROJECT of Germany has shown interest, no proposals offered
Morogoro Polyester Textile Mills	Textiles, yarn	Share sale, Republic of Korea memorandum of understanding
Tabora Textile Mills	Yarn	Share sale, awaiting investors
Ubungo Spinning Mill	Yarn	Lease or sale, awaiting investors
Tanzania Bag Corporation	Sisal bags	Share sale, awaiting investors
Ubungo Garments	Garments	Asset sale sold to VMB Investments, Limited of Tanzania, 100 per cent
Friendship Textile Mills (URAFIKI)	Textiles	Share sale to Chinese Dique Textile Company
Mwanza Tanneries	Leather	Share sale, completed 60 per cent to African Trade Development, Limited
Morogoro Tanneries	Leather	Share sale, completed 55 per cent African Trade Development Company Limited,
Tanzania Tanneries,	Leather	Share sale, completed 75 per cent to Industrial Promotion Services Limited
Morogoro Canvas Mills	Canvas	Share sale, awaiting investors
Tanzania Shoe Company Limited (BORA)	Shoes	Share sale to Nas Hauliers Limited, sale agreement signed
Morogoro Leather Goods	Leather goods	Share sale, awaiting investors
Tanga Cement Company	Cement	Share sale, sale agreement signed with Holderbank of Switzerland
Tanzania Portland Cement Company	Cement	Share sale, partial privatization, further privatization under way

Source: Ministry of Industries and Trade, *PSRC Monthly Reporting System,* March 1996.

T O G O

Macroeconomic prospects

Agriculture is the main occupation in Togo employing 70 per cent of the population. Other than food crops there is production of coffee, cocoa and cotton for national consumption and export. Phosphate mining is another major source of foreign exchange. Manufacturing accounts for only 7 per cent of GDP. The IMF has been advising Togo on stabilization measures since 1979 when the ambitious inward-oriented programme for industrialization faltered. A series of stand-by credits, debt-reschedulings and structural adjustment loans followed. Privatization has been one of the priorities and, since 1985, the State has disposed of most of its potentially profitable companies.

GDP grew by an average of 4 per cent per year in the period 1970-1980, and by 1.4 per cent annually in the period 1980-1992, which is below the rate of population growth. In this period, GDP per capita has been falling by an annual average rate of 1.8 per cent. During the last decade, GDP growth has been very volatile. In 1988 and 1989, a sharp rise in phosphate rock production increased GDP growth substantially. Then came a period of stagnation and decline, mainly caused by political turmoil, leading to a long general strike in 1992-1993. A recovery has occurred since 1994, as the political situation stabilized and currency devaluation and cotton and coffee prices boosted export earnings.

Togo's currency is the franc de la Communauté financière africaine (CFA franc), pegged to the French franc. In January 1994, the CFA franc was devalued the by 50 per cent, falling from CFAfr 50:Ffr1, which had been unchanged for 46 years, to a new one of CFAfr100:FFr 1. Devaluation was expected to restore competitiveness in these countries and to promote growth through increasing exports.

Investment in agro-industries

Agriculture, together with forestry and fishing, accounted for nearly a half of Togo's GDP in 1993. Self-sufficiency in foodstuffs has practically been achieved, the major food crops being maize, yam, millet sorghum and cassava. The political crisis of the early 1990s devastated the agricultural market system, and climate variations are a further problem.

The main cash crops are coffee, cocoa and cotton, which have increased their share in recent years. Production in all of them has fluctuated a great deal recently, due in part to government pricing policies, but mainly because of political troubles that have disrupted marketing channels diverting much of the production into unofficial trade. Livestock, forestry and fishing resources are of little importance.

The manufacturing sector accounted for 17 per cent of GDP in 1993, before the strikes of that year reduced production by an estimated 42 per cent. In the 1970s the commodities boom allowed the Government to direct many export earnings into a major industrialization drive. Persistent losses led to the closure of most of these industries in the 1980s, although the textiles factories have reopened under US-South Korean (Republic of Korea) joint ownership. According to UNIDO estimates, nearly 80 per cent of MVA comes from agro-industries, most of it from the food manufacturing and beverages branches.

In 1996, a new 50,000 tonne-capacity cotton ginning factory was opened. The $13.7 million investment was a joint venture between the Geneva-based Group l'Aiglon, Société Togolaise de Coton, Office des Produits Agricole de Togo and private shareholders who own a 37 per cent stake. The total cotton ginning capacity is now 150,000 tonnes annually, increased from 4,000 tonnes in 1970.

The Government plans to further develop its privatization plans, and it will keep holdings in only 10 of 74 firms considered to be strategic. The following are some agro-industrial projects identified by UNIDO for which the Government is seeking foreign investment:

- Construction in Atakpamé, in the plains, of a **yam processing unit** for flour production will be particularly important, because of the considerable variation in the price of yams during the course of a year. The required investment is CFAfr 220 million, of which CFAfr 190 million will be in foreign currency ($630,000). The plant will produce 400-500 tonnes annually buying yams from neighbouring regions that have surpluses.

- Construction in Kara, North Togo, of a **plant to transform sorghum** will produce a substance very close to rice, for which there is a growing urban demand and of which the production is declining. It will be able to process up to 2,500 tonnes annually and will require an investment of CFAfr126.5 million, of which CFAfr 92.5 million will be in foreign currency ($310,000).

- Creation in Kara of a **soya milk production unit** will serve the local market of 40,000 inhabitants. This type of milk, traditionally consumed in Asia and now being introduced into Africa, is cheaper and very nutritional. Production of soya seeds in the area is enough to supply the factory, which will have an annual capacity of 400,000 litres. Investment required is CFAfr106 million, of which CFAfr 96 million will be in foreign currency ($330,000).

- **Production of animal feed** in Kara will help to meet increasing demand due to insufficiencies during certain seasons. Togo has an abundance of raw materials for animal feed and even exports some of them. CFAfr 32 million investment will be needed, of which CFAfr 12 million will be in foreign currency ($40,000).

- The extension is proposed of a **plant to process fruits** in Notse-Kpalime. This is in the middle of the fruit producing region of Togo, where output is declining due to lack of markets. Pineapple production will be significantly increased with 3,000 hectares in the area having recently been designated for this purpose. The plant could process up to 25 tonnes daily for both export and domestic markets. CFAfr 148 million will be needed, of which CFAfr 113 million will be in foreign currency ($370,000).

Policy regime and incentives

Currency and trade regulations are determined by Togo's membership of the Franc Zone. Exchange controls apply to all currencies other than the CFA franc and the French franc. Import licences are required for all goods other than those from France or the Franc Zone. The import goods from the Franc Zone with a value of over CFAfr 10,000 (about $20) requires prior authorization. Imported goods are, in general, subject to both customs duty, normally assessed ad valorem and a tax fixed at 18 per cent of the landed value. Quota restrictions apply to a small number of intermediate goods. Togo guarantees the free repatriation of all investments in the country.

In order to attract foreign investment the Zone Franche, or Free Zone institution has been created. Businesses located in the Zone have the following important advantages:

- Tax reductions;
- Possibility to hold accounts in foreign currency;
- Exemption from import duties and other taxes on capital, spare parts and raw material inputs;
- Exemption from export duties and taxes;
- Legal environment and provision of infrastructure conducive to business.

A recent study by UNIDO considered that these advantages gave firms in the Free Zone an advantage in attracting foreign investment. These firms can also cope with currency crises, since they hold their assets in foreign currency.

Other important advantages of investing in Togo are:
- Natural conditions suitable for expanding cash crops;
- Ready access to a seaport;
- Good human resources and well-trained businessmen;
- Financial stability and stable banking system.

5.   Major players and institutions related to agro-business

Public: - Societé d'Administration de Zones Franches (SAZOF)
            - Ministère des Industries et des Sociétés d'Etat
            - Ministère du Plan et du Développement
            - Chambre de Commerce d'Agriculture et d'Industrie du Togo
            - International development advisers

Banks: - Central bank functions are performed by the Banque Centrale des Etats de l'Afrique de l'Ouest (BCEAO) in Dakar

- Union Togolaise de Banque (35 per cent state-owned)
- Banque Togolaise pour le Commerce et l'Industrie (50.5 per cent state-owned)
- Banque Internationale pour l'Afrique Occidental au Togo (owned by Meridian International Bank and private national shareholders)
- Banque Togolaise de Développement (50 per cent state-owned)
- Caisse National de Crédit Agricole

ZAMBIA

Macroeconomic prospects

With its reliance on copper exports declining, Zambia is no longer a single commodity economy. The share of mining declined from about 10 per cent of GDP in the mid-1980s to about 6 per cent in 1995. Against this background, manufacturing accounts for more than 25 per cent of GDP and agro-industries constitute more than three-quarters of MVA.

The Government embarked on a four-year rights accumulation programme (RAP) in 1995, whereby Zambia gained renewed access to multilateral funding on condition of further structural adjustment. To this end, the Government initiated a series of measures including the introduction of a cash budget aimed at reducing chronic overspending, often in the form of supplementary budgets. However, it has not really succeeded. A civil service redundancy programme was launched in 1992, resulting in over 10,000 redundancies, and then suspended in 1996. Since 1991 the semi-autonomous Zambia Privatization Agency (ZPA) has privatized about 60 out of 208 publicly-owned companies. The privatization of Zambia Copper Mines (ZCM) is expected to be completed in 1998.

Tax collection has been placed in the hands of another semi-autonomous body, the Zambia Revenue Authority (ZRA). The ZRA was strengthened in 1996, and was permitted to collect value added tax (VAT) from both the public and private sectors for imports, a measure designed to reduce corruption. The new stringency of the ZRA has increased tax revenues, despite the reduction in tariffs on a number of imported items.

Price controls on basic items have been completely lifted. Despite various government initiatives, inflation, although reduced, has remained at about 36 per cent. This has combined with the removal of price controls to make many basic items beyond the reach of consumers who could previously afford them. Poverty has become more widespread since 1992.

RAP was successfully concluded in December 1995. It was replaced with a three-year enhanced structural adjustment facility (ESAF), worth $1.4 billion, conditional on continued measures to reform taxation, reduce the civil service, privatize state enterprises and ensure a freely floating currency. ESAF enabled Zambia's major bilateral creditors to reduce and restructure Zambia's debt service obligations on $650 million of its external debt until 1999, reducing annual payments from $139 million to $37 million.

GDP growth continued to be negative during 1990-1995 at around -0.2 per cent on average. Growth in 1996 is estimated to increase substantially. Inflation, though reduced, remains very high at more than 35 per cent in 1995, and monetary policy has been tightened since 1996. The balance of payments position has improved. Foreign debt exceeds $7 billion, most of it owed to bilateral and multilateral donors. The precariousness of the balance of payments position reflects the fact that more than 80 per cent of export earnings came from copper. The kwacha depreciated by more than 50 per cent during the first half of 1996 but has since remained stable. Interest rates are rising and have been significantly positive during 1995 and 1996.

Financial liberalization has led to an increase in the number of financial institutions. There are 18 banks, 34 non-banking financial institutions and 36 foreign exchange bureaux in the country. Profit rates have declined within the banking sector. A stock market has been functional since 1994, and market capitalization fell from K680 billion at the beginning of 1995 to K480 billion ($370 million) at the end of March 1997.

A small group of merchant banks are supporting the securities markets. Zambia National Bank, Barclays, Standard Chartered and CitiBank are expected to expand merchant banking services. Cauvmont Merchant has been in Zambia for some time and offers a comprehensive range of merchant banking services.

Risks are associated with Zambia's continued dependence on a single source of foreign exchange earnings, very high external debt, weak domestic currency and continued bitter political conflict between the major political parties.

Investments in agro-industries

Despite political and economic difficulties, Zambia attracted some $4 million in foreign investments on the Lusaka Stock Exchange in 1996. The manufacturing sector as a whole has not fared well recently, but agro-related branches, particularly food manufacturing, textiles, and clothing, have done well. In the textile and clothing sector, export-oriented firms grew at a rate of 10 per cent during 1996 while production for the domestic market declined. Major enterprises listed on the stock exchange include Zambian Sugar (ZSUG), Rothman (tobacco) and Chilanga Cement, all agro-related enterprises. Zambian Sugar, in which foreign equity participation exceeds 35 per cent, was a particularly successful launch.

Zambian Sugar (ZSUG) had its initial placement offer (IPO) on 19 August 1996, when it issued 6.06 per cent of its shares in a full listing on the Lusaka Stock Exchange at a price of K11. ZSUG is controlled and managed by Tate and Lyle PLC, with 50.9 per cent of the equity. Other investment partners include CDC with 31.2 per cent and ZPTF with 7 per cent. ZPTF and CDC both reduced their shareholding by 3.0 per cent. At the week ending 27 March 1997, the selling price of ZSUG, then stood at K17.5.

Both Zambian Sugar and Rothman are strong, well-managed companies. Sales of their shares could prove attractive to fund managers. Rothman is the sole manufacturer of cigarettes and pipe tobacco in Zambia. In 1996, it initiated an equipment modernization programme. In 1995, it realized an after-tax profit of K2.2 billion on a shareholders equity of K9 billion. Earnings per share increased from K5.9 in 1993 to K11.7 in 1994, but fell to K10.5 in 1995. Total capital employed increased from K1.7 billion in 1994 to K13.4 billion. The company has been in existence for more than 30 years. Zambian Sugar made net after tax profits of K15.1 billion in 1996 as against K10.4 billion in 1995.

Other agro-industrial firms that may be offered on the Zambian Stock Exchange, and appear to offer good investment prospects include Zambia Breweries, Kafae Textiles of Zambia, Mustock Zambia (food manufacturing), Swarp Spinning Mills, Mpongwe Milling (grains), York Farms (food manufacturing) and Zambia Sugar (not ZSUG).

Venture capital (VC) investment should relate to the ongoing privatization programme, which is among the most successful in the African LDCs. It is evident that a wide range of opportunities exist for VC investment in Zambian agro-related industries.

Table IV.10.
Zambia: Privatized companies, 1996 and first quarter 1997

Company	Sales price
Northern Breweries	$18.5 million for 70 per cent share (Lohnro)
Luangwa Mill	K90 million ($750,000)
Zambian Consolidated Tyres	K1.6 billion (80 per cent shares) equal to $11.33 million
Zambia Cold Storage Corporation	K150 million ($125,000)
Zambia Horticultural Products	$3.65 million (Foodcorp of South Africa, 100 per cent share)
Chama Milling	K45 million ($137,500)
Kabwe Industries Fabrics	K600 million ($500,000, Tate and Lyle)
Dairy Produce Boards (3 factories)	$800,000 (Bonzam)
Mulungushi Mill	K300 million ($250,000)
Sufra Baking Company	K380 million ($317,000)
Lusaka Door Factory	$250,000
Lint Company of Zambia	$6 million (Lohnro)
Chipta Plant of Zambia Cold Storage Company	K124.9 million ($105,000)
Nkwazi Manufacturing (nets, paper)	K100 million
RPO Limited	$8.25 million (Unilever 80 per cent share)

Source: Zambian Privatization Agency.

Projects recently financed by IFC and CDC include AEF Sunblest Milling Company ($700,000), AEF Ubizane Investment Limited ($1.14 million), Value Textiles of Zambia and Swarp Spinning Mills.

A Zambian venture capital fund was established in 1995 providing financing for horticulture and fisheries. Funding will be provided in the range of $50,000 to $750,000 for a period of three to seven years, partly financed by the CDC. Project directors of the Fund are themselves expected to take 30 to 50 per cent of the equity stock in financed companies or 30 to 50 per cent of venture capital financing.

Policy regime and incentive structure

The Zambian Government is committed to liberalization and provides a wide range of incentives. There are no controls on remittances of profits and royalties or on any other form of foreign exchange transaction. The Foreign Exchange Management Committee (FEMAC), which allocated foreign exchange to importers throughout most of the 1980s, was abolished in November 1990. All imports were moved to the Open General Licence (OGL), initially with finance purchased at the market rate of the dual exchange system. Since the merging of the rates, the liberalization of the whole foreign exchange system and the creation of foreign exchange bureaux following the 1992 budget, bureaux and commercial banks now set their own daily exchange rates for the Kwacha.

Trade has also been liberalized. With the disbanding of OGL in early 1993 and the repeal of the Exchange Control Act in 1994, most importers now purchase their foreign currency directly from commercial banks and bureaux and most goods can be freely imported. Export licensing and foreign exchange retention procedures have also been eased and decentralized.

New local and foreign investment had been governed by the Investment Act of March 1986 until, just before elections, the Government hurried the 1991 Investment Code through Parliament. This Act allowed for 100 per cent retention of foreign exchange earnings, compared with 70 per cent previously, for the first three years. New investors were guaranteed exemption from customs duties and sales tax on all machinery, equipment and parts, dividend tax for seven years and company tax for three years followed by a 75 per cent exemption for the following two years. Guarantees were also given against the nationalization of companies, assets and property.

The Movement for Multiparty Democracy (MMD) Government quickly began implementing the Act and, by January 1992, the newly established Investment Committee was able to process foreign investment applications within a month of submission. Priority was given to investors in import substitution, agro-industry and tourism and to exporters of non-traditional products using local raw materials. In September 1993, a new Investment Act was enacted to replace the 1991 legislation. The main difference being that the new Act taxed new investors at 15 per cent annually on their profits from farming and non-traditional exports. An important impediment to the growth of foreign portfolio investment is that primary market offerings of the privatized companies are available only to Zambian nationals. Equity holding of foreigners and of institutions such as IFC and CDC can be purchased by portfolio investors.

There are no restrictions on foreign participation in the secondary market of the Lusaka Stock Exchange. Foreign investors can purchase secondary market shares owned either by domestic investors or other foreign investors. In practice, purchases of shares from domestic investors face some restrictions since the majority of domestic investors have very small shareholdings and thus, many individual small transactions have to take place, which is time consuming. The Lusaka Stock Exchange secondary market is essentially a dual market. There is one market for small investors, and another for large investors. Cross-over may take place between the markets, but there are delays in making purchases or sales in the small-scale investor market.

This highlights the value of the equity holdings of IFC, CDC and other multilateral/bilateral finance institutions. The value of the equity holdings resides in their financial value as well as in the usually correct financial and efficiency disciplines that such equity holdings confer. In the case of CDC and some other bilateral institutions, direct management responsibilities are sometimes undertaken. These equity holdings can also play a central role in meeting the Government's goal of stimulating foreign investment.

Opening up primary offerings of privatized companies to foreign investors can stimulate portfolio investment. Another interesting possibility is to follow Poland's lead in developing an industry- specific privatization approach for the agro-business sector. The main rationale underlying sectoral privatization is to enhance the efficiency of the privatization process. There are various economies of scale associated with working simultaneously on many units or enterprises. For example, outside advisors to assist in the development of medium- and large-sized enterprises, can capitalize on their time by working simultaneously on a number of enterprises. In addition, the advisors are likely to work more efficiently over time by accumulating knowledge about the operational, financial and marketing characteristics of the sector in a particular country setting.

Major players and institutions related to agro-business

Public

- Zambia Investment Centre: one stop investment facilitation agency
- Registrar of Companies
- Export Board
- Export Import Bank

Financial institutions

- National Commercial Bank
- Standard Chartered
- Barclays
- Stambic Bank
- CitiBank
- Cauvmont Merchant Bank
- First Merchant Bank
- The Development Bank of Zambia
- Investment Merchant Bank
- Inter Africa Corporation

Other

- Zambian Privatization Agency
- Lusaka Stock Exchange
- Zambia Revenue Authority
- Zambian Association of Chambers of Commerce and Industry

ANNEX to CHAPTER IV

Tables

Table A.IV.1. LDCs: Manufacturing activity

Region and countries	Main Industrial sectors
Africa	
Angola	Petroleum; mining-diamonds, iron ore phosphates, feldspar, bauxite, uranium and gold; fish processing; food processing; brewing; tobacco; sugar; textiles; cement; basic metal products.
Benin	Textiles, cigarettes, construction materials, beverages, feed production, petroleum.
Burkina Faso	Cotton lint, beverages, agricultural processing soap, cigarettes, textiles, gold.
Burundi	Light consumer goods such as blankets, shoes, soap, assembly of imported components, public works construction; food processing.
Cape Verde	Fish processing, salt mining, clothing factories, ship repair, construction materials, food and beverage production.
Central Africa Republic	Diamond mining , sawmills, breweries, textiles, footwear, assembly of bicycles and motorcycles.
Chad	Cotton textiles mills, slaughterhouses, brewery, natron (sodium carbonate), soap, cigarettes.
Comoros	Perfume distillation, textiles, furniture, jewelry, construction materials, soft drinks.
Equatorial Guinea	Fishing, saw milling.
Ethiopia	Food processing, beverages, textiles, chemicals, metals processing, cement.
Eritrea	Food processing, beverages, clothing and textiles.
Gambia	Peanut processing, tourism, beverages, agricultural machinery assembly, woodworks, metalworking, clothing.
Guinea	N/A
Guinea-Bissau	Agricultural processing, beer, soft drinks.
Lesotho	Food, beverages, textiles, handicrafts, tourism.
Liberia	Rubber processing, food processing, construction materials, furniture, palm oil processing, mining (iron ore, diamonds).
Madagascar	Agricultural processing (meat canneries, soap factories, breweries, refining plants), light consumer goods industries (textiles, glassware) cement, automobile assembly, plant, paper, petroleum.

(Table A.1V.1., cont'd)

Region and countries	Main Industrial sectors
Africa	
Malawi	Agricultural processing (tea, tobacco, sugar saw milling, cement, consumer goods.
Mali	Small local consumer goods and processing, construction, phosphate, gold, fishing.
Mauritania	Fish processing, mining of iron ore and gypsum.
Mozambique	N/A
Niger	Cement, brick, textiles, food processing, chemicals, slaughterhouses, and a few other small light industries; uranium mining began in 1971.
Rwanda	Mining of cassiterite (tin ore) and wolframite (tungsten ore), tin, cement, agricultural processing small-scale beverage production, soap, furniture, shoes, plastic goods, textiles, cigarettes.
Sao Tome and Principe	N/A
Sierre Leone	N/A
Togo	Phosphate mining, agricultural processing, cement; handicrafts, textiles, beverages.
Uganda	Sugar, brewing, tobacco, cotton textiles, cement.
United Republic of Tanzania	Primarily agricultural processing (sugar, beer, cigarettes, sisal twine), diamond and gold mining, oil refinery, shoes, cement, textiles, wood products, fertilizer.
Zaire	Mining, mineral processing, consumer products (including textiles, footwear, and cigarettes, processed foods and beverages, cement, diamonds.
Zambia	Copper mining and processing, construction, foodstuffs, beverages, chemicals, textiles, and fertilizer.
Arab States	
Djibouti	Limited to a few small-scale enterprises, such as dairy products and mineral-water bottling
Somalia	A few small industries, including sugar refining, textiles, petroleum refining (mostly shut down).
Sudan	Cotton ginning, textiles, cement, edible oils, sugar, soap, distilling, shoes, petroleum refining.
Yemen	Crude oil production and petroleum refining; small-scale production of cotton textiles and leather goods; food processing; handicrafts; small aluminium products, cement.

(Table A.IV.I., cont'd)

Region and countries	Main Industrial sectors
Asia and the Pacific	
Afghanistan	Small-scale production of textiles, soap, furniture, shoes, fertilizer, and cement; handwoven carpets: natural gas, oil, coal copper Agriculture: largely wheat, nuts, fruits and livestock.
Bangladesh	Jute manufacturing, cotton textiles, food processing, steel, fertilizer.
Bhutan	Cement, wood products, processed fruits, alcoholic beverages, calcium carbide.
Cambodia	Rice milling fishing, wood and wood products, rubber, cement gem mining.
Kiribati	Fishing, handicrafts.
Lao, PDR	N/A
Maldives	Fishing and fish processing tourism, shipping, boat building, some coconut processing, garments, woven mats, coir (rope), handicrafts.
Myanmar (Burma)	Agricultural processing, textiles and footwear, wood and wood products; petroleum refining; mining of copper, tin, tungsten, iron; construction materials; pharmaceuticals; fertilizers.
Nepal	Small rice, jute, sugar, and oilseed mills, cigarette, textile, carpet, cement, and brick production; tourism.
Samoa	Timber, tourism, food processing, fishing.
Solomon Islands	Copra, fish (tuna).
Tuvalu	Fishing, tourism, copra
Vanuatu	N/A
Latin America Caribbean	
Haiti	Sugar refining, flour, milling, textiles, cement, tourism, light assembly industries based on imported parts.

Source: Information from *World Almanac and Book of Facts* (Mahwah, N.J., K-111 Reference Corporation, 1997).

Table A.IV.2. Index of manufacturing output in African LDCs, 1995
(1990 = 100)

Branch	North Africa	West Africa								
	Sudan	Benin	Burkina Faso	Cape Verde	Gambia	Mali	Niger	Senegal	Togo
Food	126.7	97.5	142.5	46.7	90.3	102.0	100.4	99.5	56.7
Beverages	204.8	101.4	107.8	66.0	136.5	152.9	108.9	96.5	-
Tobacco	143.6	204.9	118.5	89.4	-	113.2	-	112.7	-
Textiles	93.2	139.1	107.0	-	199.9	122.0	107.0	130.0	103.9
Wearing apparel	99.6	104.1	107.0	43.0	-	121.8	105.3	85.0	93.7
Leather	93.2	120.9	121.2	-	103.6	102.3	96.6	139.1	83.5
Footwear	77.2	104.9	121.5	49.9	-	-	103.3	-	84.8
Wood products	64.8	94.0	119.8	84.4	-	-	52.2	-	83.7
Furniture	218.6	108.0	118.6	48.6	102.3	-	159.9	78.0	83.7
Building Materials	51.9	96.9	55.2	-	129.2	59.1	92.9	92.8	93.4
Total manufacturing	127.2	103.7	118.3	95.5	120.0	117.6	114.2	99.55	116.5

Branch	East Africa			Central Africa			
	Ethiopia	Somalia	Uganda	Burundi	Central African Republic	Rwanda	Zaire
Food	109.7	97.6	143.8	80.0	85.7	93.9	-
Beverages	108.9	134.5	153.6	80.9	91.9	92.7	-
Tobacco	111.4	108.4	168.4	80.9	85.6	-	-
Textiles	104.8	131.0	115.2	93.4	16.3	-	-
Wearing apparel	110.5	194.0	128.61	115.3	15.7	-	-
Leather	88.1	97.0	110.8	86.9	18.4	-	-
Footwear	114.4	90.9	126.7	118.3	18.1	-	-
Wood products	99.0	-	130.5	113.11	71.8	-	-
Furniture	109.6	77.4	146.9	34.9	69.8	109.9	-
Building Materials	89.0	83.4	144.6	91.6	-	161.7	-
Total manufacturing	106.8	106.5	143.8	86.0	68.9	112.2	–

Branch	Southern Africa				
	Lesotho	Madagascar	Malawi	Tanzania	Zambia
Food	162.4	99.0	97.3	96.9	77.9
Beverages	165.9	95.5	81.1	101.0	84.5
Tobacco	-	92.2	62.4	106.1	86.7
Textiles	151.3	86.0	89.5	105.0	79.8
Wearing apparel	151.2	115.3	74.6	124.1	67.4
Leather	156.0	125.7	109.0	91.6	65.0
Footwear	156.1	92.8	101.4	124.8	65.7
Wood products	-	107.4	115.1	94.2	83.2
Furniture	134.7	79.5	129.8	110.9	144.1
Building Materials	180.8	106.2	85.0	108.1	98.6
Total manufacturing	156.7	96.1	94.6	102.7	80.1

Source: UNIDO

Table A.IV.3. Mozambique: agricultural production, 1991-95
(Thousand tonnes)

Corps	1991	1992	1993	1994	1995
Export crops					
Cashew nuts	31.1	54.2	23.9	29.4	33.4
Raw cotton	40.0	49.8	47.0	49.0	51.0
Sugar cane	252.8	159.4	184.5	234.0	313.2
Copra	24.8	16.9	23.6	28.8	44.4
Tea	4.9	1.0	1.7	1.5	1.0
Sisal	24.8	24.8	24.0	24.0	24.0
Internal market crops					
Maize	74.0	75.1	142.7	149.0	173.0
Rice	23.9	16.6	17.8	29.0	14.8
Beans	14.2	13.0	23.3	16.0	31.2
Horticulture	35.1	35.4	42.5	44.1	30.5

Source: INE. *Anuàrio Estatistico*, 1995, published by the Economist Intelligence Unit Limited 1996, *EIU Country Profile 1996-97*

Table A.IV.4. Mozambique: Production of selected manufactures, 1991-95

Products	Units of measure	1991	1992	1993	1994	1995
Wheat flour	Tonnes	60,171	50,293	30,048	39,890	63,351
Raw Sugar	Tonnes	10,408	13,953	11,953	20,901	28,109
Beer	Thousand Litters	22,660	21,059	20,386	15,323	24,434
Filter cigarettes	Millions	50	288	352	60	52
Cotton Thread	Tonnes	3,843	7,279	5,894	7,725	4,504
Poplin	Thousand square metres	2,777	1,339	946	91	115

Source: INE. *Anuàrio Estatistico*, 1995, published by the Economist Intelligence Unit Limited 1996, *EIU Country Profile 1996-97*.

Table A.IV.5. Mozambique: Fishing production, 1991-95

Types of fish	1991	1992	1993	1994	1995
Shrimp	7,675	6,759	7,341	6,645	7,520
Prawns	2,351	1,652	1,833	2,250	1,770
Fish	14,996	11,557	8,552	13,489	12,620
Lobster	208	277	312	307	238

Source: INE. *Anuàrio Estatistico*, 1995, published by the Economist Intelligence Unit Limited 1996, *EIU Country Profile 1996-97*

Table A.IV.6. Mozambique: Exports, 1991-95
($ million, unless otherwise stated)

Products	1991	1992	1993	1994	1995
Shrimp	60.8	64.6	68.8	62.8	73.1
Cotton Fibre	8.8	10.8	11.1	18.9	19.2
Timber (thousand cubic metres)	0.9	0.4	1.2	2.2	9.6
Cashews	16.0	17.6	8.2	3.3	9.5
Sugar	9.8	6.7	-	11.0	7.3
Copra	4.7	4.2	2.5	3.4	6.1
Lobster	2.8	4.9	3.5	3.6	3.7
Citrus fruit	1.9	1.1	0.9	1.3	1.3
Total including others	162.4	139.3	131.9	155.4	69.4

Source: INE. *Anuàrio Estatistico*, 1995, published by the Economist Intelligence Unit Limited 1996, *EIU Country Profile 1996-97*

Table A.IV.7 Mozambique: Rate of growth of manufacturing production, 1995[a]
(Percentage)

Branches	1995
Food, beverages and tobacco	44.6
Textiles, wearing apparel and leather	-35.0
Wood and cork products	32.2
Paper, printing and publishing	-16.6
Chemicals and petrochemicals	4.1
Non.-metallic minerals	96.0
Base metal products	-5.2
Metals, equipment and transport material	-5.5
Other manufacturing industry	28.8
Total manufacturing industry	28.8

Source: INE, *Anuàrio Estatistico,* 1995, published by the Economist Intelligence Unit Limited 1996, *EIU Country Profile 1996-97.*
a   Based on a survey of 110 companies.

Table A.IV.8. Mozambique: Total accumulated investment by sector, 1985 - September 1996[a]
($ million)

Sectors	Total investment	Foreign direct investment	Domestic investment
Agricultural and agro-industry	293.25	50.99	43.71
Transport and communications	82.84	17.49	16.17
Tourism and hotels	151.61	28.34	20.83
Aquaculture and fishing	133.89	16.47	14.89
Industry	387.79	88.85	57.91
Minerals	50.28	48.43	1.66
Oil and gas	0.00	0.00	0.00
Construction	233.90	29.65	29.84
Banks, insurance and leasing	28.04	17.12	10.60
Other	39.17	5.17	8.89
Total	1,410.64	301.13	204.37

Source: Centro de Promoçao de Investimentos, *Situaçao de Projector Autorizados,* October 1996, published by the Economist Intelligence Unit
Limited 1996, *EIU Country Profile 1996-97.*
a.   Totals do not tally in source.

CHAPTER V

INVESTMENT OPPORTUNITIES IN INFRASTRUCTURE

V.1. GLOBAL ASSESSMENT OF INFRASTRUCTURE IN THE LDCs

Whether investment in infrastructure causes growth or growth causes investment in infrastructure is not fully established, but the link between development of infrastructure and economic growth certainly exists. A fully integrated economy cannot be achieved unless the country can provide and maintain adequate internal and cross-border transport systems, reliable energy sources for production, clean water and sanitation systems for the population and efficient communications technology.[17]   An overview of the existing state of infrastructure in LDCs shows that across several sectors, the need for investment is huge (see LDC infrastructure development indicators in annex II), especially in basic infrastructure, as described below.

Power supply

One of the major tasks facing LDCs today is to ensure an adequate (reliable and affordable) power supply for their growing population and for the growth of economy. Access to electricity for all households and enterprises is a prerequisite for progress. The power sector is highly capital-intensive, and substantial investment will be required to meet the rapidly rising demand for power.[18]   In LDCs, consumption of electricity per capita is generally less than 100 kilowatt-hours (kWh) per year, many countries falling even below 50 kWh per year, compared with more than 8,000 kWh in developed countries and 12,000 kWh in Canada and the United States of America.

---

[17]   "The private sector's role in infrastructure development" (Washington, D.C., World Bank, 1996).

[18]   *World Economic and Social Survey 1996* (United Nations publication, Sales No. E.96.II.C.1).

Transport

High transport costs arising from high prices of oil and fuel products, especially in net oil-importing LDCs, high costs of delivery of raw materials etc. are a major hindrance to economic development, particularly for small-scale enterprises located in remote areas far away from major centres of growth. Inadequate road systems are probably the second most acute transport problem.[19] A study of the effect of international transport costs on industrial development in LDCs (using sea freight rates) has shown that even for coastal countries, the transport factor may significantly erode the advantage offered by a cheap labour force. For landlocked countries the effect may be catastrophic.[20] Air connections in LDCs are also an issue, national airlines being either small or non-existent. The costs of connections and of air freight are another obstacle to exports and communication. In addition to the above, inadequate port facilities and railway networks also contribute to the major transport problems currently restricting the growth of manufacturing industry in LDCs.

Telecommunications

Another factor affecting growth in LDCs is the unavailability of telephones and other communications media. However, sharp differences exist between LDCs in this respect, although with the new mobile communication facilities, most LDCs are rapidly becoming accessible to telecommunication systems.

Water supply and treatment

In most LDCs, drinking water is accessible to less than 50 per cent of the population (compared with 99 to 100 per cent in developed countries). Only a negligible percentage of waste-water benefits from treatment. Water supply in many sub-Saharan African countries is of primary importance and a basic requirement for the people, cattle and agriculture. Water purification and sewage treatment is a common critical need in most LDCs, at least for major urban areas, in order to improve the quality of life and the environment, which are currently in or approaching a critical stage.

V.2. NEW TRENDS IN PARTICIPATION OF MULTILATERAL AND EXPORT CREDIT AGENCIES IN INVESTMENT IN LDCs

Historically, a large number of infrastructure projects in LDCs have been funded through multilateral agencies such as the World Bank (through IDA funds, since most LDCs are not eligible for funds and guarantees provided by the World Bank) and the International Finance Corporation (IFC), as well as the African Development Bank, the Asian Development Bank, the Commonwealth Development Corporation, the European Investment Bank and the Inter-American Development Bank. Multilateral agencies have mainly provided support to public

---

[19]   UNIDO, "Industry in the least developed countries, structure and development" (V.93-88193).

[20]   Ibid.

agencies or authorities responsible for the development of the infrastructure in LDCs, but have now changed their policy and forged new institutions and instruments to support private lenders in the financing of infrastructure projects.

Worldwide, the World Bank now provides a range of products and services to support private participation in infrastructure. While historically the World Bank and IDA have mainly financed projects in the public sector (with the managers of infrastructure projects typically being public enterprises, often with a monopoly), and IFC and the MIGA have financed industries in the private sector, the recent trends toward liberalization and privatization of infrastructure and the emergence of a global private infrastructure industry has led all the World Bank institutions to increase their support for private infrastructure projects.[21]

IFC has approved an equity investment of $50 million in the Asian Infrastructure Fund, which will invest in infrastructure projects in the private sector in the developing economies of Asia, including the Indian subcontinent. IFC will also participate in the equity capital of the Asian Infrastructure Fund Management Company, which has expertise in infrastructure and knowledge of the Asian region and will serve as manager of the Fund. The Fund will invest in utility, transport and telecommunication projects, are currently sponsored by the private sector or which are being privatized. It will focus on equity and equity-related investments.[22]

IFC has helped to finance pioneering projects in a number of countries attempting to introduce competition and private participation in infrastructure. IFC had approved $3.1 billion of financing to 148 projects worth $29 billion in 40 countries by June 1996. However, much IFC activity remains concentrated in a few developing countries and also in the power and telecommunication industries. In 1995, 11 countries, none of which were LDCs, accounted for 97 per cent of all financing approved by IFC. The IFC has approved financing for projects in LDCs (Bangladesh, Uganda, United Republic of Tanzania and Zaire) and remains committed to advancing private infrastructure in such countries. However, IFC looks to host Governments to take the initiative on deregulation and privatization to shape the local regulatory environment and overcome political and economic barriers.[23]

In recent years, the Asian Development Bank has played an important role in developing projects for infrastructure with the participation of the private sector, and has acquired a wide experience of project financing in many emerging Asian economies. Its first project undertaken in an LDC was in the Lao People's Democratic Republic, with the provision of major financing on a limited recourse loan to a 210-megawatt hydroelectric power plant on the Nam Theun River, to be built by a joint venture between Electricité du Laos, MDX Lao Co. and Nordic Hydropower. The Asian Development Bank served as a coordinating agency and provided a loan of $60 million to the Lao Government to fund the equity stake of Electricité du Laos.

---

[21]   "The private sector's role in infrastructure development".

[22]   International Finance Corporation, "IFC to invest US$ 50 million in Asian Infrastructure Fund", press release 94/76 of 15 April 1994.

[23]   *Financing Private Infrastructure Projects: Emerging Trends from IFC's Experience*, IFC Discussion Paper No. 23 (Washington, D.C., International Finance Corporation, 1994).

For Africa, the African Development Bank adopted a new strategy for the development of the private sector in May 1996. In the context of this new strategy, the Bank intends to increase substantially its activities in the private sector in the near future and to accord priority to infrastructure projects in sectors such as energy, telecommunications, water supply and transport.

The African Development Bank may assist in promoting infrastructure projects by providing the following: financial support through direct equity investment and the provision of loans; advice to enterprises on the structuring of such projects to minimize financial risks; and advice and assistance to governments in introducing an appropriate legal and regulatory framework. The presence of the African Development Bank in any deal should provide confidence and comfort for other lenders and investors, who might otherwise hesitate to participate because of the perceived risk or lack of familiarity with conditions in the host countries.

In selecting infrastructure projects, the African Development Bank pays particular attention to the process of selecting the developers and suppliers, the contract terms and the environmental aspects. The Bank will satisfy itself that host Governments are not forced by severe shortages or a desperate need for infrastructure services to pay economically unjustifiable prices providing excessive returns to developers. Equally important, the Bank will have to be assured that the host Governments are committed and have the political will to fulfil their contractual obligations.[24]

The African Development Bank is ready to assist both public and private investment projects, including those in LDCs, provided each project is technically and economically viable and in line with the primary objective of the Bank to promote the development of African countries.

The Arab Bank for Economic Development in Africa has been particularly involved in infrastructure-related projects in Africa since 1993 and has granted loans for projects (including for roads in Mozambique) as well as funds for technical assistance. Preference is given to African and Arab suppliers.[25]

In Latin America and the Caribbean, the Inter-American Development Bank has for many years undertaken several activities specifically geared to supporting the private sector in the region. In 1988, member countries established the Inter-American Investment Corporation to provide financing for small- and medium-scale enterprises. In 1992, members entrusted the Bank to manage the Multilateral Investment Fund, established to assist the countries of the region in improving their market economies through investments and grants for technical assistance to support market reform and the development of human resources and small enterprises. Since 1990, the Bank has also made sectoral adjustment loans to assist countries in reforming their institutions to create a climate more hospitable to and supportive of private initiative. In 1994, the Bank opened a new private sector lending facility that is providing direct support to private-sector activities in basic economic infrastructure in the region.

---

[24] Issac Lobe Ndoumbe, "Outlining the steps that are needed and being undertaken to facilitate project finance in Africa and assessing the realistic timescale," paper presented at the seminar Emerging Market Projects 1995, held in January 1995 in Paris.

[25] Herc van Wyk, "Examining the potential for the development of major projects in Africa", paper presented at the seminar Emerging Market Projects 1995, held in January 1995 in Paris.

Export credit agencies have historically also been amongst the main providers of finance for LDCs, providing concessional fixed rates of interest over terms that are normally considerably longer than those offered in the commercial debt markets. The main attraction of using export credit agencies in private infrastructure projects in LDCs is their capacity to mitigate country risk for commercial bankers, something that has always been a constraining factor in LDCs.

Development of regional funds

A notable development in recent years in foreign investment mechanisms has been the growth of country funds and investment trusts specialized in developing countries. This has been at least partly due to the search by investors for emerging markets in which the prospects for capital gains are expected to be greater than in developed countries. The funds have been specialized in the emerging industrial economies of Asia, such as Malaysia, Singapore, Taiwan Province of China and Thailand. For example, a new Himalayan investment fund is destined for Bangladesh, India, Nepal and Sri Lanka.[26]

Country-related funds offer one possible mechanism by which the foreign exchange earned by expatriate nationals of LDCs might be mobilized for economic development in the home country (as is currently the case with funds specialized in developing countries such as India). Most of those funds, whether mutual, global, regional or country-specific, have become the most popular form of portfolio equity investment in emerging markets, but very few are directed to infrastructure development in LDCs.

Direct investment funds for infrastructure have been created to promote investment in medium- and long-term projects (5-10 years) in developing countries, through equity (usually with a controlling stake of 10 per cent or more) or convertible debt. Foreign investors whose capital comprises direct investment funds are a diverse group that includes institutional and private investors, regional banks and multilateral organizations. Some private companies may already have considerable experience in the type of projects in which the funds plan to invest (for example, power plants). Examples of direct infrastructure investment funds are the Asian Infrastructure Fund established by AIG Investment Corp. (Asia) Ltd. (which raised over $1 billion in 1994), the Scudder Latin America Infrastructure Fund (with committed capital of $100 million) and the Asian Infrastructure Fund established by the Asian Infrastructure Fund Management Company (AIFMC) (with $500 million in capital).[27]

The AIFMC, which has received support from IFC, is likely to serve as a model for future vehicles of infrastructure financing. Several major equity investments in private infrastructure projects were identified by the Fund in recent years in emerging economies such as China, India, Philippines, Thailand and Viet Nam, and there is no reason why the Fund should not continue to participate in the growth of LDC infrastructure in the future.

The trigger for the emergence and proliferation of such funds has been the enormous financial requirements of developing countries for infrastructure. By pooling resources through direct

---

[26]   "Industry in the least developed countries ...".

[27]   *World Investment Report 1996* (United Nations publication, Sales No. E.96.II.A.14).

investment funds, foreign investors hope to lower the risk of investing in infrastructure projects in developing countries. The participation of regional or multilateral organizations with experience in financing development projects in the private sector also helps to lower the risks involved.

Despite the enormous investment potential offered by infrastructure projects in developing countries, direct investment funds have not been mobilized significantly. The costs and risks involved in infrastructure development (including those from variations in exchange rates) have discouraged them from investing large amounts of capital unless the rate of return is assured to be comparatively high by usual international standards. Most developing countries still need to clarify their regulatory and administrative procedures relating to foreign equity participation in infrastructure to alleviate the perceived country risks. Generally speaking, however, direct investment funds represent a potentially significant source of foreign capital for the modernization of infrastructure in developing countries.

Trend towards build-operate-transfer schemes

As a global trend, developing countries are being increasingly attracted by new modes of partnership between the public and the private sectors in the development of public infrastructure, such as contracting out or management contracts, private financing of public facilities, leasing, joint ventures, and build-operate-transfer (BOT) schemes. The BOT scheme is one of the most requested, including its many other variations, such as build-own-operate (BOO) and develop-build-finance-operate (DBFO).

The BOT concept for infrastructure projects consists in granting to a private company the rights to build and operate an infrastructure system for an agreed period of time during which it bears all commercial risks and financial costs associated with construction and exploitation.

What is new in the BOT scheme is that it is a form of project financing by which the essential duty of the concessionaire is to construct and finance the infrastructure with no recourse or limited recourse against the sponsors and the host Government. This contrasts with the old form of concession, which mostly concentrated on the operation and maintenance of an existing infrastructure financed by the public sector (which may, however, have included some enhancement, extension or heavy repairs to be financed by the concessionaire).

BOT projects are designed to generate enough revenue from the tariffs and fees paid by the public or by a public entity to cover the investment and operating costs of the project company plus an acceptable rate of return on capital. Project financing in all emerging economies is always a difficult exercise, and the success of a project can only be assured after financial closing. A great majority of projects never reach financial closing and have to be abandoned or financed in a different way. Indeed, the BOT method is rather new for most countries, and in particular LDCs, and quite complex from both financial and legal points of view. BOT projects require considerable expertise to develop and negotiate. The following are considered success factors for host Governments seeking to promote BOT projects.

- The project must be financially sound, feasible and affordable.
- The country risks must be manageable.

- There must be strong government political support.
- The legal framework must be stable.
- The administrative framework must be efficient.
- The project must rank high on the list of infrastructure projects of the host Government.
- The bidding procedure must be fair and transparent.
- BOT transactions should be structured so that they can be concluded within a reasonable time and at a reasonable cost.
- The sponsors must be experienced and reliable.
- The sponsors must have sufficient financial capacity.
- The construction contractor must have sufficient experience and resources.
- The project risks must be allocated rationally among the parties.
- The financial structure must provide adequate security to the lenders.
- The issues of currency, foreign exchange and inflation must be resolved.
- The BOT contractual framework must be coordinated and must reflect the basic economics of the projects.
- The public and private sectors need to cooperate on a win-win basis.
- Although there are severe constraints on the viability of such project financing in LDCs, the choice of an appropriate vehicle may help to overcome such difficulties.

V.3. MAIN CONSTRAINTS ON PRIVATE INVESTMENT IN INFRASTRUCTURE OF LDCs AND POSSIBLE REMEDIES

Private investment in infrastructure projects requires varying degrees of government support, depending on the type, size and complexity of the project and the political, economic, legal and regulatory conditions of the host Government. It is easier for a host country to attract private investment for a project in the industrial, oil and gas or mining sectors. The goods, raw materials or services produced by an industrial project can be sold, usually into established markets, and often abroad or to foreign users for foreign currency. The challenge is greater in the case of infrastructure, where the revenue stream is entirely dependent on purchase agreements with the host Government, as in the case of a power plant, or on the uncertainties of local consumer demand, as in the case of a toll road or telecommunication system. Political and economic uncertainties pose additional obstacles to privately-financed infrastructure facilities. Risks in infrastructure projects are heightened by the large capital outlays, by the long lead time associated with such projects, and - for BOT-type projects - by lenders and investors having to rely primarily, if not exclusively, on the project cash flow for their returns.

LDCs face major constraints in attracting private investment in general, and particularly in the case of private project financing for infrastructure development. The main problems encountered by potential private investors and lenders in infrastructure projects in LDCs result from political risks, inadequate legal frameworks and insufficient resources and revenues.

Political risks

One major factor that affects all foreign direct investments is the political stability of the country concerned and this is even more true for investment in infrastructure in LDCs, as the return on investment can only be expected to be long-term. In addition, the fact that the Government or other public entities will need to be a party to any project concerning public infrastructure, as well as its public nature, means that these projects will remain highly susceptible to government interference. However, recent developments show that many LDCs have recently improved their political stability and that protection against the expropriation or nationalization of foreign investments now exists in the form of bilateral treaties or international conventions.

The evolution of legislation also shows that liberalization and privatization are becoming a general trend in most if not all LDCs, and that the major political risk is no longer the risk of expropriation or nationalization but rather a non-traditional political risk of non-fulfilment by public authorities of their contractual obligations, either willingly or as a result of unavailability of funds or foreign currency.

Because of the special character of project financing for infrastructure in LDCs, specific arrangements and guarantees often need to be made for particular projects. This is particularly so where the central Government itself is not the concession-granting authority and where a municipality, a province or a state enterprise or agency is the signatory of the main agreements. Even a Government guarantee may not appear to offer sufficient security to lenders and the assistance of bilateral or multilateral institutions together with international credit agencies will be required to enhance the credit of the Government. Such international guarantees will obviously not be readily available at a competitive rate for many LDCs and will have to cover not only traditional political risk but also non-traditional risks. These latter risks may also be covered by a specific partial risk guarantee available from certain multilateral institutions or export credit agencies.

The raising of sufficient equity from sponsors may often be difficult because of the absence or insufficiency of any local capital market and lack of confidence from foreign investors. Here again, appropriate investment insurance from foreign government agencies or multilateral organizations and bilateral treaties on the protection of foreign investment may help to mitigate the difficulty of attracting part of the necessary equity. Another possibility might be the participation of a regional development fund.

Should such guarantees be available for the private financing of the project, a combination with soft loans or concessional loans from multilateral institutions and export credit agencies should help to reduce the tariffs charged by the utility to a level acceptable to its consumers.

Social risks

Infrastructure projects also face the risk that they will be rejected by the society they are seeking to benefit, "social risk". The turning of infrastructure construction or management to the private sector will, while improving the quality of the service, often induce price increases in services that previously benefited from a pricing and subsidy policy allowing the price to be set at a level that was affordable for the consumer but that was not sufficient to cover actual cost. Such a pricing policy is currently applied in many, if not in most, LDCs, particularly for the supply of water and electricity.

The private investment required for improvement of the services or rehabilitation work will generate increased costs and lead to significant price increases. Financing costs will also affect the final price of the service. The more difficult and risky the projects are (which will obviously be the case for most LDC infrastructure projects), the higher will be the rate of return expected by private investors and the rate of interest charged by the commercial banks. In all cases, the financial charge for commercial loans will be higher than the concessional loans offered to the public sector, and it is only through savings achieved in the wise selection of investment and procurement methods as well as by improving productivity and efficiency in the performance of the public service that these cost increases can be reduced.

Price increases in public services may render such the services unaffordable for part of the population and therefore politically unacceptable. One way of mitigating this aspect of social risk would be for the Government to institute the unpopular rate increases up to a level corresponding to the actual cost before the transfer to the private sector. This can then serve as a test of the acceptability of the price increase for users. Otherwise the Government may have to continue to subsidize the provision of the services by absorbing part of the economic price. However, the price factor should not be considered separately from the improvements in the service to the end-user. A real improvement in the service and the availability of the utilities may greatly reduce the potential social resistance to a reasonable price increase.

A second aspect of social risk is that involvement of the private sector in public infrastructure projects also usually results in a reduction of employment in public utilities arising from increased productivity. This may also generate social resistance. The lack of local sponsors able or willing to invest in infrastructure projects in their home country and the arrival of private foreign investors taking control of essential public services that were previously operated by the Government or a public entity may in many cases be considered by the local people as an abandonment by the State of part of its sovereignty and a loss of political power by the Government.

In addition, and due to the difficulty of selecting attractive projects where private investment is a viable solution, the private sector may be accused of "skimming off the cream", taking all the potentially profitable projects and leaving only the least economically attractive projects to be carried out by the State. In such cases, social acceptance can be fostered by encouraging the participation of competent local contractors and investors in open and transparent procurement proceedings.

All the above-mentioned factors may render the recourse to private financing for infrastructure projects difficult in some LDCs if social resistance in turn generates political or administrative resistance. Although the current environment in developing countries is favourable to private foreign investment in general, a more reserved attitude may be displayed with respect to foreign investment in public services. In such cases, the central Government must be fully convinced that such private financing will be of long-term benefit to the country and the best way to carry out necessary infrastructure investment.

Regulatory framework

To show its determination to attract foreign direct investment in general and private participation in infrastructure projects in particular, the Government will have to ensure that an appropriate regulatory framework exists that will give to potential foreign investors sufficient confidence that they will enjoy the benefit of any incentives provided by the existing legal framework or the contracts, that the project is legally valid, and that the rules applying to the investment will remain sufficiently stable for the whole duration of the project.

A review of the legal framework of LDCs shows that recently most of them have adopted new investment legislation to attract foreign capital and investment and have moved towards a liberalization and privatization of their economies. However, some of the investment codes do not always explicitly provide for investment in public infrastructure.

Apart from the specific regulations applying to foreign direct investment, of equal importance is the existence of a general stable legal framework in all areas of business law, such as corporate laws, security legislation and taxation and intellectual property rights. Even if most LDCs have recently adopted legislation providing incentives for foreign direct investment, the legal basis for all business operations may not yet be fully adapted to such projects in some LDCs, and the first step to be undertaken prior to opening infrastructure to private foreign investment would be to assist those countries in implementing, restoring or modernizing their business laws.

The effect of the regulatory framework obviously also partly depends on the efficiency of the authorities and institutions in charge of their administration. The regulatory institutions in LDCs generally do not have experience in dealing with large-scale private infrastructure projects, nor the skills required to deal with sophisticated legal instruments such as BOT contracts, concessions, bonds or similar techniques. However, the availability of technical assistance from multilateral or bilateral institutions, together with increased access to standard contracts and procedures, provides ways and means to overcome such difficulties.

A real problem is that regulatory institutions may not even be adapted to the basic philosophy of project financing of public infrastructure, which transfers the role of the major player to the private partner and its financial backers, and away from the Government, which means that the Government will have to become a partner and to restrict its authority only to laying down guidelines. It will no longer act as an owner and employer. This again will require the full understanding and support of the central Government.

The regulatory framework and preferably a specific law allowing the private financing of infrastructure investment should allow all potential sponsors or lenders to have a clear view of the legal system of the country and of the various applicable rules (regarding taxation, labour, the currency etc.). This is even more important in the absence of available case law and jurisprudence. A specific law, where it exists, has to be flexible in order to allow adaptation to different projects in a variety of sectors. It should be so framed as not to increase administrative formalities and constraints and it should specifically address sensitive issues, such as the nature of the investment contract and the possibility to arbitrate in cases of dispute.

It will need to be ascertained whether any concession or similar contracts made are of an administrative nature or can be considered as commercial and therefore not subject to local administrative laws and courts. In particular, it is strongly suggested that any LDC introducing a specific regulation for private investment in infrastructure should authorize international arbitration at least for the resolution of disputes relating to the early termination and major economic provisions of the project agreements and for the full duration of the initial loans. Without such an arbitration provision, it is doubtful whether any sponsor or lender would take the risk of financing an infrastructure project in an LDC.

The possibility of enforcing, within an LDC, arbitration awards rendered outside of the LDC will require that such a country should have ratified the Convention on the Recognition and Enforcement of Foreign Arbitral Awards, adopted in New York on 10 June 1958. It will also be a positive factor if the respective Government has signed the Convention on the Settlement of Investment Disputes between States and Nationals of Other States, adopted at Washington, D.C., on 18 March 1965, as the World Bank, with which most LDCs need to keep good relations, may have some influence on the enforcement of arbitral awards rendered under its auspices.

In many LDCs with an underdeveloped legal framework or a legal and administrative system that either dates from a period of colonization or is too new to be fully effective, major difficulties may arise in putting together a sufficiently safe security package acceptable to international lenders. The difference between common-law and civil-law systems will also generate different rules as to the security that may be granted over assets and contracts in LDCs. For example, in many civil-law countries it will not be possible to grant security over assets situated on State-owned land and used to provide a public service. Again in civil-law countries, local law may not recognize the assignment of the benefit of a contract (which might otherwise be the preferred form of security for lenders to an infrastructure project).

Difficulty may arise from the underdeveloped state of administrative frameworks, particularly in relation to securities. The identification of properties or the attachment of various assets requires that public registers should exist and that those registers should be kept up to date. This may not be the case in certain LDCs.

Putting together a proper legal and administrative framework will, therefore, in most cases be a prerequisite for the successful opening of the public infrastructure development to private financing. Without the firm support of central Governments, in particular for the building of a proper regulatory and administrative framework and for the availability of required currencies, it will not be possible to introduce pilot projects for private investment in infrastructure in many LDCs and, consequently, the chance to prove that such projects are viable and of benefit to the people will be lost.

Revenues and resources

By definition, LDCs are among the countries in the world with less revenue and they are highly dependent on external aid, usually with a huge debt burden to be repaid in foreign currency. To allow infrastructure projects to be financed in the private sector, it is essential that a sufficient and stable cash flow be generated by the project and that the necessary foreign currency is available to service any loan and pay returns to investors. The revenue may come from end-users or from the government body or public entity or a combination of the same (take-or-pay agreements, guarantee of minimum purchase of output ("offtake" agreement), guarantee of minimum revenue, subsidies etc.), but it needs to be sufficient in order to cover the operating costs of the project, to reimburse the debt and to allow a reasonable return on investment for the promoters commensurate with the level of risk undertaken.

Payment by end-users

In many LDCs, a significant portion of the population may be unwilling or unable to pay, or not used to paying, for the actual price of public services. Water is usually considered a natural resource and not paid for, especially in rural areas. In urban zones where water is paid for, the price paid to a State agency does not cover the cost of water distribution and purification. In that connection, in a country such as Angola, the majority of the population of Luanda and virtually all the poorer communities depend on private suppliers of truck-distributed water that is frequently untreated and that costs much more than the water distributed by the public agency.

To a lesser extent, the same applies to electricity in the developing world, where electricity prices have lagged behind the costs of supply and have depended heavily on government subsidies. A World Bank survey on power utilities in 60 countries found that price levels for nearly 80 per cent of the utilities did not cover the long-term average incremental cost of supply.[28]

Subsidies constitute a significant disincentive to energy efficiency in the industrial and commercial sectors, where typically 70 to 80 per cent of the total power supply is consumed. Usually, energy subsidies are advocated as a benefit to the poor. In practice, little of the subsidized electricity reaches lower-income households, as only a small segment of them have access to electricity, particularly in Africa. Because the poorest people often live in rural areas, they usually have to depend on more expensive and lower-quality forms of energy.[29]

Artificially low prices also deprive utilities of revenue and thus a measure of feasibility of the project as an autonomous economic unity. Not only does this encourage the dependence of the utility on the Government, but it limits the ability of the utility to mobilize finance under its own name for capacity expansion.

Roads offer an example of a public service that the population is not used to paying for. Ordinary roads in most countries are not perceived as service goods and there is no clear price

---

[28]   *World Bank's Role in the Electric Power Sector: Policies for Effective Institutional, Regulatory and Financial Reform*, World Bank Policy Paper (Washington, D.C., World Bank, 1993).

[29]   *World Economic and Social Survey 1996 ... .*

for roads. Road users, except for highways, which are practically non-existent in LDCs, do not directly pay for the use of roads as road expenditure is financed from the general budget. Road users pay various taxes on vehicles and fuel and this revenue is often, if not always, treated as general tax revenue and not applied specifically to the funding of road construction, maintenance and repair. Even the road funds do not, at the moment, allow the proper allocation of sufficient funds.[30]

Charges for telecommunication services and in particular for international communications are often high, with a very poor service.

Since the public services are provided by a monopoly, some form of price regulation is obviously necessary to avoid unjustified price increases that may not otherwise be controlled by market conditions. Various billing methods exist that take into account social considerations by reducing the price of the minimum necessary consumption for the poorest customers and by increasing the cost for other users. However, such distortion of pricing may lead to economically inefficient decisions on infrastructure investments.

Subsidies may be used, not only as an alternative to payment by users, but also as a supplement to allow the price to the consumer to be brought down to an acceptable level. Excessive subsidies may, however, compromise the efficiency of the public utilities and give rise to overconsumption, which may result in an overestimate of the real demand for capacity.

Availability of foreign currency

In private deals financed by foreign entities, a specific problem is also encountered with respect to the availability, convertibility and transferability of sufficient amounts of foreign currency to repay the foreign loans, to pay part of the variable operating costs in foreign currency and to pay dividends on investment to foreign sponsors. Most of the necessary basic infrastructure (energy, water and roads) does not itself directly generate foreign currencies. Telephone networks, airports and ports may on the other hand give access to foreign currencies. Even with a proper legal framework, which authorizes convertibility and transfer, the risk involved in the availability of the currency may remain high in LDCs, and an assurance from the host Government that priority treatment will be given to the project in case of a shortage of foreign currency, together with a specific insurance cover from export credit agencies or multilateral institutions, may often be required.

The involvement of agencies supporting private investors often also provides comfort to commercial banks considering participation in the financing. Such sources of finance have the advantage of offering longer maturities than commercial bank debt, and may often be at concessional rates that assist in reducing the overall cost of the project and in making the price of public service affordable.

---

[30]   Ian G. Heggie, *Management and Financing of Roads*, World Bank Technical Paper No. 275, Africa Technical Series (Washington, D.C., World Bank, June 1995).

V.4. IDENTIFICATION OF APPROPRIATE MEASURES AND OPPORTUNITIES FOR PROMOTING FOREIGN PRIVATE INVESTMENT IN INFRASTRUCTURE OF LDCs

Following the review of the main constraints faced by LDCs as a result of country risk and of the remedies available to enable infrastructure projects to be privately financed, consideration is now given to other problems specifically relevant to the majority of infrastructure projects in LDCs, which are related to the high development costs of such projects compared with their chance of success. Some of the solutions available in the market are discussed below and an indication given of some of the opportunities to be explored to foster private investment in the infrastructure of LDCs.

Attracting high-quality sponsors

Faced with fierce worldwide competition in a global economy, which is particularly true for project financing where a limited number of players are present on the international scene, it is not easy to attract investors and lenders in LDCs where the country risks may appear high compared with other developing countries that already have prior experience of private project financing.

Pre-investment and pre-construction costs for infrastructure project financing are high for potential investors and lenders in any country, but particularly so in LDCs because of the lack of readily available information on the project. Such costs will typically include, besides technical studies that have to be more sophisticated than for a classical construction contract, a study of the operation and maintenance requirements and costs for the whole duration of the concession, financial simulation and a complete analysis of the overall legal framework. Such development costs for most projects will represent several million dollars, and sponsors may prefer to invest in more developed or emerging economies where the environment is better known and the chance of a project ultimately proving to be viable is considered to be higher.

For many LDCs, sponsors are often reluctant to bear the high risks and costs associated with the *early stages* of the development process of a project that may not in fact be feasible or financeable or for which they may not have a reasonable chance of being selected. It is only if there is enough market potential that it will be possible for sponsors to spread the cost of failure of a particular project over future operations. But investors in project finance, including multilateral institutions, are now actively considering new facilities and mechanisms that may encourage the private sector to take on the development cost for worthwhile projects in small and low-income countries. Such facilities aim at reducing the development risks for private investors by, for example, arranging for successful bidders to share the costs of bidding incurred by the unsuccessful bidders. Another method consists of appointing one sponsor from among the group of pre-qualified sponsors to prepare the basic design for the project, and then requesting competitive bids on that design, granting the appointed sponsor the right to recover part of the development costs if another sponsor is selected to implemen the project.

The IFC also considers from experience that while a fully functioning regulatory framework and international competitive bidding are desirable, they may not always be possible, particularly in the early stages of promotion. In certain circumstances, for example, the first project in a country with high risk, or a small project where there is urgency or limited knowledge of the market, development by direct negotiation may be appropriate. The IFC has financed several projects on that basis.

Need for the Government to play a proactive role

As observed in many countries, the costs and time of development and negotiations and other obstacles during the pre-construction phase can be drastically reduced if host Governments take an active and structural role in supporting privately-financed infrastructure projects. Such government support may cover legislative, regulatory, administrative and sometimes even financial measures.

Obviously, there is no global recipe for a proactive government policy for private participation in infrastructure financing, as each policy must be designed for the particular country and sector involved, as well as for the type, size and complexity of the project. Fortunately, standard solutions have been worked out for problems that earlier seemed insuperable. Such standard solutions are making partnership schemes between the public and private sectors potentially applicable in most developing countries and are particularly relevant to LDCs that have no experience with respect to project financing and a huge need for infrastructure development. Some of the solutions or their essential elements are indicated below, which when in place will considerably enhance the interest of the private sector in BOT infrastructure projects in developing countries:

(a)   an explicit national development policy that clearly commits the host Government to promote participation of the private sector in infrastructure projects;

(b)   a credible legal and regulatory framework to facilitate a BOT strategy;

(c)   a credible administrative framework to expedite the implementation of BOT projects and to support such projects when they encounter the problems inherent in all large projects, no matter how they are financed or in which country;

(d)   a clear government commitment and procedure to conclude BOT deals within a reasonable time;

(e)   an orderly and transparent BOT procurement procedure.

The use of standard contracts may also reduce the preparation and negotiation time as well as the development costs, and will allow investors and lenders to feel more confident with documents that conform to international practice. Many of the essentials cannot be put in place overnight, but if the Government decides to adopt a BOT strategy and takes positive steps to encourage investment by the private sector in infrastructure, this can be a decisive factor in the face of strong international competition for private finance.

For the host Government, the preparation of project documentation and sophisticated and complex negotiations may generate huge costs. To improve the chances of success for the project and to justify that investment, the use of impartial and experienced technical, financial and legal advisors is required to structure the deal properly and in conformity with international practice and to make it bankable and acceptable to foreign investors.

Adaptation of the financing vehicle to the size of projects

Financing projects in LDCs also raises specific problems with respect to the size of the projects, which may require prohibitive development costs for sponsors or be too small to be eligible for multilateral financing. Small projects, which should prima facie be less difficult to finance, nevertheless require a level of pre-investment costs that are too high for the project to offer a viable solution for a foreign investor. Different methods have been used or are currently being experimented with to overcome this "size of project" problem. For example, the European Bank for Reconstruction and Development (EBRD) is developing a method for financing small and medium-sized enterprises in countries of eastern Europe that might very well be adaptable to small infrastructure projects in LDCs, including, in particular, a regional venture fund and funding through local banks.

Regional venture funds

Project financing needs intensive pre-investment work of a technical, legal and financial nature, whatever the size of project. The idea of regional venture funds is to use grants from multilateral organizations to pay development costs and management fees for selected countries or projects, and to assist in promoting interest in more risky infrastructure projects by reducing development risks. Normally, in a private-sector fund, development costs, including fees, expenses and appropriate incentives for managers and investors, are paid from the capital of the fund. This may reduce the participation of the fund to only those projects in a well-known environment or sector, which are most likely to be financeable from the outset, in order to preserve the profit potential of the investors. Regional venture funds overcome this obstacle by mobilizing foreign and multilateral grant funding rather than funds of investors to pay fees and expenses of professional managers and technical and industrial consultants in any selected project. The special fund is thus more likely to turn a venture capital profit while still investing in high-risk regional projects.

The initiative of the so-called regional venture fund combines classic venture capital with grant funding by a development bank. This method of combining grant and venture capital might be adapted to LDCs requiring something more than the classic venture capital fund.

The wholesale approach

Multilateral financial institutions might also use various methods of wholesale investment in local banks for subsequent onward infrastructure investment in small but repeatable projects, combining equity investment, co-financing and bank-to-bank loans. However, if such a wholesale approach is to be adapted to financing small infrastructure projects, a training programme and technical assistance will be required to enable local financing institutions to structure the project finance arrangements properly, together with the local granting authority and sponsors. For such projects, the proactive involvement of the Government will also be required, following established guidelines for procurement and a clear policy with respect to private financing of infrastructure projects.

In many respects, equity participation in local financial institutions is perhaps the simplest form of investment by multilateral or bilateral institutions. The foreign institution purchases shares in a selected bank that lends to small infrastructure projects. However, equity investment, generally, is essentially high-risk in nature, since the foreign institution as a shareholder, as opposed to a secured creditor, takes the full risk of the local institution (rather than just of the project).

Co-financing, as the name implies, involves parallel loans to an infrastructure project by the multilateral financial institution and the local bank. The wholesale approach is manifested by the delegation of project preparation, evaluation and monitoring to the local bank. When the local bank decides that the project is viable and that it also meets the criteria of the multilateral financial institution, both financial institutions invest. The co-financing bank monitors and supervises the project and reports to the multilateral financial institution. The result of such delegation of tasks is that the multilateral financial institution can invest in smaller projects.

The bank-to-bank loan is the most common financing device for small and middle-sized enterprises that may also be adapted to small infrastructure projects in LDCs. The foreign institution makes a long-term loan to a local bank for onward lending to small infrastructure projects. The local bank enters into local loans with the project company as borrowers, using the same stream of income to make a profit and to repay the foreign institution. The local bank takes the risk of non-payment by the project company. In bank-to-bank loans, the multilateral financial institution will take the full single risk of the regional banking institution selected to lend to the relevant projects and may require the traditional sovereign guarantee to cover the credit risk of the local bank.

Another wholesale approach may consist in the opening by a multilateral financial institution of a credit line to an experienced sponsor to cover various small infrastructure projects of the same nature selected by the sponsor, the multilateral institution and the host Government according to agreed criteria. The total amount of the credit line will be big enough to be handled by the multilateral institution and pre-investment costs for each project will be reduced by this global approach.

Investment opportunities

Some governments of LDCs and multilateral agencies, such as the World Bank and the Asian Development Bank, have identified the infrastructure and projects most in need of rehabilitation or implementation in several LDCs. According to a preliminary survey, 39 projects in 23 countries could be listed, covering power, transport, telecommunications and water, and amounting to approximately $9,370 million. These projects, presented in table V.1. below, indicate potential opportunities for private investment and participation (for details see annex I).

Most of these projects have been allocated funds (or are under negotiation) from multilateral and bilateral agencies, especially IDA funds and other concessional loans or grants. Some projects include co-financing with export credit agencies. Many of the projects provide for or expect to use some form of participation by the private sector, from contracting out to BOT schemes. From the outset, the allocation of multilateral and bilateral funds are meant to give more comfort to potential private investors or commercial lenders.Therefore, a first approach for promoting private investment in LDCs would be to examine the potentiality for business among the projects listed in table V.1., (see also annex II).

V.5. CONCLUSION

Given the still high political risks and difficulties to generate an adequate revenue return, infrastructure projects in LDCs cannot yet be fully privately financed. Funding under concessional terms or grants from multilateral and bilateral agencies, partial risk guarantees and special government guarantees and financial support would be needed to structure the financing of such projects. However, the situation can be much improved to attract more private investment to the infrastructure sector in LDCs, if an adequate legal framework is provided, local capital is mobilized and, through well-structured and implemented pilot projects, the confidence of investors and lenders can be stimulated.

As a general rule, well-structured projects based on an acceptable legal framework and documentation conforming to international standards can be financed in countries with low income or high risk, or both. Some projects are easier to finance in such circumstances, including smaller projects, those not facing severe market risk, those with sponsor and government support arrangements and those earning foreign exchange.[31]

Among the new pragmatic approaches, the BOT scheme and its associated forms have played a strong role for the last 10 years in the development of private participation in public infrastructure in emerging markets in Asia and Latin America, but not yet in LDCs. Meanwhile, a few experimental projects applying partnership schemes involving the public and private sectors are under way in some LDCs, such as the Lao People's Democratic Republic (hydropower plant), Cambodia (airport), Myanmar and Mozambique (port and railways).

Many LDCs have not yet acquired a good experience in project financing and in BOT types of infrastructure project. This is a handicap for the promotion of such a sophisticated type of financing. In a few cases, however, projects involving other more advanced partner countries were successfully lauched (such as the purchase of electricity by Thailand for power plants in the Lao People's Democratic Republic, the Government of Malaysia in the development of the Phnom

---

[31]   *"Financing Private Infrastructure Projects ..."* .

Penh airport in Cambodia, or South Africa in the development of the port and railways of Maputo in Mozambique), show that this type of private financing is possible in LDCs.

Even if private financing of certain infrastructure projects in LDCs is feasible, it will probably not be on a pure BOT basis (without recourse or with limited recourse). To promote foreign private financing in LDCs innovative methods are required to attract foreign investors and to engender confidence in the success of the project and in the transparency and fairness of the procurement process. Proper incentives for sponsors, by reducing risk on development costs, may also play a positive role in extending their interest to countries not currently within their main focus. Adaptation of the BOT scheme to small-scale repeatable projects through establishment of guidelines and standard procedures and contract forms can also help to develop private financing for numerous small-sized projects.

It remains essential for multilateral and bilateral institutions to act as guarantors with respect to traditional and non-traditional political risk and as major providers for concessional funds and soft loans either directly or through local banks. Such multilateral loans coupled with private lending will make it possible to keep the price for public services affordable for both the public and local enterprises.

There is no single appropriate financing vehicle for infrastructure in LDCs. The investment approach will depend on the particularities of the country and of the project. If a project is to be feasible, it will probably be through a combination of different vehicles, including soft loans, grants, equity funds and participation of multilateral and bilateral organizations together with private investors and properly motivated lenders. Other innovative techniques, such as regional venture funds, may also help to fund the necessary equity for infrastructure projects.

Proper coordination of all such multiple intervention will be possible only if a clear government policy for private financing of infrastructure exists for the country. Training and technical assistance will be required for the host Government to be able to structure the new project in a way acceptable to the international financing community. However, where there is firm determination of the Government of the host country, real partnership, innovation and the pragmatism of all players, as well as a proper allocation of risks, then an effective development of foreign private financing for infrastructure in LDCs can be made to succeed.

Table V.1. Investment opportunities in infrastructure projects in selected least developed countries

Country	Project	Sector	Total cost (millions of dollars)
Angola	Lobito Port	Transport	44.7
	Urban water supply	Water and sanitation	..
Bangladesh	Ninth power project	Power	313.7
	Jacuma Bridge access roads	Transport	196.3
	Telecommunication sector reform	Telecommunications	400.0
	Fourth Dhaka water supply	Water and sanitation	148.0
	Third road rehabilitation	Transport	500.0
Benin	Transport sector	Transport	45.5
Burkina Faso	Ouagadougou water supply	Water and sanitation	210.0
Cambodia	Siem Reap airport	Transport	17.6
	New terminals at Phnom Penh airport	Transport	..
	Phnom Penh power plant	Power	..
	Water Supply Project	Water and sanitation	34.5
Chad	Petroleum development and pipeline	Power	3 500.0
Eritrea	Ports of Masawa and Assab	Transport	42.5
Guinea	Third water supply and sanitation project	Water and sanitation	28.0
Guinea Bissau	Water supply and sanitation project	Water and sanitation	22.0
Lesotho	Highlands water project	Water and sanitation	1 500.0
Lao People's	Nam Leuk hydropower project	Power	112.6
Democratic	Theum-Hinboun hydropower project	Power	207.0
Republic	Champassak road	Transport	60.1
	Third highway improvement project	Transport	65.0
Madagascar	Restructuring of transport sector	Transport	64.2
Malawi	Water supply sector	Water and sanitation	37
Mali	Kapichira power plant - Phase II	Power	75.0
Mozambique	Regional hydropower development	Power	444.0
	Water supply and sanitation project	Water and sanitation	86.0
Nepal	Khimti hydropower project	Power	145.0
	Tribhuvan airport	Transport	47.5
	Rural infrastructure development	Transport	16.9
Niger	Rehabilitation of transport infrastructure	Transport	30.2
Rwanda	Third water supply project	Water and sanitation	40.0
Togo	Road transport project	Transport	55.0
Tuvalu	Roads, bridges and structural port	Transport	4.5
United Republic of Tanzania	Songo Songo gas development	Power	331.0
Vanuatu	Roads, port, water supply and sewerage	Transport,	12.4
Zambia	Road sector - Phase I	water and sanitation	
	Road sector programme	Transport	500.0
		Transport	640.0

Source: UNIDO

ANNEXES to CHAPTER V

I.   Infrastructure projects in selected least developed countries.

II. Infrastructure development indicators for least developed countries.

Annex I

INFRASTRUCTURE PROJECTS IN SELECTED LEAST DEVELOPED COUNTRIES

The data contained in the present annex were drawn from various sources. While every effort was made to ensure their accuracy, they are presented for indicative purposes only.

Table A.V.1. Angola: infrastructure projects

Project title	Sector and type	Description (capacity or size)	Total cost (million dollars)	Financing	Implementing or government agency	Concession company and period	Sponsors	Major lenders
Lobito Port Transport System Rehabilitation	Transport	Rehabilitation of physical assets (tracks, bridges, locomotives, wagons and communication systems) Rehabilitation of port structure, cranes and other equipment Organization and management restructuring	44.7	Multilateral: World Bank IDA $30 million, (or 67%) Bilateral/ local $14.7 million (33%), to be decided	Caminho de Ferro de Benguela (Rail component) Lobito Port Authority (Port Component)	.. Projected implement- ation period of 3 to 4 years	..	World Bank

Table A.V.1 : continued

Project title	Sector and type	Description (capacity or size)	Total cost (million dollars)	Financing	Implementing or government agency	Concession company and period	Sponsors	Major lenders
Urban Water Supply and Sanitation Project	Water supply and sanitation	Rehabilitation of the water treatment plant at Marcal Rehabilitation of water reservoirs and the related pumping stations Replacement of two main water transmission lines Replacement of about 35 km and extension of about 82 km of the primary water distribution lines Implementation of billing and collection systems Acquisition and installation of pipes, pumps and critical spare parts for provincial water-supply systems	..	Multilateral: IDA (90%) Local: Government (10%)	Provincial Government of Luanda and the National Directorate of Water	..	..	World Bank

Table A.V.2. Bangladesh: infrastructure projects

TableA.V.2: continued

Project title	Sector and type	Total cost (million dollars)	Description (capacity or size)	Financing	Implementing or government agency	Concession company and period	Sponsors	Major lenders
Ninth Power Project	Power BOT	313.7	Supply of about 575 MW of additional power to the Dhaka area and provision of about 22,000 new connections Construction of 230 kV transmission lines and substations Construction of a load dispatch center and associated communication network Construction of 280 km of distribution systems at Dhaka Engineering services	Multilateral: Asian Development Bank (ADB) ($134.4 million, concessionaire terms (40-year term, 10-year grace period, service charge of 1% per annum)) World Bank ($63.3 million) Local: Government/ electricity agencies ($116 million)	Bangladesh Power Development Board Power Grid Company of Bangladesh Dhaka Electric Supply Authority Dhaka Electric Supply Company	:	:	ADB, World Bank

Table.A.V.2: continued

Project title	Sector and type	Description (capacity or size)	Total cost (million dollars)	Financing	Implementing or government agency	Concession company and period	Sponsors	Major lenders
Jamuna Bridge Access Roads Project	Transport	Reconstruction and improvement of about 143 km of national roads, including stretches between Jamuna Bridge and Daudkandi via Dhaka, and a 20-km section between Feni and Chittagong Re-engineering of dangerous national and regional roads to prevent accidents	196.3	Multilateral: ADB ($72 million, concessionaire terms (40-year term, 10-years grace period, service charge of 1% per annum)) Bilateral: Overseas Economic Cooperation Fund of Japan and the Japan International Cooperation Agency ($122.3 million proposed) Nordic Development Fund ($2 million committed)	Ministry of Communication, Roads and Highways Department	..	..	ADB
	Cofinancing (for the Joydepur-Tangail section) Contracting out	Consultancy services for construction supervision, a road safety study and preparation of a future road project						
Teleommunication Sector Reform Project	Telecommunications	Establishment of an effective regulatory agency and a private operator (NTO) Installation network of capacity of about 300,000 telephones by NTO Rehabilitation of existing network of the Bangladesh Telegraph and Telephone Board	400	Multilateral: to be decided Bilateral: to be decided Local: Government, to be decided	Government of Bangladesh Ministry of Posts and Telecommunications	..	..	World Bank

Table A.V.2: continued

Project title	Sector and type	Description (capacity or size)	Total cost (million dollars)	Financing	Implementing or government agency	Concession company and period	Sponsors	Major lenders
Fourth Dhaka Water Supply Project	Water and Sanitation	Construction of a surface-water treatment plant including associated water intakes and major transmission mains. Preparation of comprehensive waste management to address issues in sanitation, sewerage, solid waste disposal and storm water drainage at Dhaka. Technical assistance to build capabilities in financial management, planning, operations and maintenance. A comprehensive programme for leak detection and loss control covering the entire network of the Dhaka Water Supply and Sewerage Authority	148	Multilateral: IDA ($70 million), under consideration. Bilateral: France ($33 million), under consideration. Local: Government ($45 million)	Government of Bangladesh. Ministry of Local Government, Rural Development and Cooperatives. Dhaka Water Supply and Sewerage Authority	Projected implementation period of 7 years	..	World Bank
Third Road Rehabilitation and Maintenance Project (RRMP III)	Transport	Reduction of road-transport cost on most travelled roads in Bangladesh. Construction of the Nalka-Bonpora road. Rehabilitation and improvement of the Dhaka-Sylhet road. Construction of several small but important bridges. Training of the Roads and Highways Department in project selection and implementation of the planned 3,000 km of feeder roads. Reduction of road accidents	500-600 (300 for the first phase)	Multilateral: IDA ($200 million, proposed). Bilateral: to be decided. Local: Government, to be decided	Roads and Highways Department	Projected implementation period of 4 to 5 years	..	World Bank

120

Table A.V.3. Benin: infrastructure projects

Project title	Sector and type	Description (capacity or size)	Total cost (million dollars)	Financing	Implementing or government agency	Concession company and period	Sponsors	Major lenders
Transport Sector Project	Transport	Port operations and management Road repair, maintenance, safety and network management Rural road and rehabilitation management Urban traffic management	45.4	Multilateral: IDA ($40 million, or 88%) Local: Government ($4.4 million) Project beneficiaries ($0.6 million) PAC ($0.4 million)	Ministry of Public Works and Transport	..	..	World Bank

Table A.V.-4. Burkina Faso: infrastructure projects

Project title	Sector and type	Total cost (million dollars)	Financing	Implementing or government agency	Concession company and period	Sponsors	Major lenders
Ouagadougou Water Supply Project	Water and Sanitation Co-financing with export credit agencies and commercial banks	210	Multilateral: IDA ($40 million) Local: ($20 million) Unidentified sources: ($150 million)	National Water and Sanitation Authority	..	..	IDA

Description (capacity or size):
Construction of an earth dam on the Nakambe River (capacity: 200 million m³) and a pumping station of 3,150 m³/h
Construction of a water treatment plant (capacity: 3,150 m³/h) and a pumping station of 3,000 m³/h
Construction of a reservoir at Boudtenga (capacity: 5,400m³)
Construction of a main transmission line with a total length of 47,540 metres between the dam, the treatment plant, the reservoir and the city of Ouagadougou
Primary, secondary and tertiary distribution networks including pumping stations
Provision of house connections and water meters

Table A.V.5. Cambodia: infrastructure projects

Project title	Sector and type	Description (capacity or size)	Total cost (million dollars)	Financing	Implementing or government agency	Concession company and period	Sponsors	Major lenders
Siem Reap Airport Project	Transport	Improvement and upgrading of the facilities at Siem Reap Airport: terminal, operational buildings and runway	17.6	Multilateral: ADB ($15 million, concessionaire terms) (40-year term, 10-year grace period, service charge of 1% per annum)) Local: Government ($2.6 million)	State Secretariat of Civil Aviation	..	..	ADB
New terminals at Phnom Penh Airport	Transport	Construcion of new terminal Concession of existing airport facilities	..	Multilateral: IFC Bilateral: French bank (70%) Malaysian bank (30%)	State Secretariat of Civil Aviation	..	..	IFC, French and Malaysian banks
Power Plant at Phnom Penh	Power Build-own-operate (BOO)	Construction of a 60-MW power plant	..	Multilateral: IFC	..	25 years	..	IFC

Table A.V.5: continued

Project title	Sector and type	Description (capacity or size)	Total cost (million dollars)	Financing	Implementing or government agency	Concession company and period	Sponsors	Major lenders
Cambodia Water Supply Project	Water and sanitation	Water supply facilities at Phnom Penh; water supply estimated to increase from the current 110,000 m³ per day to 175,000 m³ per day in 2000 Water storage, supply and distribution facilities at Sihanoukville; water supply to increase from 2,300 m³ per day to 6,000 m³ per day Policy and institutional development	34.5	Multilateral: IDA ($30 million, or 87%) Bilateral grant ($2.75 million, or 8%) contributor to be decided Local: Government ($1.75 million, or 5%)	Phom Penh Water Supply Authority Ministry of Industry Mines and Energy	..	..	World Bank

Table A.V.6. Chad: infrastructure projects

Project title	Sector and type	Description (capacity or size)	Total cost (million dollars)	Financing	Implementing or government agency	Concession company and period	Sponsors	Major lenders
Petroleum development and pipeline project	Power	Development of Doba oil fields of Chad	3,500	Multilateral: IDA ($1,800 million)	Company to be set up	..	..	World Bank
	Potential project for BOT scheme	Construction of 1,100 km of buried pipeline from Chad to Atlantic coast of Cameroon, and related pumping stations, ancillary facilities and infrastructure Installation of marine export terminal facilities in Cameroon and associated marine pipelines and related facilites	(1,700 for development of the oil fields and 1,800 for pipelines and marine installations)	Sponsors: $1,700 million, to be decided				

Table A.V.7. Eritrea: infrastructure projects

Project title	Sector and type	Description (capacity or size)	Total cost (million dollars)	Financing	Implementing or government agency	Concession company and period	Sponsors	Major lenders
Ports Rehabilitation Project	Transport	Assistance to the two ports at Massawa and Assab in addressing urgent capacity requirements Civil works programme at Massawa Cargo-handling equipment	42.5	Multilateral: IDA ($18 million) Bilateral Grant: Italy ($21 million) Local: Government ($3.5 million)	Ministry of Transport, Department of Maritime Transport	..	..	World Bank

Table A.V.8. Guinea: infrastructure projects

Project title	Sector and type	Description (capacity or size)	Total cost (million dollars)	Financing	Implementing or government agency	Concession company and period	Sponsors	Major lenders
Third Water Supply and Sanitation Project	Water and sanitation	*Urban water supply* Rehabilitation and expansion of the water supply network at Conakry	28	Multilateral: World Bank (IDA, $16.8 million; IBRD, $8.4 million)	SONEG: Société nationale des eaux de Guinée	:	:	World Bank
	Contracting out	Construction of about 300 km of pipelines Construction of two storage reservoirs and installation of about 10,000 household connections		Distributed as follows: SONEG: $8.4 million (IBRD), concessionaire terms (20-year term, 5-year grace period, annual interest of 7%); $8.4 million (equity)	DATU: Direction nationale d'Aménagement du territoire et de l'urbanisme			
		Urban sanitation Rehabilitate and construct on-site systems Rehabilitation and maintenance of existing sewerage system Construction of a sewerage treatment facility		DATU: $7.3 million DNH: $0.9 million	DNH: Direction nationale de l'hydraulique			
		Water resources management		Local: Government ($1.2 million) SONEG ($1.8 million)				

Table A.V.9. Guinea-Bissau: infrastructure projects

Project title	Sector and type	Description (capacity or size)	Total cost (million dollars)	Financing	Implementing or government agency	Concession company and period	Sponsors	Major lenders
Water Supply and Sanitation Project	Water and sanitation	Access to safe drinking water by increasing the number of private connections from 3,000 to 10,000 and the number of public standpipes from 50 to 150	22	Multilateral: IDA ($20 million)	Ministry of Natural Resources	··	··	World Bank
		Drilling of two 200-metre deep boreholes with an expected yield of 120 m^3/h each Construction of a 1,000 m^3 elevated steel tank		Local: Government ($2 million)	Municipality of Bissau			
		Storm water management and drainage			Electricity and Water Company			
		Development of landfills, purchase of garbage collection equipment, and management of dump sites						

Table A.V.10. Lao People's Democratic Republic: infrastructure projects

Project title	Sector and type	Description (capacity or size)	Total cost (million dollars)	Financing	Implementing or government agency	Concession company and period	Sponsors	Major lenders
Nam Leuk Hydropower Project	Power	Construction of a 60-MW hydroelectric plant Project to generate 215-GWh of renewable energy annually	112.6	Multilateral: ADB ($52 million, concessionaire terms (40-year term, 10-year grace period, service charge of 1% per annum)) Bilateral: Overseas Economic Cooperation Fund (OECF) of Japan ($38.5 million) Local: Government ($22.1 million)	Électricité du Laos	..	..	ADB OECF

Table A.V.10.: continued

Project title	Sector and type	Description (capacity or size)	Total cost (million dollars)	Financing	Implementing or government agency	Concession company and period	Sponsors	Major lenders
Theun-Hinboun Hydropower Project	Power BOO	Construction of a 210-MW hydropower plant located on the Nam Theun River	207	Multilateral: ADB ($60 million, concessionaire terms (40-year term, 10-year grace period, service charge of 1% per annum) to fund the equity stake of Électricité du Laos Nordic Investment Bank ($15 million) Bilateral: Svensk Exportkredit of Sweden ($30.3 million) Eksportfinans of Norway ($21 million) Thai-Ex-Im Bank ($10.7 million) Local: Government ($8.5 million) Other: Thai commercial bank consortium ($121.5 million)	Ministry of Finance	.. 30-year concession period (25-year power purchase agreement)	Électricité du Laos (60%) MDX Power (20%) Statkraft and Vattenfall (20%)	ADB Svensk Export-kredit Norway Eksport-finans Thai-Ex-Im Bank

Table A.V.10.: continued

Project title	Sector and type	Description (capacity or size)	Total cost (million dollars)	Financing	Implementing or government agency	Concession company and period	Sponsors	Major lenders
Champassak Road Improvement Project	Transport	Improvement of two national road sections totalling 200 km, the two sections to be upgraded to bituminous standard and 32 temporary one-lane bridges to be replaced with permanent two-lane concrete bridges of a total length of 1,355 metres. Maintenance of 400 km of national and provincial roads	60.1	Multilateral: ADB ($48 million, concessionaire terms (40-year term, 10-year grace period, service charge of 1% per annum)) Local: Government ($12.1 million)	Ministry of Communication, Transport, Post and Construction (MCTPC)	..	..	ADB
Third Highway Improvement Project	Transport	Reconstruction of route 13 between Savannakhet and Pakse, about 230 km to be improved to bituminous surface standard, including rehabilitation of about 40 bridges. Spot improvement of about 2,000 km. Periodic maintenance of 700 km, and routine maintenance of about 2,600 km. Technical assistance to the MCTPC Road Administration Division	65	Multilateral: IDA ($40 million) Bilateral: Nordic Development Fund ($7 million) Local: Government ($5 million) Other: Financial gap of $13 million may have to be provided through increased IDA funds	MCTPC	..	..	World Bank

Table A.V.11. Lesotho: infrastructure projects

Project title	Sector and type	Description (capacity or size)	Total cost (million dollars)	Financing	Implementing or Government agency	Concession company and period	Sponsors	Major lenders
Highlands Water Project (construction phase 1B)	Water supply Co-financing with export credit agencies and commercial banks	Construction of a dam at Mohale and of a tunnel to transfer the stored water from Mohale to Katse (the cost estimate also includes environmental protection measures, resettlement, technical assistance for LHDA and construction supervision)	1,500	Multilateral: IBRD ($120 million) Bilateral: Other commercial ($800 million) Other: Concessionaire ($580 million)	Lesotho Highlands Development Authority (LHDA)	..	..	World Bank

Table A.V.12. Madagascar: infrastructure projects

Project title	Sector and type	Description (capacity or size)	Total cost (million dollars)	Financing	Implementing or Government agency	Concession company and period	Sponsors	Major lenders
Telecommunication Sector Restructuring Project	Telecommunication	*Sector restructuring* Creation of a new single national telecommunications entity *Urgent equipment components* Digitalization of the central corridor, Antsirabe-Antananarivo-Toamasina, and the associated local network Setting up domestic satellite communication to connect isolated population centres and economic enclaves to the national network	64.2	Multilateral: IDA ($26 million) Caisse française pour le développement (CFD) ($26.2 million) European Investment Bank (EIB), African Development Bank and other ($4.2 million) Local: Government ($7.8 million)	Ministry of Post and Communications General Directorate of Post and Telecommunications Madagascar Telecommunications	..	..	World Bank CFD EIB African Development Bank
Water Supply Sector Project	Water supply and sanitation	Technical assistance to support the restructuring of JIRAMA Rehabilitation and extension of water supply systems in the 14 largest urban and rural centres of the country Water supply for rural communities (construction of 500 drillings in the south of the country, plus 200 gravity-pipe water systems)	37	Multilateral: IDA ($32 million, or 87%) UNICEF and non-governmental organizations ($1.2 million) Local: Government and JIRAMA ($3.8 million)	Ministry of Energy and Mines, Directorate of Water Electric Power and Water Utility (JIRAMA)	..	..	World Bank

133

Table A.V.13. Malawi: infrastructure projects

Project title	Sector and type	Description (capacity or size)	Total cost (million dollars)	Financing	Implementing or Government agency	Concession company and period	Sponsors	Major lenders
Power VI (power sector development)	Power	Installation of two 32-MW units at Kapichira hydroelectric plant (phase II) Rehabilitation of existing hydropower facilities and the standby gas turbine and diesel power plants to improve availability of the units Reinforcement and expansion of the transmission and distribution systems to reduce transmission outages and distribution losses Provision of technical assistance and computer hardware and software	90 ($75 million for Kapichira phase II, $10 million for transmission and distribution and $5 million for institutional strengthening)	Multilateral: IDA ($30 million) Bilateral: to be decided Local: ESCOM	Electricity Supply Commission of Malawi (ESCOM)	..	..	World Bank

Table A.V.14. Mali: infrastructure projects

Project title	Sector and type	Total cost (million dollars)	Description (capacity or size)	Financing	Implementing or Government agency	Concession company and period	Sponsors	Major lenders
Regional Hydropower Development Project	Power	444	Construction of 200-MW hydroelectric plant at the Manantali Dam (five units of 40 MW each and civil works)	Multilateral: IDA ($31 million)	Organization for the Development of the Senegal River	..	..	World Bank
				EIB ($46 million)		15-years concession contract		EIB
				Arab Fund for Economic and Social Development (FADES) ($29 million)	Société de gestion de l'énergie de Manantali (being set up)			FADES
			Construction of 2-kV high-voltage transmission lines to Bakamo (306 km) and to Bakar (821 km) along the Senegal River and a 132-kV transmission line to Nouakchott (219 km)	African Development Bank ($26 million)				African Development Bank
				Islamic Development Bank ($21 million)				Islamic Development Bank
			Construction of 11 substations and dispatching centres	Banque ouest-africaine pour le développement (BOAD) ($20 million)				BOAD
			Technical assistance and training	Bilateral: France ($89 million) Germany ($62 million) Belgium ($24 million) Canada ($24 million) European Community ($37 million)				France Germany Belgium Canada European Community
				Local: to be decided				

Table A.V.15. Mozambique: infrastructure projects

Project title	Sector and type	Description (capacity or size)	Total cost (million dollars)	Financing	Implementing or Government agency	Concession company and period	Sponsors	Major lenders
Water Supply and Sanitation Systems	Water and sanitation	Rehabilitation and extension of the water supply systems in five cities (Beira, Maputo, Nampula, Pemba and Quelimane) Improvement and rehabilitation of rural and small-town water treatment and distribution systems and sanitation facilities	86	Multilateral: IDA ($30 million) Bilateral: to be decided Local: to be decided	Direção Nacional de Águas	..	..	World Bank

Table A.V.16. Nepal: infrastructure projects

Project title	Sector and type	Description (capacity or size)	Total cost (million dollars)	Financing	Implementing or Government agency	Concession company and period	Sponsors	Major lenders
Khimti Hydro-power Project	Power BOOT	Construction of a 60-MW hydroelectric power plant on the Khimti Khola River, 100 km east of Kathmandu	145	Multilateral: ADB ($36.5 million), or 25%: $31 million senior loan - concessionaire terms (15-year term, 4-year grace period); $5.5 million subordinated loan - concessionaire terms (15-year term, 6-year grace period)) Bilateral: $108.5 million, or 75% to be decided	Nepal Electricity Authority (NEA)	Himal Power Limited 50-year concession (after 20 years, 50% of ownership to be transferred to NEA)	Butwal Power Co. Limited of Nepal Statkraft SF of Norway Kvaerner a.s. of Norway ABB Energi AS of Norway	ADB
Tribhuvan International Airport at Kathmandu	Transport	Expansion and improvement of the safety of the airport facilities Technical assistance to help transform the Department of Civil Aviation into a self-supporting agency to be known as the Civil Aviation Authority of Nepal (CAAN)	47.5	Multilateral: ADB ($27 million, concessionaire terms (40-year term, 10-year grace period)) Organization of the Petroleum Exporting Countries (OPEC) ($11 million) Local: Government ($9.5 million)	Department of Civil Aviation for all project components Once established, CAAN will act as executing agency	..	..	ADB OPEC

Table A.V.16: continued

Project title	Sector and type	Description (capacity or size)	Total cost (million dollars)	Financing	Implementing or Government agency	Concession company and period	Sponsors	Major lenders
Rural Infrastructure Development Project	Transport	Development of about 250 km of rural roads and related structures connecting remote villages to the national road network and market centres. Multi-purpose buildings to be constructed in 90 villages	16.9	Multilateral: ADB ($12.2 million, or 72%, concessionaire terms (40-year term, 10-year grace period, service charge of 1% per annum)) Local: Government ($4.7 million, or 23%)	Ministry of Local Development	..	..	ADB

Table A.V.17. Niger: infrastructure projects

Project title	Sector and type	Description (Capacity or size)	Total cost (million dollars)	Financing	Implementing or Government agency	Concession company and period	Sponsors	Major lenders
Transport Infrastructure Rehabilitation Project	Transport	Regravelling of 1,060 km of earth roads	30.2	Multilateral: IDA ($25.3 million)	Ministry of Equipment and Infrastructure	..	..	World Bank
		Improvement of road maintenance administration and management		Local: Government ($4.9 million)	Ministry of Transport			
		Rural road maintenance						
		Road management (road safety plan, technical control of vehicles, protection of road assets etc.)						
		Civil aviation (technical appraisal of Niamey airport and commercialization of airport management)						

Table: A.V.18. Rwanda: infrastructure projects

Project title	Sector and type	Description (capacity or size)	Total cost (million dollars)	Financing	Implementing or Government agency	Concession company and period	Sponsors	Major lenders
Third Water Supply Project	Water	Reinforcement of the water distribution network of Kigali Installation of 5,000 house connections Contribution to the new Kigali water supply through the use of underground water Completion of Mutobo water supply systems Construction of small rural water schemes	40	Multilateral: IDA (to be decided) Bilateral: to be decided Local: to be decided	Directorate for Water and Sanitation Ministry of Public Works and Energy	Projected implementation period of 5 to 6 years	..	World Bank

Table A.V.19. Togo: infrastructure projects

Project title	Sector and type	Description (capacity or size)	Total cost (million dollars)	Financing	Implementing or Government agency	Concession company and period	Sponsors	Major lenders
Road Transport Project	Transport	Rehabilitation and maintenance of national roads	55	Multilateral: IDA ($50 million)	Direction générale des travaux publics	..	..	World Bank
	Contracting out	Capacity-building and strengthening of sector institutions Road safety improvement Feeder road management, including rehabilitation and maintenance		Local: Government ($5 million: $3.7 million from the general budget and $1.3 million from the Road Maintenance Fund)	Ministry of Mines, Equipment, Transport, Posts and Telecommunications			

Table A.V.20. Tuvalu: infrastructure projects

Project title	Sector and type	Description (capacity or size)	Total cost (million dollars)	Financing	Implementing or Government agency	Concession company and period	Sponsors	Major lenders
Transport Infrastucture Project	Transport	Repair and reconstruction of roads, provision of causeways and bridges. Rehabilitation of existing coral roads on selected atolls. Funafuti port improvements (container yard, cargo shed, harbour edge, fence realignment etc.)	4.5	Multilateral: ADB ($3.5 million) Local: Government ($1 million)	Ministry of Labour, Works and Communication	..	..	ADB

Table A.V.21. United Republic of Tanzania: infrastructure projects

Project title	Sector and type	Description (capacity or size)	Total cost (million dollars)	Financing	Implementing or Government agency	Concession company and period	Sponsors	Major lenders
Songo Songo Gas Development	Power BOO	*SONGAS component* Installation of a gas-gathering system and gas-processing plant Construction of a marine pipeline and 217 km of land pipeline from Songo Songo Island to Dar es Salaam Installation of a 37-MW gas turbine with associated equipment Improvement and maintenance of the 109-MW capacity of existing gas turbines at Ubongo *TANESCO component* Installing 20,000 electricity, prepayment meters and purchasing vehicles to improve commercial operations *MEM component* Providing gas, electricity and water distribution systems	331 (SONGAS component: $231 million)	Multilateral: IDA ($199 million as investment project; $50 million from the Currency Convertibility Fund) Grant: Canadian International Development Agency ($10 million) Equity contributions: Ocelot Energy Inc. and Transcanada Pipelines Ltd. Consortium (OTC) ($50 million) Commonwealth Development Corporation (CDC) ($4 million) EIB ($4 million) IFC ($4 million) TANESCO/TPDC ($4 million) Local: to be decided	Ministry of Energy and Mineral (MEM) TANESCO (Ubongo Power Station Plant)	SONGAS Ltd. (to be created by CDC, Deutsche Investitions- und Entwicklungs-gesellschaft (DEG) IFC, OTC, a local development finance institution (TDFL) and TANESCO/ TPDC 20 years power purchase agreement between SONGAS and TANESCO	..	World Bank

Table A.V.22. Vanuatu: infrastructure projects

Project title	Sector and type	Description (capacity or size)	Total cost (million dollars)	Financing	Implementing or Government agency	Concession company and period	Sponsors	Major lenders
Urban Infrastructure Project	Transport	Urgently needed road repairs	12.4	Multilateral: ADB ($10 million, concessionaire terms (40-year term, interest-free loan))	Ministry of Finance	..	..	ADB
	Water and sanitation	Development of water supply and drainage facilities of Luganville Structural repairs of the capital's main wharf			Public Works Department at Port-Vila			
	Social infrastructure	Improvement of the Erakor causeway bridge Protection of the lagoon environment		Local: Government ($2.4 million)				

Table A.V.23. Zambia: infrastructure projects

Project title	Sector and type	Description (capacity or size)	Total cost (million dollars)	Financing	Implementing or Government agency	Concession company and period	Sponsors	Major lenders
Roads Sector Project	Transport Potential project for BOT scheme	Rehabilitation of priority trunk and main roads and bridges Resealing and regravelling programme to reduce the maintenance backlog Reconstruction and construction of feeder roads Periodic maintenance of the road network in good or fair condition	500	Multilateral: IDA ($40 million) Bilateral: to be decided Local: Government (to be decided)	Ministry of Works and Supply Roads Department	..	..	World Bank
Roads Sector Investment Programme	Transport Potential project for BOT scheme	Routine and periodic maintenance of the core network in good and fair condition Rehabilitation of selected trunk, main, district and urban roads Upgrading of selected feeder roads and improvement of feeder roads accessibility in selected provinces Community road infrastructure programme development Support to local contracting and consulting firms	640	Multilateral: to be decided Bilateral: to be decided Local: Government (to be decided)	Ministry of Works and Supply Roads Department Ministry of Communications and Transport Ministry of Local Government and Housing National Roads Board	Projected implementation period of 5 years	..	World Bank

Annex II
INFRASTRUCTURE DEVELOPMENT INDICATORS FOR LEAST DEVELOPED COUNTRIES
Table B.V.1 Electricity capacity and production, 1990

Least developed countries	Population (millions)	Capacity (thousand kilowatts)	Capacity (thousand kilowatts per million persons)	Production (millions kilowatts-hours)	Production (million kilowatts-hours per million persons)
Africa					
Angola	10.020	617	61.58	1 840	183.63
Benin	4.730	15	3.17	5	1.06
Burkina Faso	9.000	59	6.56	155	17.22
Burundi	5.300	43	8.11	106	20.00
Cape Verde	0.333	..	..	..	0.00
Central African Republic	2.920	43	14.73	95	32.53
Chad	5.680	31	5.46	82	14.44
Comoros	0.543	..	..	..	..
Djibouti	0.517	..	..	..	..
Equatorial Guinea	0.348	..	..	..	..
Ethiopia	48.360	..	..	906	18.73
Eritrea	3.080	..	..	..	..
Gambia	0.923	13	14.08	67	72.59
Guinea	5.750	176	30.61	518	90.09
Guinea-Bissau	0.964	..	..	..	..
Lesotho	1.790	..	..	..	..
Liberia	2.400	..	..	..	..
Madagascar	11.190	220	19.66	566	50.58
Malawi	9.100	106 (1980)	..	..	..
Mali	8.150	87	10.67	214	26.26
Mauritania	2.000	105	52.50	140	70.00
Mozambique	14.150	2 358	166.64	486	34.35
Niger	7.730	63	8.15	163	21.09
Rwanda	7.180	60	8.36	176	24.51
Sao Tome and Principe	0.115	..	..	..	..
Sierra Leone	3.990	126	31.58	224	56.14
Somalia	8.670	60	6.92	230	26.53

	Population	Capacity		Production	
Least developed countries	*Population (millions)*	*(thousand kilowatts)*	*(thousand kilowatts per million persons)*	*(millions kilowatts-hours)*	*(million kilowatts-hours per million persons)*
Sudan	25.750	500	19.42	1 327	51.53
Togo	3.530	34	9.63	41	11.61
Uganda	17.940	162	9.03	603	33.61
United Republic of Tanzania	24.800	439	17.70	885	35.69
Zaire	35.560	2.831	79.61	6 155	173.09
Zambia	8.070	2.436	301.86	7 771	962.95
Western Asia					
Yemen	11.270	275	24.40	910	80.75
Asia and the Pacific					
Afghanistan	16.120	..	..	..	..
Bangladesh	108.110	2 520	23.31	82	0.76
Bhutan	1.540	..	..	..	..
Cambodia	8.560	..	..	..	..
Kiribati	..	..	..	..	..
Lao People's Democratic Republic	4.200	..	..	..	..
Maldives	0.216	..	..	..	..
Myanmar	41.810	1 116	26.69	2 601	62.21
Nepal	18.110	277	15.30	739	40.81
Samoa	..	..	..	..	..
Solomon Islands					
Tuvalu	..	..	..	..	..
Vanuatu	..	..	..	..	..
Latin America and the Caribbean					
Haiti	6.480	153	23.61	475	73.30

Source: World Bank, *World Development Report 1994: Infrastructure for Development* (New York, Oxford University Press, 1994).

Table B.V.2. Electricity consumption, 1990

Least developed countries	Million kilowatts	Million kilowatts per capita
Africa		
Angola	1 840	200
Benin	194	42
Burkina Faso	192	21
Burundi	126	23
Cape Verde	36	106
Central African Republic	95	32
Chad	84	15
Comoros	16	29
Djibouti	169	346
Equatorial Guinea	18	51
Ethiopia	1 234	26
Eritrea	..	..
Gambia	70	76
Guinea	518	90
Guinea-Bissau	40	41
Lesotho	..	..
Liberia	565	219
Madagascar	592	47
Malawi	718	77
Mali	305	33
Mauritania	140	70
Mozambique	810	57
Niger	352	46
Rwanda	250	36
Sao Tome and Principe	ˉ15	126
Sierra Leone	224	56
Somalia	258	30
Sudan	1 327	54
Togo	345	98
Uganda	664	37
United Republic of Tanzania	885	35
Zaire	5 966	159
Zambia	7 291	772
Western Asia		
Yemen	1 750	147
Asia and the Pacific		
Afghanistan	1 128	75
Bangladesh	8 057	75
Bhutan	172	111
Cambodia	160	18
Kiribati	7	97
Lao People's Democratic Republic	289	69
Maldives	24	111
Myanmar	2 622	63
Nepal	768	40
Samoa	50	309
Solomon Islands	30	94
Tuvalu	..	..
Vanuatu	25	168
Latin America and the Caribbean		
Haiti	475	73

Source: *Energy Statistics Yearbook 1993* (United Nations Publication, Sales No. E/F.95.XVII.9).

Table B.V.3. Water, sanitation and telephones, 1990

Least developed countries	Access to safe drinking water (percentage of total population)	Access to sanitation (percentage of total population)	Telephone main lines (number of connections)	Telephone main lines (connections per 1,000 persons)
Africa				
Angola	40	22	70 000	..
Benin	55	55	14 778	3
Burkina Faso	70	7		2
Burundi	46	19	10 263	2
Cape Verde	..	..		..
Central African Republic	24	46	5 000	2
Chad	57	1	4 015	1
Comoros	..	..		..
Djibouti	..	..		..
Equatorial Guinea	..	..		..
Ethiopia	18	17	125 398	2
Eritrea	..	..		..
Gambia	77	67	10 700	14
Guinea	52	21[a]	12 100	3
Guinea-Bissau	25	21		..
Lesotho	47	21	13 000	7
Liberia	..	..		..
Madagascar	21	3[a]	30 000	3
Malawi	51	53[a]	26 170	3
Mali	11	24	11 169	1
Mauritania	66	31[a]	6 248	3
Mozambique	22	21	47 439	3
Niger	53	14	9 272	1
Rwanda	69	23	10 381	1
Sao Tome and Principe	..	..		..
Sierra Leone	30	39	26 550	..
Somalia	36	17	15 000	..
Sudan	34	12	62 000	2
Togo	70	22	10 516	63
Uganda	33	60	27 886	2
United Republic of Tanzania	52	77	73 011	3
Zaire	39	23	34 000	..

(Table B.V.3 8 continued)

Least developed countries	Access to safe drinking water (percentage of total population)	Access to sanitation (percentage of total population)	Telephone main lines (number of connections)	(connections per 1,000 persons)
Zambia	59	55	65 057	8
Western Asia				
Yemen	36	..	124 516	11
Asia and the Pacific				
Afghanistan	..	..	..	..
Bangladesh	78	12	241 824	2
Bhutan	34	43	..	..
Cambodia	..	..	..	..
Kiribati	..	..	..	..
Lao People's Democratic Republic	28	11	..	2
Maldives	..	..	..	..
Myanmar	74	22	..	3
Nepal	37	6	57 320	..
Samoa	..	..	..	..
Solomon Islands	..	..	..	..
Tuvalu	..	..	..	..
Vanuatu	..	..	..	..
Latin America and the Caribbean				
Haiti	41	25	47 470	..

Source: *World Bank, World Development Report 1994: Infrastructure for Development* (New York, Oxford University Press, 1994). [a]1990-1995 (United Nations Development Programme, *Human Development Report, 1996* (New York, Oxford University Press, 1996).

Table B.V.4. Roads and railways, 1990

Least developed countries	Paved roads (kilometres)	Density of paved roads (kilometres per million persons)	Railroad tracks (kilometers)
Africa			
Angola	7 914	..	2 523
Benin	1 037	233	579
Burkina Faso	1 347	21	504
Burundi	1 011	195	612
Cape Verde	..	..	..
Central African Republic	486	155	0
Chad	378	56	0
Comoros	..	..	..
Djibouti	..	..	..
Equatorial Guinea	..	..	..
Ethiopia	13 198	84	781
Eritrea	..	..	..
Gambia	590	..	0
Guinea	4 424	240	940
Guinea-Bissau	..	..	..
Lesotho	530	359	..
Liberia	..	..	..
Madagascar	10 503	475	1 030
Malawi	2 320	278	782
Mali	5 959	308	642
Mauritania	800	804	650
Mozambique	4 949	343	3 150
Niger	4 000	383	0
Rwanda	720	149	0
Sao Tome and Principe	..	..	..
Sierra Leone	1 510	194	84
Somalia	6 199	375	0
Sudan	3 149	98	4 784
Togo	1 833	444	514
Uganda	2 416	118	1 241
United Republic of Tanzania	3 506	156	2 600
Zaire	2 800	..	5 088
Zambia	6 198	751	1 894
Western Asia			
Yemen	2 360	951	0
Asia and the Pacific			
Afghanistan	..	..	..
Bangladesh	6 167	59	2 892
Bhutan	..	..	..
Cambodia	..	..	..
Kiribati	..	..	..

Least developed countries	Paved roads (kilometres)	Density of paved roads (kilometres per million persons)	Railroad tracks (kilometers)
Lao People's Democratic Republic	..	..	..
Maldives	..	..	..
Myanmar	6 153	210	4 664
Nepal	2 805	139	52
Samoa	..	..	..
Solomon Islands	..	..	..
Tuvalu	..	..	..
Vanuatu	..	..	..
Latin America and the Caribbean			
Haiti	629	..	..

Source: *Energy Statistics Yearbook 1993* (United Nations publication, Sales No. E/F.95.XVII.9).

Appendices

I.   Investment Opportunities.

II.   List of Investment Promotion Agencies and contact addresses in LDCs

III.   Foreign Exchange Regulation-LDCs.

APPENDIX I

Investment Opportunites reported to UNCTAD by LDCs

The following information on investment opportunities in eight LDCs was provided to UNCTAD by the respective government authorities in these countries in response to a Questionnaire sent to them in December 1996. The language and format of these replies have been reproduced as received by UNCTAD from:

Lesotho
Mozambique
Myanmar
Niger
Sierra Leone
Tchad
Uganda
Zambia

LESOTHO

INVESTMENT OPPORTUNITIES

1. **Manufacturing Sector** (Refer to Annex I for Project Profiles)

This sector has been the area of priority for investment in Lesotho and has been the major contributing sector in the economic growth for the past years. Investors take advantage of Lesotho's membership of the Southern African. Customs Union (SACU) which gives duty and quota free access to the region's market. Membership of Lome Convention, access to North America, Europe and other developed countries' markets is also an added advantage for foreign investors. The implementation of the Southern African Development Community (SADC) Trade Protocol will also widen the market.

In order to support the export market, labour intensive manufacturing products are encouraged. Prospects on international market are good for products in clothing, footwear, pharmaceuticals, television/radio receivers, electro-mechanical tools, toys, electronic products, household goods etc. To support the textile industries there is need for the establishment of spinning, weaving and dyeing processes since the bulk of fabric products are currently imported. Other industries encouraged include production of zip fasteners, collar supports trimming, elastic braids, buttons etc.

The Lesotho Highlands Water Project estimated at M4 billion and covering an implementation period of over 30 years, require some engineering material and other indirect supplies for building and construction such as drainage pipes, corrugated iron, window frames etc.

Infrastructure

The Lesotho National Development Corporation (LNDC) has ready built factory shells available for rental at competitive rates in different industrial areas of the country. All industrial estates are roughly 20 minutes away from the South African First World Class roads connecting with Durban, South Africa's busiest harbour.

2. **Tourism** (Refer to Annex II for Proposed Projects)

The Lesotho Highlands Water Project has enhanced potential for tourism in Lesotho. Several sites suitable for development have already been identified and facilities, services as well as infrastructure are in place. The most profitable investment areas are in Lodges, hotels and camping sites. There is a need for the development of labour force that will enter the tourism industry hence the need for investment into vocational training at managerial as well as skilled and unskilled labour levels. In order to feed the construction workers, the project requires services such as catering, meat processing, poultry, milk related products etc. Other related services like handicrafts and vehicle service workshops are also necessary.

3. **Privatization** (Refer to Annex III for list of companies and Progress)

The Privatization and Private Sector Development Project was approved by the government of Lesotho in 1995 and the Privatization Unit has already been set up within the Ministry of Finance. The aim is to privatise several state-owned enterprises and parastatals. The principal objective is to facilitate technical partnership with foreign investors for the enhanced management and performance of enterprises. Privatisation of about nine enterprises in brick making, oil processing, fruit and vegetable) canning, pharmaceutical etc., has already been approved by the government and many more are in the pipeline. The Privatization Unit together with the Central Bank are in the process of developing the Capital Market. LNDC provides equity funding to foreign investors who are in company with the locals.

ANNEX I - PROJECT PROFILES FOR FOREIGN INVESTMENTS IN MANUFACTURING

Maloti Oil and Cake Mills (PTY) Ltd.

1.0 BACKGROUND:

Maloti Oil and Cake Mills is a medium sized plant located at the Thetsane Industrial Estate, seven (7) kilometres south-east of the Maseru city centre, the Capital of Lesotho. It was established in 1993.

2.0 PRODUCTS

The company produces edible sunflower oil.

3.0 MARKET

The company has successfuily penetrated the targeted market viz. the Lesotho domestic markel. It also supplies South African companies. The managemenI is currently investigating the marketing opportunities within the wider Southern African Development Community (SADC) and the Common market for Eastern and Southern Africa (COMESA).

4.0 TOTAL COST OF INVESTMENT

	(in thousands of Malotis)
Building(1,868 M2)	M1,300 (Actual)
Machinery and Equipment	M1,800 (Actual)
Vehicles	M0,185 (Actual)
Working Capital	M0,637
Total	M3,922

5.0 ESTIMATED TOTAL CAPITAL INVESTMENT AT APPRAISAL:

Total investment is estimated at M6.3 million

6.0 EMPLOYMENT: 50 (Current)
                                    150 (Estimated at full production)

7.0 REQUIRED

An international investor with the following attributes:

(i)   Good management and technical expertise to fully exploit the market potential.
(ii)   Financial strength.
(iii)   Willingness to form a joint venture with a reputable local regional private investor.

Project Profile - Loti Brick (PTY) Ltd.

1.0 BACKGROUND

Loti Brick is the major manufacturer of burnt clay bricks in Lesotho. The company is based the Thetsane Industrial Estate, seven (7) kilometres south-east of the Maseru city centre. the Capital of Lesotho. The company was established in 1980; it currently has rights to a total surface area of 39 hectares of good quality clay deposits. These deposits are conservatively estimated to last for at least a further forty (40) years at the rate of current exploitation.

2.0 PRODUCTS

Good quality bricks for the residential and non-residential construction sectors.

3.0 PRODUCTION CAPACITY:

The company has recently introduced new technology in the form of a tunnel kiln and additional dryers are being installed to synchronise drying capacity with that of the new tunnel kiln. Capacity is at present pegged at twenty (20) million bricks per annum. The management is contemplating increasing this capacity to thirty (30) million bricks by 1988/99 due to the rapidly growing demand in the industry.

4.0 MARKETS:

The target markets are Lesotho and South Africa. The company currently supplies 75% of the Lesotho market and has plans to increase this to 85% within a year based on quality and price competitiveness of its product.

The South African market is estimated to be worth R1 billion or six (6) billion bricks per annum. Prospects for the budding sector are very good driven mainly by the economic turn-around and the launching of the Reconstruction and Development.

5.0 CURRENT SHAREHOLDING:

The current shareholding of the company is as follows;

LNDC	73%
Lesotho Bank	23%
Lesotho Energy Enterprise	4%
	100%

6.0 EMPLOYMENT

The company has a total staff complement of 164.

7.0 HIGHLIGHTS OF RECENT FINANCIAL PERFORMANCE (in Million Maloti)

Year	Turnover	Gross Profit	Net Profit
1993/94	5.4	0.27	0.13
1994/95	6.2	2.6	1.78

Thus the company has been able to ride on the crest of the improving economid conditions and has satisfactory growth prospects.

8.0 REQUIRED

As part of the privatization programme, the LNDC is required to sell off its shareholding in successful companies Like Loti Brick so as to enable to corporation to development new businesses. An international investor is therefore required who has the following attributes;

(i)	Technical know-how
(ii)	Financial strength
(iii)	Management know-how
(iv)	Willingness to form a Joint Venture with a local private investor.

Project Profile - Rockwool Project

1.0 BACKGROUND

This project idea is about production of an insulation material know as rockwool or Basaltwool or Mineral wool. It is a resultant product of the smelting of basal or dolerite both of which are found in abundance in Lesotho.

2.0 ESTIMATED INVESTMENT

For the annual output of 75,000 tons, the projected investment required, including land and buildings, plant and equipment, pre-operating expenses and working capital amounts to US$15 million.

3.0 PROPOSED FINANCIAL STRUCTURE (IN M'000)

	Equity	Loan	Totals
LNDC/Local Investor	US$3,000	US$0.0	US$3,000
International Investor	US$3,000	US$0.0	US$3,000
Lending Institution	US$0.0	US$9,000	US$9,000
Totals	US$6,000	US$9,000	US$15,000

The above structure is tentative and can therefore be altered to suit the requirements of the potential international investor.

4.0 MARKET

The target market for rockwool is the mining and construction industries as well as oil refineries within the Southern African Development Community (SADC), whose demand is currently being met form imports from Europe.

5.0 CURRENT STATUS

There is a need to conduct raw materials testing and market studies, the European Union agency, the Centre for Development of Industry (CDI) is willing to contribute towards the funding of both studies.

6.0 REQUIREMENTS

An international investor is therefore required who has the following attributes;

(i)   Technical know-how
(ii)   Financial strength
(ii)   Management know-how
(iv)   Willingness to form a Joint Venture with a local private investor.

Mineral Water Bottling Plant

1. BACKGROUND

This project proposal seeks to take advantage of Lesotho's most abundant natural resource, water. Lesotho being richly endowed with rivers and springs, possesses an abundance of water, providing an attractive opportunity for commercializing this naturally occurring drinking water.

The process involves bottling this naturally occurring mineral water at source to sell within the regional market.

2. SPRING SOURCE

Moits'upeli spring located in Moits'upeli village, near Roma, has been identified as the most lucrative spring for commercial expoiltation. The spring was found to have the following comparative advantage: high yield; easy accessibility and close proximity to the capital and commercial centre, Maseru; and compliance with the South African Bureau of Standards (SABS) requirements.

3. CAPITAL INVESTMENT

For a conservative initial estimate of 20,000 litres per day production target for the South African market, investment was estimated at US$1.2 million. This includes equipment, transportation, sea freight, insurance, customs clearing and forwarding charges.

4. MARKET

The primary target market is South Africa because of demand and high purchasing power. However, the overall target market is Southern Africa taking advantage of the favourable location to compete with international brands.

5. CURRENT STATUS

There is a need to conduct in-depth market research on the target market especially the South African market as demand influences investment decisions. Although, initial analysis of the spring water has had exceedingly positive results, thorough anaiysis is still recommended.

6. REQUIREMENTS

An international investor with the following attributes:-

(i)   Financial Strength
(ii)   Technical know-how
(iii)   Willingness to form a joint-venture with local private investor.

ANNEX II - PROJECT PROFILES IN TOURISM DEVELOPMENT

Project Profile - HA Theko Peninsula

1.0 BACKGROUND

The project is located in the northern part of Lesotho, within the lower Bokong Special Development Area of the Highlands Water Project as seen from the attached map. The project site already easily accessible with an excellent and a high quality tarred road linking it with Maseru and other neighbouring towns in South Africa.

2.0 OBJECTIVES

The project aims at providing a 150 bedroomed luxury hotel to fully capitalize on the substantially increasing, tourism generated by the most sophisticated, engineering water development project in Africa, the Highlands Water Project.

3.0 COMPONENTS OF THE PROJECT

This project will encompass the following:

- A 150 bedroomed luxury hotel.
- A lakeland marina with river cruising operations (e.g. lake sailing and rowing club).
- A winter house containing an alpine botanical garden and leisure facilities.
- Pony trekking, hiking and nature tracks.
- A trout farm tourist centre.

4.0 PRODUCTS

Visitors to the project will enjoy a wide range of attractions, namely:

- Naturally, historic and cultural assets.
- Scenic beauty of the Highlands-mountain-range
- Pollution free and environmentally sensitive recreation and relaxation.
- Traditional lifestyle.
- Water sporting activities that will be enhanced by the Highlands Water Project.
- "Green product" - attractive flora and fauna.

5.0 MARKET

As a result of changes in Southern Africa, the region has become the heartland of tourism. Lesotho will exploit its favourable location and attraction to its unique tourist product to capture a large share of the long-haul visitors to the region, as well as tourists from the region.

6.0 TOTAL COST OF INVESTMENT

Investment for the project has been estimated at MS, 250 000..

7.0 REQUIRED

An international investor with the following attributes:

(i)   Good management and technical expertise.
(ii)   Financial strength.

Project Profile - Malibamats'o Bridge Resort

1.0 BACKGROUND

The project is located in the northern part of Lesotho near Malibamats'o river bridge. Malibamats'o river runs along the way to Katse dam, and it is within Ha Lejone Special Area of the Lesotho Highlands Water Project. The crossing access of the river is by the biggest bridge ever seen in the country, and as seen from the attached map, the bridge cuts across the extended dam. In addition, the project site is already accessible with a good tarred road linking it with Maseru and other neighbouring towns in South Africa.

2.0 OBJECTIVES

The project aims at providing an 80 room hotel to accommodate many tourists currently visiting the area and its surroundings. The project seeks to exploit the attractiveness of the Lesotho Highlands Project, the magnificent and most sophisticated engineering water development scheme in Africa.

3.0 COMPONENTS OF THE PROJECT

The project comprises of the following:

- An 80 room hotel.
- Mooring and cruise boat facilities.
- A 9 hole practice golf course and equestrian centre.
- A driving range.
- Sports and health club facilities.

4.0 PRODUCTS

Visitors to the project will enjoy the following attractions:

- Natural, historic and cultural heritage assets.
- Scenic beauty of the Highlands-Mountain-Range.

- Pollution free and environmentally sensitive recreation and relaxation
- Traditional lifestyle.
- Water sporting facilities that will be enhanced by the Highlands Water Project.
- "Green product" - attractive flora and fauna.

5.0 MARKET

As a result of changes in Southern Africa, the region has become the heartland of tourism. Lesotho will exploit its favourable location and attraction to its unique tourist product to capture a large share of long-haul visitors to the region, as well as tourists within the region.

6.0 TOTAL COST OF INVESTMENT

Investment for the project is estimated at M5,250,000.

7.0 REQUIRED

An international investor with the following attributes:

(i)   Good management and technical expertise.
(ii)   Financial strength

Project Profile - Family Holiday Centre

The project is situated at the Thaba-Tseka/Katse village junction. The project area is easily accessible with an excellent tarred road linking it with Maseru and other neigbouring town in South Africa.

2.0 OBJECTIVES

The project aims at providing an 80 roomed resort to accommodate tourists currently visiting the area and the considerable amount of patronage from club members living in the capital, Maseru, and surrounding regions. The resort will furnish an upmarket country, sports and health club facility.

3.0 COMPONENTS OF THE PROJECT

The project comprises of the following:

- An 80 roomed sports and health club facility.
- A marina with pontoons, lake sailing and rowing club.
- Mountain botanical gardens and winter house.
- The Bokong pony-trekking centre which will be the Pony-Trekking Association's headquarters in the highlands.
- Hiking trails, nature trails, environmental reserve and trails to fishing areas.

4.0 PRODUCTS

Visitors to the Family Holiday Resort will enjoy the following:

- Natural, historic and cultural heritage assets.
- Magnificent scenery of the Highlands-Mountain-Range.
- Pollution free and environmentally sensitive recreation and relaxation.
- "Green product"- attractive flora and fauna.

5.0 MARKET

As a result of changes in Southern Africa, the region has become the heartland of tourism Lesotho will exploit its favourable location and attraction to its unique tourist product to capture a large share of long-haul visitors to the region, as well as tourists from the region.

6.0 TOTAL COST OF INVESTMENT

Investment for the project has been est/mated at M2,450 000.

7.0 REQUIRED

An international investor with the following attributes:

(i)   Good management and technical expertise.
(ii)   Financial strength.

Lesotho Highlands Development Area

The following are proposed projects for the development of tourist facilities within the phase l(a) of the LHDA programme outside of it.

Project Title	Cost Estimates (M'000)
1. Eagle Rock Country Club	
Stage 1: Country club + sports facilities	5,000
Stage 2: Golf course & Time Share Homes	7,500
Stage 3. Time Shares, homes	9,000
Sub-total	**21,500**
1. Mahlasela Resort (Ski Resort)	5,000
3. Mt. Aux-sources Resort	5,000
4. Ha Lejone Family Resort	
- Marine/sailing centre	1,200
5. Ha-Lule & Poli Reach Country Hotel Facilities	
- moorings, berths & cruise-boats	1,200
- golf driving range & 9-hole golf course	3,500
Sub-total	**4,700**
6. Malibamatso Bridge Resort	
- moorings, berths & cruise boats	1,750
7. Malibamatso island living village and harbour	600
8. Ha-Seshote Special Development area	
8.1 18-hole "Roof of Africa" International golf course	6,000
8.2 Timeshare Mountain Lodge estate	9,000
Sub-total	**15,000**
9. Lower Bokong Special Development Area	
9.1 Ha-Theku Peninsula Hotel	
- Marine & lake sailing & rowing club	4,000
- Mountain Botanical gardens & winter house	1,250
Sub-total	**5,250**
10. Molikaliko family resort	
10.1 Adventure camp & Sports park	1,000
10.2 Angling and boating centre	350
Sub-total	**1,350**
11. Likalaneng Lake resort	
11.1 Sports & health club	3,500
11.2 Sailing & equestrian	4,500
Sub-total	**8,000**
Grand Total	**M69,350**

It is believed that the natural environment in the particular case of Lesotho Highlands is of paramount importance to tourism; it follows that the maintenance of a good environment is essential for its sustainability. The following environment projects will therefore be implemented by the government to demonstrate its commitment to the tourism sector and also to enhance the tourism product, especially within the Katse catchment area and Moteng valley tourism area:

1. Alpine Natural reserve (Moteng)	3,750,000
2. Muela Environmental & Nature reserve	686,000
3. Development of picnic sites	600,000
4. Hiking & fishing trails	400,000
5. Pony trekking and nature trail	600,000
6. Mphosong (Mafika Iisiu): Afro-alpine environment & tourist Information gateway	
6.1 Reserve, bird sanctuary & lodge	M825,000

4. Government Policies on Market and Investment Promotion

The promotion of tourism is an important part of the tourism policies of the government of Lesotho. It have not left this activity in the hands of the private sector.

The Lesotho Tourist Board which is the national tourist marketing agency receives around US$2.2 million annually. While this may seem rather low, it is to be seen together with other activities Lesotho involved in.

In order to encourage tourism investment within Lesotho, the government is working on the following investment incentive packages directed at the sector:

   i) Subsidised loan finance.
   ii) Corporate tax deduction form 45% to 15%.

MOZAMBIQUE

INVESTMENT OPPORTUNITIES

LARGE SCALE INVESTMENT OPPORTUNITIES

1. **Companhia do Buzi, SARL** - in Buzi (Sofala Province) approximately 2 hours river trip by boat from Beira;
   Current Situation: Not operational
   Ownership: Mozambican Government (67%). Banco de Mozambique (30%);
   Investment Potential: The cost of rehabilitating this estate has been estimated at USS 85 million in a 1994 feasibility study financed by the African Development Bank (ADB) which is the major interested party, currently seeking co-financing. Other activities which are currently being developed on the estate include cotton production, alcohol distillation, livestock rearing and a sawmill.

2. **Sena Sugar Estates Ltd.** This is the former British-owned company that has now extinguished. It comprises two estates on the opposite sides of the Zambezi River:

   (i)Marrorneu (Sofala Province);
   (ii) Luabo (Zambezia Province);
   Current situation: Not operational
   Investment Potential: Negotiations are ongoing with Alcantara (representative of Tate & Lyle UK) with regard to potential rehabilitation of these two estates. The major constraint is the lack of functioning infrastructure to transport the sugar from the estates. Various options are being considered including transporing sugar by barge down the Zambezi River and the reconstruction of the railway line to Beira.

3. **Acucareira de Moçambique, SARL (Mafambisse)** - In Dondo district (Sofala Province) about 45 kms from Beira;
   Current situation: Operational, but producing *at* only 25% of installed capacity (production levels of 19000 tomes in 1994;
   Ownership: Banco de Moçambique (67%), others (23%), Government (10%);
   Investment Potential: Currently in its fifth year of rehabilitation under an ADB loan. A 12 month management contract has been signed with Tongaat Hulett who have an option to buy a controlling share in the company, subject to approval of their performance by the Board of Directors.

4. **Marracuene Agricola Acucareira, SARL (Maragra)** - situated in Manhica district about 70 kms north of Maputo;
   Current Situation: Not Operational

Ownership: Petiz family, Portugal (40%), Banco de Moçambique (25%), Government (15%), Others (20%);

Investment Potential: Booker Tate (UK) is currently carrying out a feasibility study on the rehabilitation of the estate and is also involved in negotiations for a future management contract.

5. **Acucareira de Xinavane, SARL (Incomati)** - also situated in Manhica district about 110 km north of Maputo.
    Current Situation: Operational - producing at 25% of installed capacity (9,997 tonnes in 1994);
    Ownership: Mozambican Government (51%), Soc. Agricola do Incomati - Portugal (49%);
    Investment Potential: A feasibility study for the rehabilitation of the estate has been carried out estimating the total cost of rehabilitation *at* USS 45.5 million. Various international financing institutions are being approached to fund this project, including the Kuwait Fund, OPEC Fund, BADEA and ADB.

    Contact: Instituto Nacional do Aucar, Maputo
    (National Sugar Institute)
    Tel: 258-1-420478; Fax: 258-1-425387

    NOTE: The information in this section is designed to inform potential investors the existing situation in the sugar industry in Mozambique. Specific opportunities for private investors can be discussed with the National Sugar Institute.

6. **Carbornoc E.E**: With coal reserves of more than 2 billion tons, offering opportunities to participate in the rehabilitation, expansion and modernization of the Moatize Coal Mines.
    Total investment: US$25 million

    This project can facilitate the opening and development of other new mines and the rehabilitation of the coal extraction line, increasing the total amount of investment to around USS 1.2 billion.
    Contact: Ministry of Mineral Resources and Energy
    Tel: 258-1-430849; Fax: 258-1-430850

7. **Aquaculture:** Aquaculture projects (along the coast line of Mozambique). With excellent ecological and climatic conditions in various places situated near to the Ports of Maputo, Beira, Quellmane and Angoche, unique opportunities are offered for the development of projects involving aquaculture of prawns, lobster and other fish resources of high commercial value.

    Estimated minimum investment for every project: US$30 million
    Projected annual income: US$17 million
    Contact: Ministry of Agriculture and Fisheries
    National Directorate of Fisheries

Tel: 258-1 30961/34885
Fax: 258-1 420335
Maputo, Mozambique

SMALL AND MEDIUM SCALE INVESTMENT OPPORTUNITIES

Agriculture

1. National entrepreneur looking for a partner for the production of rice, maize, cashew nuts and other crops in Chokwe, with an area of 3.000 ha.
   Contact: Ms. Laurinda Allredo Maholela, Tel: 021 20118

2. National entrepreneur looking for a partner for the production of cotton and tobaco in Chokwe, with an area of 60 ha.
   Contact: Mr. Vazir Osseman Dazi Bana, Tel: 258-1-752841 - Bairro da Liberdade, Maputo.

3. National entrepreneur looking for a partner for the production of pineapple and copra in the region of Matilde, Chinde and Zambezia. Exist various plantation of coco, shops and other infrastructure for rehabilitation.
   Contact: Mr. Joao Levessene, Av. Paulo Kankhomba n° 1034, 2°, Maputo, Tel: 258-1-424324/5; Fax: 424311.

4. National entrepreneur looking for a partner for the development of cattle farming, with an area of 5.000 ha in Cabo Delgado.
   Contact: Mr. Anatasio Makala, Tel: 417390, C.P 160, Maputo.

5. National entrepreneur looking for a partner for the production of maize, beans, sunflower and other vegetables, cattle and pig farming in Beira.
   Contact: Mr. Domingos Pascoal CP 81 - Beira, Tel: (03) 323972/322318.

6. Partner or financing sought for the expansion/rehabilitation of livestock and cropping activities on I 500 ha farm in Maputo.
   Contact: Mr. Henrique P. da Costa, Soc. Pecuaria e Agricola, Av Filipe S. Magaia 970, 9° floor, Tel: 31653.

7. Partner sought for development of mixed crop/livestock in Maputo province.
   Contact: Mr. Filipe Simba, C.P. 1364 Tel/Fax: 493280.

8. Partner sought for the development of 105 ha mixed crop/livestock in Moamba, Maputo province.
   Contact: Mr. Medeiro, Av Guerra Popular 1365 - Maputo.

9. Joint venture partner sought for existing 10.000 ha farm for development of crop/livestock and wildlife, in Manhoca Administrative post of Zitunde, Matutuine district in Maputo Province.
   Contact: Mr. Joao Gonçalves Perdigao, Tel: 29049 Maputo.

10. Joint venture partner sought for existing 200ha mixed farm producing maize, beans, sunflower, potatoes, beef, pork and animal feed near the city of Beira Sofala Province. Estimated Investment: US$1,000,000.
Contact: Mr. Antonio J. Ferreira, C.P. 171, Manga, Beira.

11. Joint venture partner sought for the development of a farm of nearly 600 ha in the city of Beira (Sofala Province), currently producing pigs, rice and various fruits and vegetables. Livestock-rearing outhouse, drainage systems, and animal-food processing equipment existing.
Estimated Investment: US$100,000
Contact: Mr. Americo B. da Costa, Agro-Pecuaria de Nhassassa Tel: 322318 Beira.

12. Joint venture partner sought for cotton production on an existing plantation of over 400 ha in Mutarara. Land also has high sunflower and gergelim potential.
Contact: Mr. Joao Levessene, Av. Paulo Kankhomba n° 1034, 2°, Maputo, Tel: 258-1-424324/5; Fax: 424311.

13. Partner sought for development of 8.000 ha mixed crop/livestock farm in Sena, Sofala Province.
Contact: Mr. Issufu. Av Z. Manganhelas 754, Maputo, Tel: 33706

14. Partner sought for the recultivation of 1,000 ha for the production of cashew nuts and coconuts in Mutucuti, Nampula Province.
Contact: Mr. Gil B. Rosario C.P 711 Tel: 214676 Nampula.

15. Joint venture partner sought for the recultivation of *an* existing horticulture farm of 100 ha in *Moamba/Maputo* province.
Contact: Ms. Ernesto, Tel: 258-1 431921, Fax: 258-1 42 76 67, Maputo

16. National entrepreneur looking for a partner for the production of cotton, sunflower, gergelim, corn, rice etc. in Marromeu/Sofala Province
Contact: Mr. Abdul Cedar Mussa, Tel: 03 326254, Fax: 03 323229

Fisheries sector

Mozambique produces an estimated 100,000 tons of fish annually worth US$116 million in 1993, of which US$73 million was exported In value terms, the principal fisheries are those for shallow and deep-water prawns which are mainly exploited by large industrial trawlers, producing 8000 tons of prawn annually. Prawns and other crustaceans represented over 50% of Mozambique's total export earnings in 1994.

As an overall strategy for the development of Mozambique's fisheries sector, the following resources have been identified in the good development potential:

- Collection handling and export of mangrove crab (Scylla serrata);

- Shark fishing and processing

- Capture, freezing and export of high-value finfish in the northern part of Mozambiaque and Inhambane province;

- Collection and export of rock lobster (Panilurus ornatus, Panilurus momarus and Panilurus penicilatus);

- Harvesting of pelagic species (mackarel, sardine and scad) for local consumption and to supply existing canneries;

- Collection, processing and export of seaweed and sea cucumber or beche de mer;

- Collection, purification and processing of molluscs including clams (Venus species), oysters (Crassostrea species and mussels (Perna perna);

- Collection and processing of precious shells - mother of pearl, cameos, ornamental shells;

- Capture and export of ornamental fish; and

- Development of prawn aquafarming projects in several suitable locations along the Mozambican coast.

For more information about the fisheries sector in Mozambique, kindly contact:

Ministry of Agriculture and Fisheries
National Directorate of Fisheries
Rug Consiglieri Pedroso, 343 - 2°
Maputo, Mozambique
Tel: (258 -1) 30961/34885
Fax: (258-1)420335

Industry

1. Looking for a partner for the introduction of a new line of production of sport and recreation materials and other plastic articles (relegious articles cruz etc.), in Maputo. **Contact:** Mr. Miguel portugal, Mipogal, Tel: 400920 - Maputo.

2. Looking for a partner for the modernization and rehabilitation of a factory for ship construction and repair in Beira.

   Contact: Mr. Raul Diaz, C.P 2344, Maputo.

3. Looking for a partner for the establishment of a processing meat company and various canning activities in Maputo.

Contact: Mr. Victorina Malete, Av. Karl Marx 1902 R/C, Maputo, Tel: 258-1 125389, Fax: 258-1-422477.

4.   Looking for a partner for the production of low cost teaching material, with local materials for domestic sales.
Contact: Mr. Maia, Buko Ltd, Av. Arebed Sekou Toure, Tel: 258-1 417055, 258 475310, 258-1-429715.

5.   National entrepreneur looking for a partner for the rehabilitation and modernization of an existing infrastructure for the manufacturing of furniture in Machava/Maputo province.
Contact: Liacat All Hussene, Tel: 258-1 752999, Fax: 258-1 752999

6.   A company, SOMOPESCA, Ltd. is looking for a partner for shallow water shrimp fisheries in Beira/Sofala province.
Contact: J.B Flores, Telefax: 03 31 15 15

Construction

1.   Three local partners are looking for a foreign partner to invest in know-how for the rehabilitation of roads.

    Contact: TimoteoManganhela, ProfuroLtd.,Tel:258-14912061491251; Fax: 492701.

2.   A company, CIPREL, Lda is looking for a partner for the production of construction materials (beams, blocks, grills, etc.) in Machava/Maputo province.

    Contact: Mr. Mussagy, Tel: 258-1 753151, Fax: 258-1 422186

3.   A company, CERAMICA DE UMPALA is looking for a partner to modernize its existing infrastructure for the production of construction materials and potteries in Boane/Maputo province.

    Contact: Mr. C. Quadros, Tel: 258-1 422185, Fax: 258-1 422186

Tourism

1.   Joint venture partner sought the construction of a tourist resort in Vilancula/Inhambane.

    Contact: Mr. Timoteo Feliz Pinto, Tel: 258-1 421732, Fax: 258-1 422315, Maputo

2.   SOCINVEST Ltd, a company is looking for a partner to build a hotel in Beira/Sofala province.

Estimated Investment: USS 2.000,000
Contact: Mr. Joaquim B. Flores, Telefax: 03 311515

Transport

1.   A maritime transport company for the transportation of goods and passengers, TRANSPORTES MARITIMOS JUSSUFO, Ltd is looking for a partner for the expansion of its activities in Quelimane.
Contact: Issufa J.T. Mohamed, Tel: 04 213721, Fax: 04/214423

INDUSTRIAL FREE ZONES
(export processing zones)

Industria Ceramica de Moçambique (ICM) -   proposed site for the development of a multi-user industrial free zone (IFZ)

Industria Ceramica de Moçambique (ICM) site, EN2, Boane. The site is on the main road between Maputo and Boane which continues on to Namaacha (Swaziland border) and Ressano Garcia (South Africa Border). Is 30 km from Maputo port and is adjacent to a concrete railway sleeper factory on one side and empty land on the other. The railway sleeper factory has an existing rail siding clinking into the Goba line between Maputo and Swaziland. The ICM existing factory belongs to the Mozambican Government, and is suitable for rehabilitation and conversion into IFZ units. The factory has approximately 11,000m2 of existing covered space and an additional 10 ha of land available for development.

The ICM company is currently being privatised by the Ministry Of Public Works and Habitation. Conversion of the existing facilities to IFZ usage is estimated to cost US$2.6 million, yielding 11,820m of lettable IFZ space.

Other areas in consideration for the development and exploration of IFZ in the country are Sofala province near to the port of Beira, Nampula Province and Nacala.

For more information on Industrial Free Zones, please contact:

CPI -INVESTMENT PROMOTION CENTRE
Av. 25 de Setembro N° 2049, 1 st floor, PO Box 4635
Maputo, Mozambique
Tel: (258-1) 422456/7
Fax: (258-1) 422459
Telex: 6-876

INVESTMENT OPPORTUNITIES IN THE STATE PRIVATISATION PROCESS

As part of the artgoing privatisation programme, the Government of Mozambique has put forward on an annual basis, a series of companies for sales. The method of privatisation used involves a public tender preceded by pro-qualification of interested buyers resulting in the transfer to private hands which may take the following modalities:

- sale by public tender;
- public offer of share:
- private negotiations (preceded by prospecting for investors) or restricted tender preceded by pre-qualification;
- joint venture through an injection of private capital;
- transfer or sale of shares to managers and employees; and
- granting of management or lease concessions.

For further information on enterprises to be privatised by UTRE, please contact:

UTRE: Technical Unit for Enterprise Restructuring
(Ministry of Planning and Finance)
Av. 25 of September 1230 7° Andar, Maputo
Tel: 258-1-426514/5/6; Fax: 258-1- 421541, or
Email <rani@utre.uem.mz>

For further information on enterprises to be privatised by GREI, please contact:

GREI: Office for Restructuring of Industrial
Commercial and Tourism Enterprises
Av. 25 de Setembro I 167 3rd Floor, Maputo
Tel: 258-1-423884; Fax: 258-1-420245

In each particular case the respective dates of pre-qualification and tender are announced in advance. Enterprises or individuals who express interest in the privatisation process are directly contacted by fax or telephone.

PRIVATISATION PROGRAMME FOR 1996 (UTRE)

1. **Pedreira Estevel:** Stones quarry and processing of stones.

2. **Pescorn Nacional, E.E:** Company involved in the processing and sale of fish products with branches throughout the country.

3. **Steia: 4 Units:** Company repairing construction equipment.

4. **Equipesca, E.E (Maputo):** Company producing fishing equipment in Maputo with delegations in Beira and Nampula. Sales in 1993: US$300 million.

5. **Cogropa (Maputo)**: Company for consumer goods distribution. Sales in 1992: US$12.2 million.

6. **Imbec, E.E:** Company for consumer goods distribution and other products.

7.   **Anfrena, E.E:** Sea freight and navigation agent, with headquarters in Maputo end delegations in the provinces.

8.   **Navinter, E.E:** Sea freight and navigation agent.

9.   **Construtora de regadios do Limpopo, E.E:** Irrigation systems and civil works.

10.   **Marmonte, E.E:** production of marble.

11.   **Geomoc:** Company which undertakes drilling and geological studies.

12.   **Gemas e Pedras Lapidades:** Cutting, polishing and sale of precious and semi-precious gemstones.

13.   **Vidreira:** Glass and glass product manufacture.

14.   **Fabrica de Cervejas Reunidas:** Brewery in Maputo.

15.   **Dalo:** Enterprise for civil construction.

16.   **Emose:** Insurance company.

17.   **Linhas Aerea de Moçambique (LAM):** Civil Aviation.

18.   **Adena:** Customs clearing.

19.   **Navique:** Coastal shiping line.

20.   **Empressa Nacional do Tourism, E.E:** Tourism and Hotels

21.   **Geralco:** Producing cooking oil from copra.

PRIVATIZATION PROGRAMME FOR 1996 (GREI)

Industry

1.   **Fapel/Fapacar:** Paper and carton factory. Occupying a covered area of 10234m2 out of a total area of 47000m2. Installed capacity of 18400 ton/year, with FAPEL 12000 ton/year and FAPACAR 6400 ton/year.

2.   **Enafrio**
Location: Maputo
Principal activity: production of freezers and fridges.

3.   **Equitec**

176

Location: Maputo
Principal activity: Distribution of industrial machines.

4. **Metal Box (Quota)**
    Location: Machava/Maputo province
    Principal activity: Production of metal products.

5. **Extrasal**
    Location: Matola/Maputo province
    Principal activity: Production of salt.

6. **Frigo Services (Quota)**
    Location: Beira/Sofala province
    Principal activity: Production of cold storage equipment and wagons.

7. **Van Leer Moçambique**
    Location: Matola/Maputo province
    Principal activity: Production and sales of metal packaging and drums.

8. **Ceres (Quota)**
    Location: Matola/Maputo province
    Principal activity: Production of biscuits and pasta.

9. **Fernando Raul da Silva**
    Location: Beira/Sofala province
    Principal activity: Manufacturing of furniture and sales of woods.

10. **Fabrica de Brinquedos**
    Location: Beira/Sofala Province
    Principal activity: Manufacturing of furniture and sales of woods.

11. **Bertino/Galeria Ducai**
    Location: City of Maputo
    Principal activity: Production of curtains and furniture.

12. **Indel**
    Location: Maputo
    Principal activity: Assembling of radios, TV and production of electric lamps.

13. **Ermoto**
    Location: Beira/Sofala Province
    Principal activity: Repairing engines.

14. **Belita**
    Location: Beira/Sofala Province
    Principal activity: Manufacture of ready made clothing.

15. **Emma**
    Location: Chimoio/Manhica Provience
    Principal activity: Manufacture of knitwear articles.

16. **Metecna**
    Location: Beira/Sofala Province
    Principal activity: Production of agricultural instruments.

17. **Celmoque**
    Location: Beira/Sofala Province
    Principal activity: Production of cables and electric conductors.

18. **Empresa Moderna**
    Location: Maputo
    Principal activity: Edition of books and other articles.

19. **Projecto Ikarus**
    Location: Beira/Sofala province
    Principal activity: Assembling of vehicles.

20. **Facol**
    Location: Beira/Sofala province
    Principal activity: Manufacture of ready made clothing.

21. **Fatemol**
    Location: Beira/Sofala province
    Principal activity: Manufacture of ready made clothing.

22. **Cegraf**
    Location: Maputo/Sofala Province
    Principal activity: Production of school books.

23. **Filiarte**
    Location: Beira/Sofala
    Principal activity: Manufacturing of furniture.

24. **Quimica Geral**
    Location: Matola/Maputo
    Principal activity: Production of pesticides.

25. **Loumar (Quota)**
    Location: Maputo
    Principal activity: production of juices and confectionaries.

26. **Mailer (Quota)**
    Location: Matola/Maputo
    Principal activity: Shoes manufacturing.

27. **IMA**
     Location: Maputo
     Principal activity: Production of galvanized tubes and zinc.

28. **CSM (Quota)**
     Location: Maputo
     Principal activity: Production of wooden rods for building construction.

29. **Isotal/Carpintaria**
     Location: Maputo
     Principal activity: Production of roof ceiling.

Tourism

1. **Pensao Martins:** Boarding house in Maputo.
2. **Hotel Central:** Hotel in Maputo.
3. **Complexo Silva:** Hotel in Bilene, Gaza Province.
4. **Hotel Tourism:** Hotel in Maputo.
5. **Complexo Estoril:** Hotel in Beira, Sofala Province.
6. **Hotel Kassuende:** Hotel in Tete.
7. **Hotel Vera Cruz:** Hotel in the city of Quelimane, Zambezia Province.

Commerce

1. **Interquimica:** A company importing chemical products, with headquarters in Maputo and delegations in Beira and Nacala.

2. **Interelectra:** A company distributing electrical materials, with headquarters in Maputo and delegations in Beira and Nacala.

3. **Diprom:** Warehouse company in Maputo with delegation in Magude and Manhica.

4. **Imbec:** A company importing foodstuffs, with headquarters in Maputo and delegations in Beira and Nacala.

5. **Facirn:** A company for the organization of annual trade exhibition in Maputo.

MYANMAR

INVESTMENT OPPORTUNITIES

Myanmar is the largest country on the mainland South-East Asia with a total land area of 676,577 sq. km. sharing total international borders of 5858 km. with Bangladesh and India on the North-West, China on the North-East, Laos on the East and Thailand on the South-East. It has a total coastline of 2832 km. It stretches 2090 km. from north to south and 925 km. from east to west at its widest points.

Myanmar's population spread over seven States and seven Divisions is estimated at 44.74 million in 1995-96. Myanmar is inhabited by many ethnic nationalities, as many as 135 national groups with the Bamars forming the largest group comprising about 68.96 per cent of the population.

Agriculture

The agricultural sector being the mainstay of the Myanmar economy with about 38 per cent of the total GDP and about 40 per cent of foreign exchange earnings is accorded priority.

Myanmar is rich in agricultural land resources and agricultural labour is relatively cheap. Investment in this sector is a promising one. Local and foreign investors are welcomed to invest in the form of Joint Venture or 100 per cent investment and profit sharing basis in the following areas:

- Agriculture
- Trade
- Agro-based Industries
- Other Business Opportunities

Agricultural Land Utilization - with a view to develop agriculture, livestock breeding and other affiliated enterprises, the State Economic Enterprises, joint ventures, co-operative societies and other organizations and private individuals will be granted the right to cultivate/right to utilize culturable, fallow and waste land upon application. Central Committee for the management of culturable land, fallow land and waste land has been formed and the duties and rights of the Committee has been prescribed. The Committee had prescribed the procedures for the right to cultivate land/right to utilize land for agriculture and livestock breeding purposes. Foreigners or organizations consisting of foreigners may also apply for the utilization of land to the Myanmar Investment Commission.

Persons who desire to invest in commercial enterprises concerning such activities will be granted the right to cultivate/right to utilize culturable land, fallow land and waste land up to the maximum area mentioned below:

(a) Agriculture
    (i)   Plantation Crops   5000 acres
    (ii)   Orchard   3000 acres
    (iii)   Seasonal Crops   1000 acres
(b) Livestock, Poultry Farming and Aquaculture
    (i)   Aquaculture   2000 acres
    (ii)   Livestock & Poultry Farming
        (aa) Buffalo, cattle, horse   5000 acres
        (bb) Sheep, goat   1000 acres
        (cc) Poultry, pig   500 acres

Duration has been fixed for a maximum period of thirty years for cultivation and utilization of land for plantation crops and orchard, livestock and poultry farming and aquaculture purposes. The period may be extended upon negotiation. In case of cultivation for seasonal crops the duration shall continue as long as there is no breach of conditions.

Exemption from payment of land revenue shah be granted for a period of 2 to 8 years from the granting of the lease depending upon the type of agricultural crops, livestock breeding and aquaculture; and at least 3 years of income-tax exemption may be granted from the year of commencement of commercial run of the business carried out on land developed and invested. An order permitting the right to cultivate/right to utilize land shall be granted after a deposit of 10% of the investment as guarantee fee has been paid.

Livestock and Fishery

Foreign investors can undertake economic activities in the following areas.
- Cattle breeding
- Pig and poultry production
- Pig, poultry and pets vaccine production
- Veterinary pharmaceutical production
- Construction of ice plant
- Construction of cold storage complex
- Construction of fish meal plant
- Construction ofc~nning plant
- Development of Slkfimp hatchery
- Establishment of shrimp farm
- Bee keeping and bee products production
- Industries related to fisheries, such as construction of fishing vessels, fishing nets etc.

Forestry

Myanmar is indeed very rich in forest resources, as the forest covers about 50.87 per cent of the total land area. According to its climatic zones from temperate to arid and tropical, several variant forests types exist. They are the temperate forests in the north, the deciduous forests and dry forests in the central part and semitropical rain forests in the south. There are over

8570 different plant species, including 2300 tree species, 850 kinds of orchid, 97 varieties of bamboo and 32 different types of cane. In 1994/95 reserved forest area totalled 103312 sq. km.

The forest policy of Myanmar has been formulated according to the forestry principles adopted by the United Nations Conference on Environment and Development. The Government gives priority to protect the soils, water catchments, eco-systems, bio-diversity, plant/animal resources, scenic reserves and national heritage sites. At the same time sustainable management of the forests is practised simultaneously so as to ensure perpetuity the level of benefit both tangible and intangible for future generations. It also employs the maintenance and rational use and enhancement of the forest resources base, to ensure ecological resilience and its contribution to socio-economic growth on a continuous basis.

Teak - The forest area with significant teak resources covers about 6.1 million hectare, accounting for about 10 per cent of growing stock in some places. Teak is highly reputable in the world market. Myanmar enjoys the largest share of the world teak trade. The total annual allowable cut (AAC) for teak is around 0.3 million hoppus tons (0.6 million cubic meters). Export items are veneer, plywood, furniture, carving, joinery, flooring products, mottiding etc.

Hardwood- There are different species of hardwood such as Padauk (Pterocarpus macrocarpus), Pyinkado (Xylia dolabriformis), Kanyin (Dipterocarpus species), Taungthayet (Swintoma floribunda), Pine (Pinus insularis) etc. The total annual allowable cut (AAC) for hardwood is 1.3 million hoppus tons (2.34 million cubic meters).

Bamboo - Bamboo grow mostly mixed with other tree species while in the Rakhine State there is a single patch of Kayin-Wa (Mellocanna bambusoides) growing in pure strands stretching over about 7770 sq. km. On a cutting cycle of 10 years, the annual yield is 2.0 million tons, an equivalent of about 0.8 million tons of bamboo pulp. In the Tanintharyi Division, there are single pure bamboo patches and also some mixed with other tree species. The growing stock covers an area of 1860 sq. km. On a cutting cycle of 10 years, the annual yield is about 0.6 million tons, an equivalent of about 0.2 million tons of bamboo pulp.

Cane - Cane grows in abundance in Myanmar, and there are about 32 species having been identified and recorded. The annual potential yield of various species is estimated at about 70 million pieces. At present, only a few species are exported. However, with the present extent of cane resources, there is ample scope for expansion of its extraction and for exports.

Others - Other products are cutch for tanning and dyeing of fish nets, canvas, tarpaulins and leather with an annual production of about 200,000 kilograms; tan-bark for tanning with an annual output of about 650,000 kilograms, and lac used for varnishes, polishes, sealing wax etc., with an annual output of about 70,000 kilograms.

Myanmar has refrained from practising concessioning, and has adhered to the tendering system. Timber harvesting has been undertaken solely by the Myanma Timber Enterprise (MTE) but investors can negotiate with MTE to extract on a contractual basis.

Mining

Minerals - Myanmar is well endowed with mineral resources and has many famous mines. To explore, develop and exploit the mineral resources of the country and to make partnership in bilateral co-operation, the Ministry of Mines is welcoming the foreign investors interested to invest in joint ventures with the economic enterprises under the Ministry. Two State Enterprises under the Ministry are responsible for the production of metallic minerals and one Enterprise deals with Industrial minerals as well as iron and steel products. The production of precious stones, such as gems, jade and diamond are handled by another State Enterprise. The main minerals produced are refined lead, refined silver, zinc concentrate, copper concentrate, refined tin, tin concentrate, tin-wolfram-scheelite concentrate and gold. The precious stones produced are ruby, sapphire, diamond and jade. Industrial minerals produced inclued coal, gypsum, baryte, limestone, dolomite, bentonite, chromite, fireclay, fluoride, granite and various other items.

Investments can be made through production sharing or profit sharing arrangements. Production sharing type of investment could be either straight split on total production or with consideration of recovering production cost. In the cost recovery type of production sharing, it is usually done in such a way that a certain percentage of total revenue is reserved before consideration of recovering the production costs. Straight production split type is preferred in large volume, low price and low cost of production types of minerals such as dimension stones, coal and other industrial minerals. In case of more valuable metallic minerals such as gold and copper, production sharing with cost recovery type of cooperation may be possible. The ratio of production split may be fixed for the term of contract or on a sliding scale depending on the level of production. Profit sharing type of arrangement is intended principally to be used for existing mines and plants. To give a fair chance before investing major portion in both types of arrangements, it is usually preceded by evaluation and feasibility phase.

Mineral prospecting - The government is inviting foreign firms to conduct prospecting and exploration for gold and copper in Myanmar. First round competitive bidding will involve a total of (16) blocks, each having an area of 1400 square kilometers. The initial stage of activity will be prospecting and during a period of one year, a mineral occurrence should be identified using various disciplines of prospecting. It is to be followed by exploration stage. However 50% of the original area of the block has to be relinquished at the end of prospecting stage. Exploration stage can be extended twice of one year period each at end of initial one year and subsequent extensions, mandatory relinquishment is 50% each time. It is to be followed by a feasibility stage of one year and if found economically feasible, joint venture agreement will be signed. Recovery of exploration costs will be considered during the first five years of production, up to and extent of 25% of total revenue. The competitive bidding will be on bonus, dead rent and minimum committed expenditure during each stage of activities. Second round bidding will be announced in mid 1995 including lead and zinc prospects.

Lead Zinc - Over three million tons of lead blast furnace slags accumulated over a long period of operations exists at Namtu in the Northern Shan States containing approximately 20% zinc and 13 grams of silver per ton. A suitable metallurgical method such as Siro Smelt or new hydrometallurgical process may be applied to recover the above minerals. Survey work has also indicated the existence of lead zinc at Mahochaung. The No. (1) Mining Enterprise is looking for foreign partners to work these prospects on joint venture basis. Feasibility study has been undertaken by ANIDEL of Australia for this zinc slag project.

Dimension Stone Industry - With the intention of producing dimension stones for use in construction and decoration works, systematic geological survey and prospecting has shown an abundant occurrences of granite and marble deposits in Myanmar with various colours and patterns. Six granite deposits are located in Kyaikto and Ye townships in the Mon State and eighteen deposits are located around Myeik and Dawei archipelagos in the Tanintharyi Division. An estimated ore reserve of these deposits in the Mon State are 3.7 billion tons. The total estimate ore reserves in the Tanintharyi are 57 billion tons.

Limestone in Myanmar has been mostly deposited in rock formation during the Palsozoic and Oligocenc age. The limestone quality is good enough to produce ornamental stones and the estimated ore reserve in the whole country is about 563 million tons. It is the intention of the Ministry to promote and establish the dimension stone industry jointly with interested foreign companies to produce granite and marble blocks in Slabs as final products.

Iron and Steel - The present production capacity of iron and steel from existing mill is not sufficient for domestic needs which is growing very rapidly with the development of Myanmar's economy. Revamping of the Ywama Steel Mill at Yangon including addition of new production lines such as plate and roofing sheets is one of the potential projects. There is also one iron ore deposit of considerable quantity (approximately 100 million tons) at Pengpet near Taunggyi in the Southern Shan States which could be developed for a new iron and steel plant.

Nickel Project - Mwetaung nickel deposit is situated in Tiddim township, Chin State, approximately 380 km. north-west of Mandalay. It is accessible by car up to the foot of Mwetaung hill from Sakagyi village (on the Kale - Tamu road), about 16 km from Kalemyo. There is airway services from Yangon to Kalemyo as well as from Mandalay.

According to the preliminary geological investigation in 1964-65 there exist six ore bodies within (10) km in Mwetaung. Among these ore bodies, ore body No.4 and No.6 are the most significant ones. In ore body No.4 it was estimated that a probable ore reserves of (30) million tons averaging 1.19% Ni exists whereas ore body No.6 has indicated (80) million tons of potential ore reserves averaging 1% Ni. Mwetaung nickel deposit is a nickeliferrous laterite ore deposit.

No.(3) Mining Enterprise is presently producing coal to supply local consumers. A draw back for further expansion of coal production is difficulty in transportation to consumers. As Mwetaung nickel deposit is located close to the Kalewa coal mine (only about 40 km) most of the coal produced can be arranged to be utilized not only as material for reduction and combustion but also as energy source for nickel smelting. Therefore, the development of Mwetaung nickel deposit and expansion of Kalewa coal production will lead to an integrated facility of nickel mining and smelting operation.

Jewellery Manufacturing and Jade Carving - With the intention of acquiring new technology in Gem cutting, polishing, manufacturing of jewellery and also to earn added value

Myanma Gems Enterprise is willing to expand its joint co-operation in jewellery manufacturing with suitable partners.

Energy

Crude Oil and Natural Gas - The Myanrna Oil and Gas Enterprise (MOGE) is the only State enterprise which carries out exploration, drilling, production and transportation of crude oil and gas in the country. Its exploration operations have extended from inland to offshore since 1971, and the largest gas deposit was discovered in the Gulf of Moattama as early as 1982. In 1989, the Ministry of Energy had invited foreign oil companies for exploration and development.

Petroleum - With the opening of the market, the demand for fuel in Myanmar is increasing. It is planned to meet the increasing demand by importing fuel or by offering private entrepreneurs the opportunity to share the surplus capacity at the Thanlyin refinery. The refinery is equipped with secondary refining facilities for efficient refining and production of high quality fuel.

Petrochemical - Since Myanmar is an agricultural based country, fertilizers are in great demand. The present production of urea fertilizer is about 1200 m. tons per day, which is far behind the country's estimated demand of 600,000 m. tons annually. The Ministry of Energy is in consultation with interested foreign investors for the feasibility study of establishing a 1750 m. tons per day urea plant or a floating methanol plant of 1000 m. tons per day near Dawei.

Establishments of the following plants are under consideration.

	Plant	Capacity
1.	Carbondioxide Plant	40 m. tons/day
2.	New Methanoi Plant	600 m. tons/day
3.	Polypropylene	30,000 m. tons/year
4.	Polyethylene	30,000 m. tons/year
5.	Methyl Tertiary Butyl Ether	300,000 m. tons/year
6.	Olefins	10,000 m. tons/year
7.	Petrochemical	
	a) Melamnine	50,000 m. tons/year
	b) Polyester	20,000 m. tons/year
	c) Nylon (6)	25,000 m. tons/year

Electric Power - Much emphasis and priority is placed on the development of the electric power sector because of its vital importance to the nation's social and economic development.

The Ministry invites foreign participations for joint development of the following major hydropower projects which are under irnplementation and planning stages:-

	Project	Capacity (MW)
	Shan State	
1.	Zawgyi	20.0 Under Construction
2.	Nam Mae Sai	12.5 Feasibility Study
3.	Nam Kok	100.0 Office Study
4.	Salween (Tasang),	3,000.0 Pre-feasibility
	Bago Division	
5.	Zaungtu	18.0 Under Construction
6.	Yenwe	16.2 Feasibility-study Completed
7.	Kun	84.0 Preliminary Study
8.	Pyu	65.0 Preliminary Study
9.	Kabaung	30.0 Preliminary Study

The present inland gas reserves will be sufficient enough for two new more 100 MW gas turbine power station which are currently under construction in Yangon. Myanma Electric Power Enterprise is willing to operate these two power stations on joint venture basis with any foreign investors.

Also, a number of existing gas turbine plants already in operation, including the two new 100 mw plants will be converted to combined cycle operation in the near atture. Private sector participation in the form of joint venture is also permitted in these Combined Cycle Power Plants.

Furthermore, the Ministry of Energy is considering installing a 1500 MW Combined Cycle Power Plant near Dawei utilizing the offshore gas of Yetagon Gas Field which Texaco is developing under Production Sharing Contract in Tanintharyi offshore Blocks of the Union of Myanrnar. One of the market possibilities is to sell electricity across the border to Thailand.

Manufacturing

The Ministry of Industry (1) is now, forming more and more joint ventures with foreign partners in the field of textile and apparels, foodstuff and beverages, pharmaceutical, ceramics, pulp and paper, packaging, rubber and leather industries for the mutual benefit of both panics. The areas of investment available for mutual corporation are mentioned below:

a) **Myanma Textile Industries (MTI)** - 26 factories comprising 3 spinning and weaving factories, 2 spinning, weaving and fini.~hing factories, 1 dyeing and printing factory, 3 garment factories, 10 textile factories, 3 blanket factories, 3 towel factories and 1 sewing thread factory.

b) **Myanma Foodstuff Industries (MFI)** - 20 factories including 1 beer factory, 3 alcohol factories, 9 soft drink and ice factories, 1 wheat products factory, 1 tapioca factory, 1 monosodium glutamate factory, 1 coffee product industry, 1 virginia tobacco industry, 1 cigarette factory and 1 sauce and vinegar factory.

c) **Myanma Pharmaceutical Industries (MPI)** - 12 factories - 1 pharmaceutical factory, 1 pharmaceutical raw materials factory, 1 toilet goods factory, 3 soap factories, 3 plastic factories, 1 hydrogenated oil factory, 1 refined oil factory and 1 coconut industry.

d) **Myanma Ceramic Industries (MCI)** - 15 factories - 3 cement mills, 3 brick factories, 1 firebrick factory, 1 concrete product plant, 2 asbestos cement plants, 2 pottery plants, 1 sheet glass factory, 1 glass factory and 1 marble factory.

e) **Myanma General and Maintenance Industries (MGMI)** - 10 factories - 2 footwear factories, 1 rubber factory, 1 leather factory, 1 leather goods factory, 2 packing factories, 1 fountain pen factory, 1 thermos flask factory and 1 work and maintenance factory.

f) **Myanma Paper and Chemical Industries (MPCI)** - 11 factories - 3 paper mills, 2 paint factories, 2 match factories, 1 chemical industry, 2 gas factories and 1 Hmawbi pilot plant.

Industrial Estate

(1) Thanlyin Industrial Estate located just across the Bago River and half an hour drive from Yangon have 3 garments factories, shoe, packaging, glass and thermos flask factories.

(2) Hmawbi Industrial Estate is about 35 miles from Yangon. There are the brick, plastic, noodles, biscuit, asbestos, cement and pharmaceutical raw materials factories.

(3) Daik-U Industrial Estate 25 miles north of Bago and about 77 miles from Yangon. This estate is meant for food industries because tapioca starch plant, monosodium glutamate factory and meat canning factory are set up there.

(4) Bago Industrial Estate is 4 miles south of Bago and 46 miles north of Yangon. Infrastructure is already established in this estate where a garment factory has already been leased out and a towel factory is established.

(5) Sagaing Industrial Estate is situated in upper Myanmar, 17 miles north of Mandalay. A wheat flour mill and a garment factory have been established in this estate.

Hotels and Tourism

There is a growing need for international class hotels in major tourist sites like Mandalay. Bagan, Inle and Ngapali. There are also many newly opened areas like Mawlamyine, Myitkyina, Kyaing Tong, Pyay where there are no hotels of international standard.

Many opportumties for the investment in developing golf courses, beach resorts, tourist village, amusement parks, recreational centres, service apartments, condominiums and office complex are also available.

Myanmar therefore has many diverse attractions and is also an ideal place for investors who are interested in property and estate development.

A sound infrastructure (airports, roads, rails, hotels, telecommunication, etc.) is highly crucial for the promotion of tourism and so investors who are looking for investment opportunities in these areas are also welcome.

NIGER

I. OPPORTUNITÉS D'INVESTISSEMENT.

1. Les secteurs et les projets qui offrent les meilleures possibilités d'investissement étranger

Les secteurs et les projets qui offrent les meilleures possibilités d'investissement étranger sont essentiellement ceux de:
- l'agro-industrie: cuirs et peaux (Tannerie), lait et produits dérivés (petites unités de production), abattage des animaux, transformation de la viande, produits vétérinaires, alimentation animale, conditionnement et conservation de l'oignon, transformation de céréales locales (niébé, mil, sorgho, maïs...), produits maraîchers (tomate..), tubercules (manioc, pomme de terre, patate douce);
- les petites mines et carrières: orpaillage production de sel, extraction du natron, production de phosphate, prospection et exploitation de la tourbe, production de pierre à lécher;
- la production d'emballages et articles en plastique.

Par ailleurs plusieurs sociétés d'Etat sont en voie de privatisation parmi lesquelles les entreprises industrielles suivantes: la Société Nigérienne de Cimenterie (ciment), l'Office de Lait du Niger (lait et produits dérivés), L'Abattoir frigorifique de Niamey (viande). Ces entreprises à privatiser sont sous la tutelle du Ministère de l'Economie et des Finances.

Plusieurs entreprises privées existantes recherchent des partenaires extérieurs notamment techniques et/ou financiers. Il s'agit des entreprises de transformation de céréales locales, de fabrication de briques, de tannage de peaux brutes, d'aviculture, de production d'huile d'arachide, de transformation de riz paddy etc...

2. Contraintes et entraves majeures affectant le développement de ces secteurs

Les potentialités majeures étant dans les secteurs de l'agriculture et de l'élevage, les contraintes principales sont:
- l'insuffisance des structures d'encadrement et des moyens mécaniques pour augmenter la production agricole et pastorale;
- l'importance des cycles de sécheresse et la dépendance de la production agricole des aléas climatiques;
- le manque de technologies appropriées pour la transformation des produits agro-pastoraux;
- la réticence des banques locales pour le financement des entreprises industrielles;
- l'absence d'une véritable institution spécialisée pour le financement d'entreprises industrielles;
- l'absence de fonds d'étude pour apprécier la faisabilité de plusieurs idées de projets;
- le manque de fonds de roulement pour la plupart d'entreprises existantes;
- la vétusté ou l'obsolescence des équipements de certaines unités industrielles;

189

- le problème de maintenance d'équipements industriels;
- la lourdeur des coûts des facteurs (énergie et transports notamment).

3. Mesures prises pour encourager l'investissement étranger

Actuellement le Niger est en train de mettre en place un vaste programme de promotion du secteur privé dont les objectifs sont entre autres:

- la simplification des procédures administratives et réglementaires;
- l'adaptation de l'environnement juridique;
- l'amélioration de l'environnement fiscal;
- l'amélioration de la compétitivité des opérateurs privés;
- la création et le renforcement des capacités institutionnelles et d'encadrement;
- la création d'un fonds de promotion économique;
- l'amélioration de l'information en direction et en provenance des entreprises.

Il existe aussi un code des investissements qui offre d'importants avantages fiscaux et douaniers pour soutenir le démarrage des entreprises. Il ne fait aucune discrimination entre investisseurs nationaux et étrangers.

a.   *Politiques des changes, y compris les politiques de transferts des capitaux et des dividendes*

Le Niger est membre de la Banque Centrale des Etats de l'Afrique de l'Ouest (BCEAO) dont la monnaie est le franc CFA.

Il existe une réglementation en matière des changes qui ne fait pas de restriction pour les investisseurs étrangers. D'ailleurs, le code des investissements en son article 5 stipule que "les personnes physiques ou morales non résidentes au sens de la réglementation des changes, qui réalisent un investissement au Niger financé en devises convertibles, peuvent obtenir conformément à cette réglementation, des transferts de revenus de toute nature provenant des capitaux investis et du produit de la liquidation de l'investissement.

Peuvent également être effectués tous transferts à des personnes physiques ou morales non résidentes correspondant à des paiements normaux et courants pour des fournitures et prestations effectives.

b.   *Accès au financement local.*

Au niveau local il est difficile d'obtenir des financements. Les banques commerciales interviennent très peu dans le secteur industriel. Il existe toutefois une Agence de financement (Agence de Financement de la Libre Entreprise au Niger) dont les activités ne couvrent pas du tout les besoins des unités industrielles.

4.   **Les sociétés actuelles dans lesquelles les investissements étrangers sont faits sont les suivantes:**

-    la Société des Produits Chimiques du Niger (SPCN)
-    la Société des Brasseries du Niger (BRANIGER)
-    la Société Nigérienne d'Aluminium (NIGERAL)
-    les Moulins du Sahel (M.D.S.)
-    l'Entreprise Nigérienne des Textiles (ENITEX).

Taille et performance de ces entreprises.

Sociétés	Secteur	Taille	Capital (CFA)		Performance (données de 1996) (CFA)		
			Total	Part Etrangers	CA	V.A	R.E.
SPCN	produits chimiques (savons,détergents)	grande	1,46114 000	64,9%	3 634 000000	1 020 000000	
BRANIGER	agro-alimentaire (boissons)	grande	1400100000	94,46%	3 418 676456	1 103 830686	
NIGERAL	équipement (tôles)	moyenne	190 00 000	95,00%	-	-	
MDS	farine de blé	moyenne	-	-	-	-	
ENITEX	textiles	grande	1000000000	80,00%	2 360 449654	-	

II.   **AUTRES FORMES D'INVESTISSEMENT PRIVÉ ÉTRANGER EN PLUS DES INVESTISSEMENTS DIRECTS**

a)   Le Niger ne dispose pas de bourse de valeurs.
b)   Il n'existe pas encore de société ou entreprise dont les actions sont cotées à l'étranger.
c)   Il n'existe pas encore de fonds national de marché émergent.

Au niveau régional, une bourse de valeurs est en voie de création au sein de l'Union Économique et Monétaire Ouest Africaine (UEMOA) dont le Niger est membre. Le démarrage des activités de cette bourse de valeurs est prévu pour le début de l'année 1998.

Les autres fonds régionaux sont le Fonds de Solidarité Africain (F.S.A), le Fonds Africain de Garantie et de Solidarité (FAGACE).

d)   Seule la Banque Ouest Africaine de Développement a créé une société de capital-risque depuis 1995, appelée Cauris-Investissement.

Au niveau national, il n'existe pas encore de limite réglementaire d'achat d'actions de société domestiques.

III. DÉVELOPPEMENT ET RÉGLEMENTATION DES MARCHÉS FINANCIERS.

Le marché financier régional (bourse de valeurs) de I'UEMOA est en projet. En effet, la bourse est juridiquement créée mais les activités ne commenceront qu'en début d'année 1998.

La bourse de valeurs de I'UEMOA a son siège à Abidjan(Côte d'Ivoire). Il s'agira d'un marché centralisé où seules les Sociétés de Gestion et d'intermédiation(SGI) peuvent transmettre des ordres de négociation. Les ordres sont irrévocables dès lors que le processus de cotation est entamé. La méthode de cotation sera le *Fixing*.

Annuellement, un contrôle des règles et procédures appliquées par la bourse sera opéré.

Du point de vue organisationnel, le marché financier comporte:

- un Conseil Régional de l'Epargne Publique et des Marchés Financiers qui réglemente l'exercice de l'activité des marchés financiers;

- la Bourse et le Dépositaire central qui sont des sociétés anonymes. La Bourse assure la cotation et le Dépositaire central gère les titres. Chaque Etat membre aura une représentation locale de la bourse;

- des SGI, démarcheurs et apporteurs d'affaires. Ils interviennent respectivement pour la transmission des ordres, l'orientation des clients vers la bourse ou les SGI et la négociation des clients ou la transmission des ordres.

IV. COOPÉRATION AVEC LA CNUCED ET RELATION EXTÉREURES

1. La CNUCED pourrait adopter des mesures concrètes pour aider le Niger à promouvoir le flux d'investissement étranger. Pour ce faire, la CNUCED pourrait:

- apporter une assistance technique ou financière pour la réalisation des études de faisabilité de projets industriels dans le domaine par exemple: de la fabrication d'emballages en plastique, la déshydratation d'oignon, la production d'aliments pour bébé, l'exploitation de phosphate, le machinisme agricole, la transformation de céréales locales, la cimenterie, la production de pesticides, la production de sucre, le recyclage de déchets d'Abattoir, le recyclage d'ordures ménagères, la production de concentré de tomate etc..

- rechercher des partenaires pour la réhabilitation d'entreprises existantes telles : la Société de Transformation du Mil (SOTRAMIL), la Société Nouvelle de Briques de Saga (SNBS), la Société Nigérienne de Tannerie (SONITAN), La Société Industrielle et Commerciale du Niger (SICONIGER : huilerie), le Riz du Niger (RINI), la Société Nigérienne de Cimenterie (SNC), la Société Nigérienne d'Allumettes (SNA), etc..

- rechercher des promoteurs pour le projet de mise en bouteille d'eau minérale;
- créer un Centre de Promotion des Investissements;
- implanter le réseau d'information INNET

- appuyer la Direction du Développement Industriel par la formation des cadres et la dotation des moyens matériels; etc..

2. Avec la création de l'UEMOA, plusieurs mesures sont en train d'être prises pour assainir l'environnement et favoriser les investissements étrangers. Il s'agit:

- de la création d'un marché commun;
- de l'harmonisation des fiscalités, des codes d'investissements, des tarifs douaniers, des politiques économiques, des droits des affaires.

3. Au plan national, il n'existe pas d'organisations ou institutions spécialisées de recherche gouvernementales ou non gouvernementales qui s'occupent des flux d'investissements. Toutefois, la Direction du Développement Industriel au Ministère du Commerce et de l'Industrie joue ce rôle en ce qui concerne les investissements industriels. A ce titre, la personne à contacter est:

M. TRAPSIDA JEROME OUMAROU
Directeur du Développement Industriel.
B.P. 480 Niamey - Niger
Tel: (227) 73-58-25
Fax: (227) 73 21 50

ANNEXES

- 5 fiches de projets de réhabilitation d'entreprises existantes (SOTRAMIL, SNBS, SONITAN, CENTRE AVICOLE DE GOUDEL, SICONIGER).

- 1 fiche de projet pour recherche d'investisseur (eau minérale);

- 4 fiches d'idées de projets pour études de faisabilité (plastique, oignon, sucre, aliment pour bébé);

PROJET DE REHABILITATION

NOM OU RAISON SOCIALE SOTRAMIL
ANNEE DE CREATION 1967
LIEU D'IMPLANTATION Zinder
CAPITAL SOCIAL
    Montant 170.000.000F CFA
    Répartition *Etat 0%
        *Privés nationaux 100%
        *Etrangers 0%

PRODUITS FABRIQUES **CAPACITE DE PRODUCTION**

    *Pâtes alimentaires 2.000 tonnes/an
    *Farine de céréales 4.300 tonnes/an
    *Biscuits 400 tonnes/an

INDICATEURS DE PERFORMANCE En raison des difficultés
Niveau de production d'approvisionnement en matières premières (manque de fonds de roulement) et de la mauvaise qualité des produits, les activités de la société sont très faibles.

PART DE MARCHE
    - Local - Le marché existe au plan national
    - Export -

MATIÈRES PREMIÈRES **SOURCE D'APPROVISIONNEMENT**

    * Blé Europe
    * Mil, Maïs ,Sorgho Local

ETAT DES EQUIPEMENTS Usine en bon état de marche
SITUATION ACTUELLE Activités ponctuelles

    Difficultés rencontrées - Qualité des pâtes alimentaires contestée
    - Manque de fonds de roulement

OBJECTIFS DE LA RÉHABILITATION - Relance des activités de production et de commercialisation.

BESOINS * Assistance Technique pour améliorer la qualité des produits
    * Assistance Financière: besoin en fonds de roulement estimé à 103.000.000 de FCFA.

DOCUMENTATION DISPONIBLE
PROJET DE REHABILITATION

1. **Identification de la Société (SNBS):**

   - **NOM:** Société Nouvelle des Briques de Saga: S.N.B.S.
   - **ADRESSE:** B.P. 10 536 Niamey - Niger
   - **No. Tél:** (227) 73 21 49
   - **No. Fax:** (227) 73 21 49

2. **Forme Juridique et Capital:**

   - Société Anonyme
   - Capital de 152 Millions de FCFA
   - Privés Nigériens: 100%

3. **Année de Création - Démarrage des activités:**

   - Création Juridique SNBS: juillet 1995
   - Activités Industrielles non encore démarrées.

4. **Estimation des Investissements:**

   - Investissement prévisionnel de réhabilitation: environ 500 Millions de FCFA.

5. **Production:**

   - Produits:
     * Briques: 5 x 20 x 33. 7 x 20 x 33. 10 x 20 x 33. 15 x 20 x 33 et 20 x 20 x 33
     * Hourdi: 16 x 29 x 33
     * Poutrelles: 6 x 12 x 33

   - Capacité de production nominale prévisionnelle: 30.000 t par an
   - Chiffre d'affaire prévisionnel annuel: 700 Millions de FCFA
   - Principaux marchés
     * Construction de logements privés
     * Construction de logement sociaux
     * Infrastructures publiques et privées

6. **Description des Equipements:**

   - Voir Annexe

7. **Matières Premières:**

- Argile extraite à 5 km de l'usine
- Consommation annuelle prévisionnelle: 34 800 tonnes
- Valeur livraison usine: 55,7 Millions de FCFA

8.   Personnel Structure Prévisionnelle: 35 agents dont:

- I Directeur
- 4 Techniciens
- 30 ouvriers et employés

9.   Production *Concurrente*:

- Pas de concurrence formalisée, car il n'existe pas de briqueterie industrielle;
- Existence de petits artisans avec moins de 10% du marché;
- En général briques fabriquées sur chantier par les promoteurs eux-mêmes.

10.   Description des Problèmes:

- Technique:
  * Mise en oeuvre de la réhabilitation de l'usine;
  * Importants problèmes d'économie d'énergie: combustible et électricité.;
  * Inexistence d'un manuel opération du procédé;
  * Problèmes liés au redémarrage de l'usine: maintenance et procédé;

- Financier:
  * Difficulté de financement du Projet;

- Formation:
  * 1 partie du personnel est jeune d'où stage pratique à prévoir;
  * Visites de briqueteries industrielles;

- Commercial:
  * Etude de marché;

11.   Etude de faisabilité:

Il existe une étude de faisabilité réalisée en 1996.

12.   Intérêt de l'Etat:

Dans le cadre de sa politique d'urbanisation et de l'amélioration des conditions de vie des populations. L'Etat soutient le programme de construction des logements sociaux, de routes en pavés, et aussi dés infrastructures publiques. Pour la réalisation de tous ces projets, la création d'une unité industrielle est nécessaire afin de satisfaire les besoins en briques.

PROJET DE REHABILITATION

NOM OU RAISON SOCIALE SOCIETE NIGERIENNE DE TANNERIE (SONITAN)

ANNEE DE CREATION 1969
LIEU D'IMPLANTATION Maradi
CAPITAL SOCIAL
    Montant 80.000.000 FCFA
    Répartition * Etat 0%
        * Privés nationaux 100%
        * Etrangers 0%

PRODUITS FABRIQUES   **CAPACITE DE PRODUCTION**

    *   Wet Blue 1.000.000 peaux/an
    *   Stain

INDICATEURS DE PERFORMANCE
Niveau de production Avant l'arrêt, l'usine traitait 400.000 peaux/an
PART DE MARCHE
    -    **Local** 5%
    -    **Export (Europe)** 95%

MATIÈRES PREMIÈRES   **SOURCE D'APPROVISIONNEMENT**

    *   Peaux brutes Local
    *   Produits chimiques Europe

ETAT DES EQUIPEMENTS Vétustes
SITUATION ACTUELLE En arrêt
    Difficultés rencontrées -   Niveau d'endettement trop élevé
        -   Insuffisance dans la gestion financière et technique.
        -   Réseau de collecte de peaux brutes désorganisé.
        -   Manque de politique appropriée de marketing.

OBJECTIFS DE LA RÉHABILITATION -   Relance des activités de production et de commercialisation.

BESOINS *   Assistance Technique
        *   Assistance Financière

DOCUMENTATION DISPONIBLE

PROJET DE REHABILITATION

NOM OU RAISON SOCIAL	CENTRE AVICOLE DE GOUDEL
ANNÉE DE CRÉATION	1981
LIEU D'IMPLANTATION	Goudel/Niamey
CAPITAL SOCIAL	Etablissement Public à caractère Administratif
Montant	617.292.000
Répartition	Etat 100%

PRODUITS FABRIQUE

* poussins
* poulettes de ponte

CAPACITÉ DE PRODUCTION

* 1.400.000 poussins par an
* 200.000 poulettes

MATIÈRES PREMIÈRES

* aliments
* poussins à 1 jour

SOURCE D'APPROVISIONNEMENT

* local et importé
* local

ETAT DES EQUIPEMENTS
SITUATION ACTUELLE
Difficultés rencontrées

Bon état

* concurrence du Nigéria
* amateurisme et manque de technicité
* approvisionnement irrégulier en intrants
* demande fluctuante
* durée d'élevage non maîtrisé

Objectifs

* Reconquérir le marché national
* Privatisation du Centre
* Installation d'une petite unité du production d'aliments

BESOINS

* Partenariat Technico-Financier

DOCUMENTATION DISPONIBLE

* Etude de JOURDAIN INTERNATIONAL (Sept. 1994)

POINT DE CONTACT
Direction du Développement Industriel
B.P. 11700 Niamey - Tel (227) 73 59 07

PROJET DE REHABILITATION

NOM OU RAISON SOCIALE SICONIGER
ANNÉE DE CRÉATION 1942 et agrandie en 1975
LIEU D'IMPLANTATION Maradi
CAPITAL SOCIAL
    Montant 400 million
    Répartition * ETAT/SONARA 90%
            * Privés Nigérien 10%

PRODUITS FABRIQUES   **CAPACITÉ DE PRODUCTION**

*   Huile d'arachide   * 19.000 tonnes d'huile soit 40.000 tonnes
                              d'arachide coques

MATIÈRES PREMIÈRES   **SOURCE D'APPROVISIONNEMENT**

*   Arachide coupe   Local

ETAT DES EQUIPEMENTS   Bon état
SITUATION ACTUELLE
    Difficultés rencontrées * Prix de revient de la matière première trop
                élevé
            * Vente du produit fini à perte
            * Forte concurrence des huiles du Nigéria et
                de la Côte d'Ivoire

OBJECTIFS DE LA RÉHABILITATION * Relance de la production arachidière
            * Assurer une meilleure couverture des
                besoins nationaux (50%)

BESOINS * Assistance Financière
DOCUMENTATION DISPONIBLE

POINT DE CONTACT
Direction du Développement Industriel
B.P. 11700 Niamey - Tel: (227)73 59 07

FICHE DE PROJET

1	**INTITULE DU PROJET**	MISE EN BOUTEILLES D'EAU MINÉRAL NATURELLE

2   **OBJECTIF**
- Fabrication de bouteilles vides en PVC
- Mise en bouteille de l'eau minérale
- Commercialisation de l'eau minérale

3   **PROMOTEUR**   A rechercher

4   **CAPACITÉ DE PRODUCTION**
- 600 bouteilles vides en PVC/heure
- 1800 bouteilles d'eau minérale/heure

5   **COÛT DES INVESTISSEMENTS**   537,6 millions FCFA avant dévaluation

6   **MARCHE**

	1990	**2001**
* **National (nb de cols)**	500.000	1.500.000
* **Régional**		

7   **MATIÈRES PREMIÈRES**   **SOURCES D'APPROVISIONNEMENT**

* eau minérale	local
* PVC	extérieur
* bouchons	extérieur
* étiquettes	extérieur

8   **DONNÉES ECONOMIQUES**
- Chiffre d'affaires   : 124 millions
- Cash Flow   : 59,99 millions
- TRI   : 10,45%

9   **OBSERVATIONS**   L'étude, réalisée en 1990, mérite d'être réactualisée

10   **COOPÉRATION RECHERCHÉE**
- Partenariat Technico-Financier
- Réalisation d'une étude sur les perspectives d'exportation

POINT DE CONTACT
Direction du Développement Industriel
B.P. 11700 - Tel: (227) 73 59 07

FICHE DE PROJET

1	**INTITULE DU PROJET**	PROJET D'UNE USINE DE SUCRE
2	**OBJECTIF**	Production de sucre à partir de la canne à sucre locale.
3	**PROMOTEUR**	A rechercher
4	**CAPACITÉ DE PRODUCTION**	450.000 T de canne/an soit 45.00T par an de sucre
5	**COÛT DES INVESTISSEMENTS**	106.630.000 $US dont 3.000.000 de fonds de roulement

6 **MARCHE**
* **National**
* **Régional**   Nigéria, Mali

7 **MATIÈRES PREMIERS**   **SOURCES D'APPROVISIONNEMENT**

Canne à sucre principalement   * Locale

8 **DONNÉES ECONOMIQUES**
* création de 880 emplois industriels et agricoles
* économie de devises
* création d'une valeur ajoutée sur place

9 **OBSERVATIONS**
* chiffre d'affaires : 31.200.000 $US
* consommations intermédiaires : 10.098.650 $US
* T.R.I. : 20,4%
* VAN : 53.551.384 $US

Une étude de préfaisabilité à été réalisée en 1995 pour l'implantation d'un complexe sucrier.

10 **COOPÉRATION RECHERCHÉE**   * Partenaires Techniques et Financiers

POINT DE CONTACT
Direction du Développement Industriel
B.P. 11700 Niamey - Tel: (227) 73 50 07

ETUDE DE PROJECT

---

1. **Titre de Projet:**   Production industrielle de Produits en Plastique
(emballages et articles divers).

2. **Justification:**

Le Niger consomme de plus en plus de produits en plastique tant au niveau des ménages, qu'au niveau des entreprises industrielles. Par rapport à ces dernières, le coût des emballages en plastique pèse lourdement sur les coûts de production, particulièrement dans l'agro-industrie.

Par ailleurs, le niveau de consommation des ménages estimés à 20 Millions par an pour les sacs de 50 kg et 60 Millions par an en ce qui concerne les sachets, provoquant ainsi de sérieux problèmes d'environnement à cause de l'importance des déchets.

Ces déchets en plastique dus à l'utilisation grandissante des emballages plastiques polluent l'environnement et constituent aujourd'hui un véritable fléau pour les villes et campagnes. L'absence d'une unité industrielle de fabrication d'articles en plastique capable de recycler ces déchets et l'ampleur des importations de ces types d'articles fait que la situation demeure une grande préoccupation pour les autorités. Pourtant des opérateurs économiques sont intéressés par ce projet. Mais ils souhaitent, avant toute intervention, la réalisation d'une étude de faisabilité qui déterminera le choix technologique et la rentabilité financière du projet.

3. **Assistance souhaitée**

Réalisation d'une étude de faisabilité d'articles en plastique (technique, financière et économique).

4. **Intérêt du Gouvernement**

Le Gouvernement accorde un grand intérêt pour le projet à cause de ses effets positifs:

- effets positifs sur l'environnement,
- effets positifs sur la balance commerciale,
- réduction des coûts de production dans l'industrie.

5. **Existence d'une documentation**

Aucune, sauf les statistiques d'importation des articles en plastique.

ETUDE DE PROJECT

1.   Titre du projet

Production d'aliment pour bébé

2.   Justification du projet

Avec quelques 9.000.000 d'habitants, le Niger compte environ 49,4% de jeunes de o à 14 ans. Les taux de mortalité infantile est de 346 pour mille pour les enfants de 0 à 5 ans. L'une des causes principales de ce fort taux de mortalité est la malnutrition. Après le sevrage, la plupart des enfants sont nourris à la bouille (à base de céréales locales) dont la densité énergétique est très faible.

Or, il existe au niveau des productions locales des légumineuses et céréales dont la combinaison pourrait offrir aux bébé une alimentation riche et équilibrée. Il s'agit entre autre de niébé dont la production tourne autour de 400.000 à 500.000 tonnes par an. La transformation du niébé en combinaison avec d'autre céréales en aliments pour bébé permettrait de fournir à ces derniers des aliments de qualité.

Aujourd'hui le niébé est transformé par une petite unité de transformation qui appartient à l'O.N.G. CARITAS - NIGER. Malheureusement, il se pose un problème d'acceptabilité du produit au niveau des bébés. C'est pourquoi, il est important d'implanter une unité de production d'aliment pour bébé pour contribuer à améliorer l'état nutritionnel des bébé à l'intérieur du pays et dans les autre pays, particulièrement ceux qui connaissent des guerres civiles.

3.   Assistance souhaitée

Réalisation d'une étude de faisabilité.

4.   Intérêt du Gouvernement

Assurer l'équilibre des bébés et réduire le taux de mortalité infantile.

5.   Existence d'une documentation

Il existe des informations qui sont dispersées entre les différentes structures qui s'occupent de la situation des enfants.

ETUDE DE PROJECT

---

1.   **Titre du Projet**

Unité de Déshydratation d'Oignon

2.   **Lieu d'implantation**

Malbaza ou Galmi (TAHOUA)

3.   **Justification**

Le Niger est un grand pays producteur d'oignons. L'oignon est cultivé sur presque tout le territoire, principalement dans le département de Tahoua. La production actuelle est de l'ordre de 200.000 tonnes par an. Toutefois le potentiel de production est estimé à 800.000 tonnes par an. Trois variétés sont cultivées au Niger: le violet de Galmi, le blanc de Galmi et le blanc de Soumarana. La qualité de l'oignon fait que le Niger est le principal pays exportateur dans la sous-région. C'est l'une des cultures pour laquelle le Niger dispose d'un avantage comparatif.

Aujourd'hui, il n'existe pas un système moderne d'exploitation de ce produit. De grosses quantités sont perdues pendant la conservation, ce qui pousse les producteurs à brader leur production juste après les récoltes. Des techniques de conservation ont été introduites dans les zones de culture sans pour autant avoir un impact significatif sur les taux des pertes et le niveau de la production. C'est pourquoi il est préconisé la mise en place d'une unité de déshydratation d'oignons afin de:

-    minimiser les pertes après les récoltes;
-    valoriser le produit et garantir un prix rémunérateur aux producteurs;
-    organiser la filière et accroître la production;
-    développer les exportations.

4.   **Assistance souhaitée**

Réalisation d'une étude de faisabilité du Projet.

5.   **Intérêt du Gouvernement**

Valorisation d'une production locale; création de valeur ajoutée et d'emplois; augmentation du revenu des paysans; amélioration de la balance des paiements.

6.   **Existence d'une documentation**

Il existe plusieurs documents sur la production de l'oignon au Niger.

SIERRA LEONE

Investment Opportunities

The sectors/projects enumerated below have been identified as having the best opportunities for the utilization of foreign investment:

1a. <u>Agricultural Sector: opportunities exist for</u>:

- The establishment of large scale farms to cultivate; mango, pineapple, cashew, chilli, ginger, sesame seeds, coconuts, kolanuts, flows etc.

<u>Current Level of Development and Growth potential of sector</u>

- Activities in the agricultural sector has been severely devastated by over 5 years of rebel wars which has now come to an end. The war resulted in the displacement of the rural population who have now started returning.

- Pre-war activities in this sector were dominated by subsistence agriculture with farm sizes averaging about 5 acres per farm family.

- Low input/output technology packages predominate.

- Farm labour is available in sufficient quantities at an average wage rate of about one United States dollar a day.

- Sufficient farm land available with long-term lease options.

- Foreign investors encouraged to invest in this sector.

- No restriction on ownership of enterprises in this sector by foreign nationals.

- No corporate taxes are charged on enterprises investing in the agricultural sector for the first 10 years of operation.

1b. <u>Agro-industrial Sector: Foreign investors are encourages to invest in the following areas</u>:

- Processing and canning of fruits and vegetables

- Processing and canning of meat products
- Production of feeds for livestock and poultry
- Processing of forest products into timber, plywood, veneers and furniture

<u>Current level of development and Growth potential of Sector</u>

- Most of the existing enterprises in this sector are operating below capacity due to the war which caused devastation to existing enterprises located in the rural areas and/or making the plants and raw materials inaccessible.

- No processing and canning facilities for fruits, vegetables and meat products.

- The raw materials and labour required to establish enterprises in this sector are available in sufficient quantities locally.

- Foreign investors are encouraged to invest in this sector and there is no restriction on ownership of enterprises by foreign investors.

1c. <u>Fisheries sector: Opportunities exist to develop the fishing industry through</u>:

- Increased fish/shrimp production for export of value added fish/shrimps.

<u>Current level of Development and Growth Potential of Sector</u>

- Recent performance of the marine sector has been poor with production estimates for 1995 estimated at only 27% of its 1989 value.

- Total industrial catch rose continuously from 78,824 metric tons in 1983 to 184,520 metric tons in 1989 while artisanal catch stayed virtually constant at 45,000 metric tons. The situation has continued to deteriorate since 1991 when the war started.

  Since 1991 foreign investment in the marine sector has dwindled leading to the poor performance of industrial fishery.

  The sector has also been characterized by poor management and weal surveillance and control mechanisms.

- The Fisheries Act together with associated regulations were revised in September 1994 and provides for the implementation of a durable fisheries management regime comprising management, surveillance and control.

1d. <u>Export manufacturing sector</u>: <u>Opportunities exist for</u>:

- The development and promotion of cottage industries with export potential.

<u>Current level of development and Growth potential of sector</u>

- This sector is characterized by widely dispersed small and informal activities and a small urban-based modern enclave of medium and large scale enterprises.

- Most enterprises in this sector are single unit monopolies, which depend on imported raw materials, employ capital intensive technology and have little backward and/or forward linkages.

- Skilled and semi-skilled labour is available.

- No restrictions on foreign ownership of enterprises operation in this sector.

- Government Policy in this regard gives priority to: improvement of the overall investment climate, reviewing the investment code and tax structures, improving the incentive structure for private investment and lessening the level of administrative intervention in the industrial sector.

1e. <u>Business Services</u>: <u>Opportunities exist for</u>:

- The establishment of import/export companies for the promotion of international trade.

- The establishment of industries for the production of appropriate technology.

- The establishment of off-shore banking and financial services.

- The establishment of companies to promote exports such as packaging for export labelling etc.

<u>Current level of Development and Growth Potential</u>

- This sector has tremendous room for growth especially now that the war has come to an end.

1f. <u>Tourism</u>: <u>Opportunities exist for</u>:

- The establishment of tourist hotels/motels, lodges, airline and tour operators.

- The development of tourism infrastructure generally including acquisition and operation of aircraft, helicopters, pleasure boats, marinas, tour buses etc.

Current level of Development and Growth Potential of Sector

- The war has affected this sector adversely as most of the tourist installations have been directly hit by rebels. This sense of insecurity has discouraged tourists and subsequently forced many hotels to fold up especially those around the peninsula in the western area including the capital Freetown.

- Total arrival of tourists almost doubled from 15,390 in 1986 to 28,858 in 1990 but declined further to 13,701 in 1995 at the height of the insurgency.

1g.   Mining sector: Opportunities exist to develop the Mining Sector in the following areas:

- Prospecting and establishing companies for export of bauxite, chromite and platinum.

- Prospecting new areas and establishing companies for diamonds, gold, iron-ore and rutile.

- Rehabilitation of Bauxite Mines.

- Rehabilitation of Marampa Mines for the production of iron-ore.

- Processing of mineral products where feasible.

Current Levels of Development and Growth Potential of Sector

- By 1989, diamonds, bauxite, rutile and gold accounted for 80% of official exports. However the security situation in the country after 1991 (when the war started) and smuggling has badly affected the contribution to the economy of particularly gold and diamonds.

- Official mineral exports amounted to US$123.2 million in 1989/90 (pre-war) however with the on-set of the war, important mining locations in particular the Kimberlite Mining Installations and other important alluvial mining centres were occupied by rebel forces thereby reducing the level of official exports to US$58.6 million in 1994/95.

- Foreign investors are encouraged to invest in this sector and there are no restrictions on such investments.

<u>Measures</u>

a.   Foreign exchange regulations, including policies on transfer of capital and dividends.
Foreign exchange regulations including transfers of capital and dividends.

b.   Access to local finance.

Registered foreign businesses are allowed to borrow funds from the local banking system subject to the existing rules.

c.   Other active promotion activities to approach potential investors

The Government of Sierra Leone has set up an autonomous corporation SLEDIC with responsibility for the promotion of investments and exports in all sectors. Furthermore, an investment code is been developed to assist with investment promotion.

An Investment Guide will be enacted shortly.

Agency/Organization	Contact persons
1.Sierra Leone Export Development and Investment Corporation	Mr. Chris Jasabe
2. Bank of Sierra Leone	Dr. Raymond Gilpin
3. Institute of Public Administration and Management (IPAM)	Dr. May-Parker
4. Sierra Leone Trade and Investment School	Mr. L.B. Rogers-Wright
5. National Development Bank	Mr. Santon Conteh
6. Union Trust Bank	Mr. Sanpha Koroma
7. Ministry of Trade, Industry and State and State Enterprises	Mr. Tom M. Kargbo Permanent Secretary
	Mr. Joseph W.A. Jackson Ag. Director of Industries

TCHAD

Institutions/ personnes à contacter:

- Mr. Komandi Patrit
  Sous-Direction du Budgét d'investissement
  BP.144 N'Djaména - Tchad
  Tel: 52 24 85
  Fax: 51 61 15

- Chambre de Commerce, d'Industrie, d'agricultrue, des
  Mines et d'Artisanat
  Avenue Colonel Moll
  BP.458 B'jaména - Tctad
  Tel: 52 52 64
  Fax: 52 58 84

I. OPPORTUNITÉS D'INVESTISSEMENT

Le Secteur primaire offre les meilleures possibilités d'investissement étranger. Les domaines les plus porteurs sont:

Agriculture

La situation climatique du Tchad permet une activité sur environ 20 millions d'hectares. Ce qui suppose une importante superficie potentiellement exploitable. Actuellement seulement 5% de la superficie des terres arables sont exploitées. Il existe donc de larges possibilités d'extension et d'intensification de la production agricole. Malgré les multiples handicaps liés aux aléas climatiques, les atouts existent pour voir l'avenir avec optimisme.

La production alimentaire dans le cadre de la petite propriété telle que la production de céréales (mil, sorgho, maïs, riz, blé) et autres produits agricoles (arachide, sésame, oignons, ail, haricot, et tubercule) représente les principales activités économiques.

En matière des fruits et légumes, l'expansion rapide des grands centres fait que cette filière prend de l'ampleur et a un avenir promoteur. Les produits de cueillette ne sont pas négligeables. Il serait intéressant de repertorier notamment: la gomme arabique, la siprulime (algue bleue), la noix de karité, le balantex egyptiaca et le néré.

Arachide

Elle est cultivée dans toutes les zones aussi bien soudanienne que sahélienne.

Evolution en 6 ans (1990-1996)

- la superficie cultivée est passé de 184 996 à 318 673 hectares;
- le rendement en Kg par hectare est passé de 586 à 918Kg;
- la production est passée de 108 423 à 292 581 tonnes.

Sesame

Il est cultivé dans toutes les régions du pays.

Situation en 6 ans d'activités (1990-1996).

- superficie cultivée évolue en dents de scie mais elle est passée de 35 825 hectares à 45 040;
- rendement: réduction progressive de 325 Kg/hectares à 230 Kg/hectare;
- la réduction de la production de 11 652 tonnes à 10 440.

PRODUCTION MARAICHERE ET FRUITIERE est en plein expension.

LES CULTURES INDUSTRIELLES qui sont essentiellement le Coton, la Canne à sucre et le Tabac et dont les productions sont suivies par les entreprises qui les transforment (CONTONTCHAD, SONASUT et M.C.T.).

Elevage

L'élevage constitue la 2ème source de devises du Tchad. En effet les production animales occupent une place importante dans l'économie du pays en contribuant pour 28% au PIB agricole.

Le Tableau qui suit donne l'évolution du Cheptel pendant les 20 dernières années:

ANNEES	BOVINS	OVINS-CAPRINS	CAMELINS
1971	4.690.000	5.150.000	355.000
1976	3.954.000	4.460.000	392.000
1986	3.886.000	4.400.000	488.000
1991	4,400.000	4.906.000	565.000
1994	4.653.000	5.800.000	662.000
1995	4.546.400	6.252.000	613.440

La productivité reste faible pour les raisons suivantes:

- L'élevage est de type extensif, évoluant dans un milieu hostile où la survie du troupeau, et le niveau de productivité dépendent essentiellement de la pluviométrie et le mode d'exploitation du troupeaux reste encore traditionnel;

- Le déplacement long lors de transhumance et des ventes, cependant le potentiel de production est très élévé;

- ressources fourragères (paturages naturels et sous-produits agricoles) sont importantes et l'état sanitaire des animaux est relativement satisfaisant grâce aux efforts de vaccination opérés par les services du Ministère de l'Elévage (50 à 60% de têtes seraient vaccinées chaque année).

- les débouchés extérieurs restent largement ouverts.

Les sous produits de l'élevage tels que les peaux et cuirs ne sont pas encore valorisés et constitue donc un potentiel non négligable.

MINES

Le sous sol Tchadien renferme d'énormes potentialités minières non exploitées ou partiellement exploitées et de manière artisanale, hormis le pétrole dont la commercialisation est pour bientôt.

Des nombreux indices mineralisés ont été signalés sur le territoire tchadien au cours des derniers décennies alors que d'autres sont identifiés par le Projet PNUD/DRCM en cours, notamment les substances industrielles.

Dans l'état actuel des connaissances, les indices minéralisés qui semblent les plus promoteurs pour une valorisation et un éventuel développement sont:

- Métaux précieux (Or, Argent, Platine)
- Métaux de base (Cuivre, Plomb, Zinc)
- Chrome et Nickel
- Fer, Titane et Manganèse
- Etain et Tungstène
- Niobium, Tentale et Beryllium
- Aluminium
- Matière radioactives (Uranium)
- Pierres Gemmes (Diamant)

Substances minérales industrielles:

- Calcaires
- Marbres et Pierres ornementales

- Materiaux de construction
- Graphite
- Teleschites
- Kaolin
- Sable de verrerie
- Diatomites
- Gypse

Formation saline

- Natron
- Sel gemme

Recherche petrolière

Les recherches petrolières ont commencé depuis 1970 et ont abouti à des résultats positifs.

I. CONTRAINTES ET ENTRAVES

Effectivement le manque de financement est l'obstacle majeur.

A l'exception de la B.D.T. (Banque de Développement du Tchad), les institutions financières de la place ne sont pas disposées à financer le moyen et le long terme et moins encore les projets de développement. Il se pose également le problème de garantie étant entendu qu'il n'y a pas de fonds de garantie. Les lignes de crédits pour financer des projets de développement ne sont pas mises en place. Il n'y a pas de Sociétés de capital risque ni, d'institutions de financement spécialisées.

III. MESURES INCITATIVES

Le Gouvernement tchadien a opté pour un nouveau modèle de développement économique qui fait du secteur privé le moteur de croissance depuis 1990.

a)   la liberté en matière des changes et libre transfert de capitaux et de dividendes;

b)   libéralisation de l'économie et réduction sensible des obstacles tarifaire et non tarifaires;

c)   le désengagement progressif de l'Etat des entreprises publique et para-publique en vue de la promotion du secteur privé (ci-joint liste des entreprises à privatiser).

Les investissements étrangers sont réalisés dans les grandes et les petites et moyennes entreprises:

CONTONTCHAD, **SONASUT** (Société Nationale Sucrière du Tchad), **M.C.T.** (Manufacture des Cigarettes du Tchad), **BDL** (Brasserie Du Logone), **BGT** (Boisson et Glacière du Tchad), **TCHADIPEINT, SIMAT** (Société Industrielle de Matériel Agricole du Tchad), **SIPT** (Société Industrielle des Produits Pharmaceutique du Tchad), **SOPCOTOD** (Société de Production et de Commercialisation de Toles et Divers).

* **COTONTCHAD** (Société Cotonnière du Tchad) S.A au capital de 4.256.000.000 FCFA dont 51% sont détenus par l'Etat Tcbadien. La CotonFranc, la CFDT et la Caisse Centrale de Coopération Economique (CCCE) se partage respectivement 30%, 17%, 2%.

* **SONASUT** (Société Nationale Sucrière du Tchad) S.A d'économie mixte au capital de 4.711.000 FCFA détenu à 83% par l'Etat Tchadien et 17% par le Secteur Privé étranger.

* **BDL** (Brasserie Du Logone) S.A au capital de 800.000.000 FCFA. Elle est exclusivement entre les mains du Secteur Privé Etranger dont le principal actionnaire est United African Compagny

* **M.C.T** (Manufacture des Cigarettes du Tchad) C'est une Société mixte au capital de 312.000,000 FCFA détenu à 85% par le Sectecr Privé Etranger et 15% par l'Etat Tchadien.

* **B.G.T** (Boisson & Glacière du Tchad) S.A au capital de 110.000.000 FCFA détenu entièrement par le Secteur Privé dont 81% par le Secteur Privé Etranger.

* **SIMAT** (Société Industrielle de Matériel Agricole au Tchad) S.A au capital de 200 millions de FCFA réparti à 65% pour l'Etat Tchadien et 35 % pour le Secteur Privé Etranger.

Le taux de rendement en moyenne est autour de 20 %.

Il n'y a aucune restriction, aucune discrimination concernant l'achat d'action dans notre pays.

LISTE DES ENTREPRISE EN COURS DE PRIVATISATION

1. SNER (Société Nationale d'Entretien Routier)
2. STEE (Société Tchadienne d'Eau et d'electricité)
3. BTCD (Banque Tchadienne de Crédit et des Dépot)
4. SONASUT (Société Nationale Sucrière du Tchad)
5. AIR TCHAD (Compagnie Nationale des Transports Aériens)
6. BDT (Banque de Développement du Tchad)
7. ONPT (Office National des Postes et Télécommunications du Tchad)
8. TIT (Télécommunications du Tchad)
9. Hotel du Chari (Hotel du Chari)
10. AFF (Abattoire Frigorifique de FARCHA)
11. COTONTCHAD (Société Contonnière du Tchad)
12. Seerat (Société d'etude et d'exploitation de la Raffinerie du Tchad)

UGANDA

INVESTMENT LICENSING AND ONGOING INVESTMENT ACTIVITIES

Natural Resources Division

A total of 20 applications for investment licences were received and 27 investment licences were issued during November and December 1996.

Summary of Agricultural licensed Projects

Sub-sector	No. of Projects	US$ Planned Investment	Planned Employment
Forestry and Wood Processing	3	1,658,000	172
Crop Resources Based	11	19,609,000	3,240
Livestock and Fisheries	3	5,358,000	432
Foods and Beverages	4	1,607,000	48
Tourism	6	2,832,000	144
Total	**27**	**31,064,000**	**4,027**

The total planned investment is US$31,064,000 and total planned employment is 4,027.

The key projects licensed include:

Company	Nature of Business	US$ Planned Investment	Planned Employment
Lonrho Limited	Cotton Ginning	6,300,000	104
Kishita Young Farmers Ltd.	Meat Slaughter and Processing	3,500,000	38
Hortuga Limited	Production of Asparagus	1,500,000	457
Uganda Forest Industries Ltd.	Timber processing	1,300,000	111
Ladhani Industries Ltd.	Growing and Processing of beans and maize	1,646,000	2,028
Uganda Young Plants	Propagation of African Plant Cuttings for export	642,000	75

Manufacturing Division:

The Division received 16 applications for investment licences in November and December 1996 and 20 licences were issued.

Summary of Manufacturing licensed projects.

Sub-sector	No. of Projects	US$ Planned Investment	Planned Employment
Manufacturing (General)	9	33,153,000	515
Property Development	6	18,297,000	594
Transport	3	5,055,000	132
Fabrication	2	813,000	111
Total	**20**	**57,833,000**	**1,352**

The total estimated investment is US$57,833,000 and planned employment is 1,352.

The Key projects icensed include:

Company	Nature of Business	US$ Planned Investment	Planned Employment
Republic Air	Air transport	3,095,000	83
Intex Developers (Africa) Ltd.	Property Development	8,700,000	307
Uganda Pharmaceuticals (1996) Ltd.	Pharmaceuticals manufacture	2,901,000	40
Super Bargains (U) Ltd.	Manufacture & assembly of motor cycle/vehicle batteries	1,017,000	40
East African Glass Works Ltd. (1995)	Manufacture of glass bottles and tableware	18,800,000	216

Investor Facilitation Division

A total of 9 project applications for investment licences were received and 5 were licensed during November and December 1996. Four projects are still pending submission of additional information.

Summary of Services licensed.

Sub-sector	No. of Projects	US$ Planned Investment	Planned Employment
Consultancy Services	1	50,000	12
Printing & Light packaging	1	1,230,00	60
Airport handling services	1	2,400,00	73
TV broadcasting	1	980,000	54
Education	1	1,225,000	48
Total	**5**	**5,885,000**	**247**

The total planned investment is US$5,885,000 and total employment is 247.

The Key projects icensed are:

Company	Nature of Business	US$ Planned Investment	Planned Employment
ULL Printing & Packaging Ltd.	Printing & Light packaging	1,230,000	60
Dairo Air Services Ltd.	Airport Handling services	2,400,000	73

Certificates of Incentives

Certificates of incentives are granted by UIA to projects that have been fully implemented and have reached commercial production. Holders of certificates of incentives are entitled to a tax holiday of between 3-6 years from payment of corporation tax, dividend tax and withholding tax at an agreed percentage, as stipulated in the Investment Code, 1991. A total of 18 projects were granted certificates of incentives in November and December 1996 with a total actual investment of US$21,985,000.

Name of Company	Sector	Value of Investment on ground US$
Uganda Paper Products Ltd.	Paper Conversion	757,000
Medical Products Ltd.	Gauze & Bandage manufacture	1,862,000
Britania Foods Ltd.	Confectioneries	2,050,000
Royal Flowers	Cut Flowers	708,000
A.K. Oils and Fats	Edible Oil	2,455,000
Alhamed Hides & Skins Ltd.	Tannery	187,000
Golf Course Investmets Ltd.	Real Property Development	2,061,000
Delux Printing & Paper Ltd.	Printing	765,000
A.K. Plastics	Assorted Plasticware manufactue	3,779,000
Casements (A) Ltd.	Casements Windows manufacture	184,000
Entebbe Handling Services	Airport Ground handling services	298,000
Shumuk Enterprises Ltd.	Rolling aluminium	1,082,000
Wananchi (U) Ltd.	Coffee Processing	75,000
Rwenzori Beverages Co. Ltd.	Mineral Water	403,000
Uganda Inflight Services	Inlight & Airport Services	298,000
The Monitor Publications	Publication	55,000
Afriplast Industries	Plastic shoe soles	336,000
Middle East Hospital & Shopping Complex Ltd.	Hospital & Shopping Complex	264,000
	Total	**21,985,000**

Aggregate Project Proposals received and Approved

Total Application Forms Issued

A total of 139 potential investor contacts were made with UIA during the months of November and December 1996. The cumulative number of forms issued since July 1991 increased from 5,734 in October 1996 to 5,873 in December 1996 (see exhibit I).

Total applications received

A total of 45 formal investment applications were received during the months of November and December 1996. Cumulative projects received since July 1991 rose from 2,392 in October 1996 to 2,437 in December 1996 (see exhibit II).

Total projects approved

The total approved projects since July 1991 reached 2,057 at the end of December 1996 with a planned investment of US$3.343bn and planned employment of 143,371 jobs. (see exhibit III).

ZAMBIA

INVESTMENT OPPORTUNITIES

The Government of the Republic of Zambia since 1991 has put in place a very enabling economic and political framework that is conducive for the development of private entrepreneurship. The macroeconomic indicators are stable and the economy grew by 6.4 % in 1996 compared to a decline of 4.3 % in 1995.

SECTOR	DESCRIPTION OF OPPORTUNITIES	CONSTRAINTS
AGRICULTURE	Opportunities for investments in the Zambian agriculture abound. Zambia has: • 75 million hectares of land; 45 million of which is arable land. There is also a substantial amount of developed land previously operated as state farms being privatised. • Highly diversified soil and climate base where various cash crops (tropical and sub tropical) can be grown. • Abundant water resource for irrigated agriculture. • Ideal climate; 6 hours of sunshine per day and average annual temperatures of 20 degrees celcius. • Pro-business agricultural policy, which encourages primary commodities for agro-industry and the development of an internationally competitive sector in line with our international comparative advantage. • Agricultural exports as a proportion of Non Traditional exports stood at 22.9% in 1995. • There is readily available skilled and semi skilled agricultural workers in rural areas at very competitive rates. The agricultural sector contributed 28.9% to GDP in 1996 .	• Lack of fully developed physical infrastructure such as roads and storage sheds in rural areas. • Shortage of investible capital.
	Specific incentives include: • 15% on income derived from farming and non traditional exports. • Dividends derived from farming are exempt from tax for the first five years. • There is a 20% improvement allowance for expenditures on capital improvements for the first five years. • There is farm works allowance of 100% for expenditure on farm land such as stumping, clearing, prevention of soil erosion, bore holes, wells, water conservation and aerial or geophysical surveys.	

SECTOR	DESCRIPTION OF OPPORTUNITIES	CONSTRAINTS
Soyabeans	• Good policy which encourages production of exportable crops. • Abundant market; both locally and abroad. • Abundant fertile land and enabling agricultural policy. • Production during 1996 was 40,050 Mts. compared with 21,129Mts. In 1995.	• Shortage of investible capital.
Cotton	• Abundant fertile land coupled with an enabling agricultural environment. Clark Cotton, a South African company is expecting about 17 million kgs. of cotton from Eastern Province alone this year. Production during 1996 was 37,074,200kgs. compared with 16,578,240kgs. in 1995.	• Shortage of machinery and installation skills
Rose Flowers	• There is a big market for Zambia's rose flowers in Europe, particularly in the Netherlands.	• Shortage of investible capital. • Lack of processing infrastructure
Castor seed	• The commercial value of the crop has only been recognised recently in Zambia. • Castor oil has a variety of uses in industry. The crop has 45% oil content.	• Under-developed infrastructure.
Tobacco	• Zambia has one of the best soils and climate for tobacco in the Region. • Infrastructure for the crop is being developed.	
Tobacco	• Currently Zambian tobacco is processed abroad and re-imported for cigarette manufacturing. Opportunities therefore exist for investment in this area. • In 1996 1,892,100kgs. of Barley and 1,560,000kgs. of Virginia tobaccos were produced compared with 811,111kgs. of Barley and 862,960kgs. of Virginia tobaccos in 1991.	
Wheat	• Current wheat production in Zambia does not meet National demand. • In 1994 60,944Mts. of wheat was produced.	• Shortage of capital for irrigation equipment. • Under-developed infrastructure.
Coffee	• High quality Arabic coffee grows very well in Zambia. • In 1995, 1700Mts. of coffee was produced in Zambia.	• Shortage of investible capital. • Under-developed processing infrastructure.

SECTOR	DESCRIPTION OF OPPORTUNITIES	CONSTRAINTS
MINING	• Highly diversified mineral resource based which include **Base metals** (Copper, Cobalt, Zinc, Silver, Lead, Manganese, etc.) **Gemstones** (Aquamarine, Amethyst, Emeralds and Diamonds) and **Precious Metals** (Gold and Silver).	• No funding base for mineral exploration.
Exploration & Prospecting	• Good and progressive mines and minerals act with procedural simplicity in administration and acquisition of mineral rights that is transparent and equitable. Abundant supply of hydro electricity. ZCCM which is Zambia's largest mining establishment is being privatised. Plentiful supply of skilled and experienced labour force. Developed infrastructure for Base Metals. Lapidary opportunities abound in cutting and polishing gemstones. Good policy which calls for competitive operation and development of the mining sector by private entrepreneurships. By end of last year Government issued a total of 35 licences to 20 international investors.	
TOURISM	• Zambian tourism potential is largely unexploited. On average 125,000 foreign tourists vist Zambia yearly. Zambia has a variety of natural attractions, such as the Victoria Falls, Wildlife, and one of the largest man-made lakes in the world and over 400 bird species. There is no history of civil or political strife in Zambia. Untapped and undisturbed fauna and flora. With increasing awareness by international tourists, a lot of room exists for more lodges and hotels.	
	• Zambia is strategically logated in COMESA and SADC where there are over 300 million consumers. Strong emerging private sector led economy.	
ECONOMY	Economy is fully liberalized with no controls on foreign exchanges, prices, etc. Labour laws are pro-business and labour rates are competitive. There is an industrial policy which provides greater freedom of action to entrepreneurs. Active privatization programme since 1992. The Stock Exchange has been established. For listed compaines, corporate tax is lower by 5% and there is no capital gains tax and there is no restrictions on shareholding levels. Tax regime is far and equitable.	

SECTOR	DESCRIPTION OF OPPORTUNITIES	CONSTRAINTS
MANUFACTURING		
Textiles	• Cotton yarn is locally produced on very competitive terms. The sub-sector is expanding. The value of exports grew by 36% in 1995.	• Shortage of capital for irrigation equipment. • Under-developed infrastructure.
Iron & Steel	• There is no iron and steel industry in Zambia despite its significance to the economy. Zambia is endowed with quality iron ore deposits and coal.	• Shortage of investible capital. • Under-developed processing infrastructure. • No funding base for mineral exploration. Limited geological data. Low technological capacity operating with inferior infrastructure. Small scale miners lack capital equipment for excavations.

FOREIGN PORTFOLIO INVESTMENTS

Apart from creating an enabling environment for Foreign Direct Investment flows, the Zambian Government has put in place legislation and Institutions to promote and attract other forms of private foreign investments. These include Foreign Portfolio investments.

There is already a stock market in Zambia which became operational in 1994. Foreign investors are free to directly participate in the market.

There are already issues of shares abroad by companies in Zambia. 35% of the shares in the primary market and 92% in the secondary market are owned by foreigners.

Foreign issues relating to privatisation schemes include:

South Africa	-	US$29.6 Million
U.K	-	US$40.7 Million
Zimbabwe	-	US$23.8 Million
Others -		US$8.0 Million

Countries which invest in Zambian market include United States of America, U.K, Republic of South Africa, France, Cayman Islands, India, Indonesia, Singapore, and Zimbabwe.

Foreign investments have been made in the following companies as at the end of 1996.

Primary Market

Company	No. of successful applicants	Volume of Shares	Value (US$)
Zambians			
1. Chilanga Cement	3,909	54,750,970	4,211,613
2. Rothmans Pall	876	14,057,000	596,900
3.Zambia Sugar	1,965	228,710,00	1,962,410
Sub--Total	6,750	297,517,970	6,770,923
Foreigners	48	160,393,607	1,378,382
Grand Total	6,798	457,911,579	8,149,305
Activity Analysis (%)			
Zambians	99.29	64.97	83.08
Foreigners	0.71	35.05	16.92

Secondary Market

	No. Of Trades	Volume of Shares	Value(US$)
Zambians			
1994	976	3,126,739	349,772
1995	896	4,017,400	203,558
1996	1370	10,253,457	262,720
Sub--Total	3,242	18,297,596	816,049
Foreigners			
1994	1	807,281	18,612
1995	2	3,000,000	25,343
1996	6	231,128,443	2,380,426
Sub- Total	9	234,935,724	2,424,381
Grand total	3,251	253,233,320	3,240,430
Activity Analysis (%)			
Zambians	99.70	7.20	25.20
Foreigners	0.30	92.80	74.80

Appendix II

**List of Investment Promotion
Agencies/contact addresses in LDCS**

Mr. Raul Pinto
Director
Angolan Gebinete de Investimento Estrangeiro
Rua Cerqueira Lukoky, 25/9
P.O. Box 6862
Luanda
ANGOLA
Tel: (244 2) 39 26 20/39 27 42
Fax: (244 2) 39 33 81

Mr. Penjore
Chief, Research and Statistics Division
Royal Monetary Authority of Bhutan
Post Box No.154
Thimbu
BHUTAN
Tel: (975 2) 23 110
Fax: (975 2) 22 847

Mr. Ith Vichit
Secretary General
Cambodian Investment Board
CDC-Government Palace, Sisowath Quay,
Wat Phnom
Phnom Penh
CAMBODIA
Tel: (855 23) 50 428/26 909
Fax: (855 23) 61 616

Mr. Joao Santos
Investment Director
PROMEX
P.O. Box 89, Avenida Qua
Praia
CAPE VERDE
Tel: (238) 61 57 52
Fax: (238) 61 14 42

Mr. Zahid Hossain
Member
Board of Investment
Shilpa Bhaban, 91
Motijheel C/A
Dhaka
BANGLADESH
Tel: (880 2) 956 1430/1431/7541
Fax: (880 2) 956 2312

Ms. Marie Blanche Bado
Responsable
Direction Générale du Développement
    Industriel
01 B.P. 258
Ouagadougou 01
BURKINA FASO
Tel: (226) 30 73 05/30 73 42
Fax: (226) 30 73 05

Mr. José Luis Sà Nogueira
Director
PROMEX
P.O. Box 89, Avenida Qua
Praia
CAPE VERDE
Tel: (238) 61 57 52
Fax: (238) 61 14 42

Mr. Henri Claude Jueremba
Président
Chambre de Commerce, de l'Industrie,
    des Mines et de l'Artisanat
B.P. 252
Bangui
CENTRAL AFRICAN REPUBLIC
Tel: (236) 61 16 68
Fax: (236) 61 38 37/61 54 05

Mr. Abakar Alhadj Ousmane
Responsable
Chambre Consulaire du Tchad, Division no.III
Promotion Industrielle, Commerciale,
   Agricole, Artisanale et des Services
B.P. 458
N'djamena
CHAD
Tel: (235) 51 52 64
Fax: (235) 525 884

Mr. Abdoulkader Doualeh Wais
Secrétaire Général
Cellule Secteur Privé
Ministère de l'Economie et du Commerce
B.P. 121
DJIBOUTI
Tel: (253) 35 25 40
Fax: (253) 35 4376

Mr. Guillermo Nguema Ela
Secretary General
Ministry of Economy and Finance
Malabo
EQUATORIAL GUINEA
Tel: (240 9) 21 51/ 31 05
Fax: (240 9) 32 05

Mr. Abdi Hussein
Ethiopian Investment Authority
51 30 00 Addis Ababa
ETHIOPIA
Tel: (251 1) 15 04 43
Fax: (251 1) 51 43 96

Mr. Said Youssouf Mondoha
Secrétaire Général
Ministère des Finances et du Budget
B.P. 324
Moroni
COMOROS
Tel: (269) 73 26 76/73 19 83
Fax: (269) 73 11 59

Ms. Odette Gema Diloya
Président-Délégué Général
Fonds de Promotion de l'Industrie
Place du 27 Octobre
Nouvelles Galeries Présidentielles
B.P. 11696 Kin 1
Kinshasa
DEMOCRATIC REPUBLIC OF CONGO
Tel: (243 12) 21 489/26 190
Fax: (243 12) 87 1874

Mr. Tekie Beyene
Managing Director
Eritrea Investment Center
P.O. Box 921
Asmara
ERITREA
Tel: (291 1) 12 42 93
Fax: (291 1) 11 88 22

Mr. Kebba Njie
Executive Secretary
The Gambia Chamber of Commerce &
   Industry
Banjul
GAMBIA
Tel: (220) 22 96 71
Fax: (220) 22 70 42

Mr. Fofana Ibrahima Kassory
Administrateur des Grands Projets
Présidence de la République de Guinée
Conakry
GUINEA
Tel: (224) 41 22 39
Fax: (224) 41 11 19

Mr. Bureti Williams
Chairman
Foreign Investment Commission
Ministry of Commerce, Industry & Tourism
P.O. Box 510, Betio
Tarawa
KIRIBATI
Tel: (686) 26 157/8
Fax: (686) 26 233

Mr. S. Rapapa
Lesotho National Development Corporation
Private Mail Bag A96
Maseru 100
LESOTHO
Tel: (266) 31 20 12
Fax: (266) 31 00 38

Mr. Tovonanahary Rabetsitonta
Minstre
Ministère de l'Economie et de la Promotion
 des Investissements
P.O. Box 674
Anosy, Antananarivo 101
MADAGASCAR
Tel: (261 2) 20 647
Fax: (261 2) 28 508

Mr. Henry Robert Sévère
Responsable de la Direction de
l'Entrepreneur
 et du Developpement Industriel
26, rue de Légitime, Champs de Mars
Port au Prince
HAITI
Tel: (509) 23 40 30/22 33 46
Fax: (509) 23 84 02

Mr. Bounomme Southichak
Director
Foreign Investment Management
 Committee (FIMC)
Luangprabang Road
Vientiane
LAO PEOPLE'S DEM. REPUBLIC
Tel: (856 21) 21 66 62/4
Fax: (856 21) 21 54 91

Mr. Lusinee Kamara
Minister
Ministry of Commerce and Industry
P.O. Box 10-9041
1000 Monrovia 10
LIBERIA
Tel: (231) 22 14 37/22 21 17
Fax: (231) 22 62 83

Mr. James Pnin
CEO
Malawi Investment Promotion Agency
Aquarius House
Private Bag 302
Lilongwe 3
MALAWI
Tel: (265) 78 17 16
Fax: (265) 63 54 29/78 17 81

Mr. Ahmed Naseem
Director
Foreign Investment Services Bureau
Ministry of Trade and Industries
Ghazee Building
Male
MALDIVES
Tel: (960) 32 38 90
Fax: (960) 32 37 56

Mr. Kelly Oumar Sada
Chef
Le Services du Secrétariat de la Commission
    Nationale des Investissements
Ministère du Plan - Direction de la
Planification, B.P. 230
Nouakchott
MAURITANIA
Tel: (222 2) 51 913/50 349
Fax: (222 2) 54 617

Mr. Binod Prasad Acharya
Section Officer
Ministry of Industry
Singhe Durbar
Kathmandu
NEPAL
Tel: (977 1) 21 66 92/21 28 65
Fax: (977 1) 22 03 19

Mr. Afonso da Graça Valera da Silva
Secrétaire Général
Ministère des Affaires Economiques et
    Financieres
B.P. 591
SAO TOME AND PRINCIPE
Tel: (239 12) 22 182
Fax: (239 12) 22 945

Mr. Alhassane Ag Hamed Moussa
Directeur
Direction Nationale des Affaires
Economiques
Ministère des Finances et du Commerce
B.P. 201, Quinzambougou
Bamako
MALI
Tel: (223) 22 23 14
Fax: (223) 22 01 29/22 35 77

Mr. U. Maung Maung Yi
Director-General
Directorate of Investment and Company
    Administration
651/691 Merchant Street
Pabedan, Yangon
MYANMAR
Tel: (951) 272 052/009/855
Fax: (951) 282 101

Mr. Jerome Trapsida
Directeur du Développement Industriel
Ministère des Mines, de l'Industrie et de la
    Technologie
P.O. Box 11700
Niamey
NIGER
Tel: (227) 72 38 51
Fax: (227) 73 27 59

Mr. Alfred II Demby
Director of Investment and Small/Medium
    Scale Enterprises
Sierra Leone Export Development and
    Investment Corp. (SLEDIC)
18/20 Walpole Street
Freetown
SIERRA LEONE
Tel: (232 22) 229 760/227 604
Fax: (232 22) 229 760/227 604

Mr. Joseph W.A. Jackson
Acting Director of Industries MTISE
Ministry of Trade, Industry and State
    Enterprises (MTISE)
Ministerial Building
George Street
Freetown
SIERRA LEONE
Tel: (232 22) 224 747/226 045
Fax: (232 22) 228 373

Mr. Mohamed Ahmed Osman
Head
Investment Promotion Centre (IPC)
P.O. Box 6286
Khartoum
SUDAN
Tel: (249 11) 77 01 56/77 04 54
Fax: (249 11) 77 07 30

The Director
Ministry of Finance, Economic, Planning,
Commerce and Industries
Private Mail Bag
Vaiaku
TUVALU
Tel: (688) 20 207
Fax: (688) 20 210

Mr. Japin C. Tari
Director
Department of Industry, Trade & Commerce
Port Vila
P.M.B. 030
VANUATU
Tel: (678) 22 770
Fax: (678) 25 640

Mr. Allan Billy Arafoa
Permanent Secretary
Ministry of Commerce, Industries and
    Employment
P.O. Box G26
Honiara
SOLOMON ISLANDS
Tel: (677) 21 849/21 850
Fax: (677) 25 084/21 651

Mr. Egbarè Yazas Tchohou
Directeur Général
Société d'Administration des Zones
    Franches
Bvd. Eyadema - Tokoin Forever, B.P. 3250
Lomé
TOGO
Tel: (228) 26 13 74
Fax: (228) 26 52 31

Mr. Issa Mukasa
Manager
Uganda Investment Authority
P.O. Box 7418
Kampala
UGANDA
Tel: (256 41) 23 41 05/9
Fax: (256 41) 242 903

Mr. Tunaimatia Falani Chan Tung
Secretary
Department of Trade, Commerce and
    Industry
P.O. Box 862
Apia
WESTERN SAMOA
Tel: (685) 20 471
Fax: (685) 21 646

Mr. C.G. Kahama
Director General
Investment Promotion Centre
P.O. Box 938
Dar-Es-Salaam
UNITED REPUBLIC OF TANZANIA
Tel: (255 51) 46 848/850
 Fax: (255 51) 46 851

Mr. Abdulkareem Mutair
General Manager
General Investment Authority
26 Al-Kods St. Southern Al-Safia
P.O. Box 19022
Sana'a
YEMEN
Tel: (967 1) 262 962/963
Fax: (967 1) 262 964

Mr. L.S. Chanda
Zambia Investment Centre
P.O. Box 34580
Lusaka
ZAMBIA
Tel: (260 1) 25 23 30/33/52
Fax: (260 1) 25 21 50

APPENDIX III

**Foreign exchange
regulations in LDCs**

Appendix III

Foreign Exchange Regulations, 1996

Country	National currency	Exchange rate arrangement	Payments restrictions — for current transactions	Payments restrictions — for capital transactions	Special controls applied on: Other capital movements	Special controls applied on: Foreign Direct Investment(FDI)	Special controls applied on: Foreign investments in some sectors	Restrictions on repatriation of capital and profits	Preferential status/incentives to foreign investments	Forex bureaus	Surrender and repatriation requirement for export proceeds	Access to local finance (local banking system)
Afghanistan	n.a.	n.a.	n.a.	n.a.	n.a.	n.a.	n.a.	n.a.	n.a.	n.a.	n.a.	n.a.
Angola	Adjusted Kwanza	Flexible arrangement : managed floating. No taxes or subsidies on purchases or sales of foreign exchange. No arrangements for forward cover against exchange rate risk.	Yes	Yes	Over borrowing abroad		Defense, law and order, education, health, utilities, communications and transportation infrastructure	Dividends and Capital may be repatriated upon liquidation with the prior approval of the Ministry of Finance.	In the oil sector		Repatriation and surrender requirement of foreign exchange with the exception of the foreign oil companies.	
Bangladesh	Bangladesh Taka	Pegged to a basket of currencies. Forwards contracts available.	No	Yes. Approval required on inward capital transfers other than foreign investments (FI) in the industrial sector	The issuing and transfer of shares and securities in favor of nonresidents against FI or the transfer from one nonresident holder to another are allowed without prior approval.	FDI other than in industrial sector require approval	With the exception of a few reserved sectors, private foreign investment are freely allowed	Proceeds from sales including capital gains and dividends earned on the shares or securities may be remitted abroad in freely convertible currency. Repatriation of investment is guaranteed	Foreign Private Investment Act provides protection and equitable treatment of foreign private investment, indemnification, protection against expropriation and nationalization.		Repatriation and surrender requirement. Proceeds from exports must be received within four months of shipment unless otherwise allowed by Bangladesh Bank.	Nonresident persons and institutions may buy Bangladesh shares and securities through the stock exchange against freely convertible foreign currency remitted from abroad through banking channels. No restriction on the import of securities
Benin	CFA Franc*	Pegged to the French franc. No taxes or subsidies on purchases or sales of foreign exchange. Forward exchange contracts may be arranged with the prior authorization of the Minister of Finance.	No	Yes. Limited exchange control measures	Over borrowing abroad. Prior approval required in some cases. See note a/	On inward FDI (that must be declared) and all outward investments in foreign countries.			In industry, mining, fisheries, agriculture and tourism. The preferential regime consists of 3 categories depending of the enterprise's size		Repatriation and surrender requirement.	
Bhutan	Ngultrum	Pegged to the Indian rupee. No subsidies or taxes on exchange transactions. No arrangements for forward cover against exchange rate risk.	Yes	Yes					Working towards introducing Foreign Investment Policy and Regulations		Repatriation and surrender requirement. Proceeds of exports in currencies other than the Indian rupee must be surrendered to the Royal Monetary Authority	No direct participation by foreign investors in the stock market.
Burkina Faso	CFA Franc*	Pegged to the French franc. No taxes or subsidies on purchases or sales of foreign exchange. Forward exchange contracts may be arranged with the prior authorization of the Ministry of Finance.	No	Yes. Limited exchange control measures	Over borrowing abroad. Prior approval required in some cases. See note a/	On inward FDI (that must be declared) and all outward investments in foreign countries.	Foreign firms are required to have national participation in their capital of at least 51% in vital or priority sectors and of at least 35% in all other sectors	Full or partial liquidation of either type of investment requires prior declaration.	Preferential treatment for foreign investments except for enterprises whose capital stock belongs entirely to foreigners		Yes, surrender requirements for export proceeds.	

Country	National currency	Exchange rate arrangement	Payments restrictions: for current transactions	Payments restrictions: for capital transactions	Special controls applied on: Other capital movements	Special controls applied on: Foreign Direct Investment(FDI)	Special controls applied on: Foreign investments in some sectors	Restrictions on repatriation of capital and profits	Preferential status/incentives to foreign investments	Forex bureaus	Surrender and repatriation requirement for export proceeds	Access to local finance (local banking system)
Burundi	Burundi Franc	Pegged to a basket of currencies reflecting the pattern of Burundi's international trade.	Yes	Yes. Exporters of coffee and commercial banks are allowed to borrow foreign exchange to hedge against exchange rate risks.				The repatriation of invested capital in the event of sale or shutdown is guaranteed.	Under the Investment Code, new investments that fulfill specified conditions as to amount and economic importance may be granted priority status to which specified privileges are attached (e.g. exemptions from import duties and taxes)		Repatriation and surrender requirement.	Burundi guarantees each foreign investors the right to move into the country. They are assured an allocation of foreign exchange for the purchase of raw materials abroad as well for the repayment of loans.
Cambodia	Cambodian Riel	Flexible arrangement: managed floating. No taxes or subsidies on purchases or sales of foreign exchange. No arrangements for forward cover against exchange rate risk.	No	Yes	Special control on State-owned enterprises engaging in export/import : on borrowing abroad by public sector	Foreign investors are required to submit investment applications to the Cambodian Investment Board for review and approval under the Investment Law.					Repatriation and surrender requirement.	
Cape Verde	Cape Verde Escudo	Exchange rate determined on the basis of a weighted basket of currencies. No taxes or subsidies on purchases or sales of foreign exchange. No arrangements for forward cover against exchange rate risk.	Yes	Yes	Any private capital transaction must be approved in advance. The exportation of resident-owned capital is not normally permitted			Legally imported capital, including FDI, may be re-exported without limitation.			Export proceeds must be repatriated within three months.	
Central African Republic	CFA Franc***	Pegged to the French franc. No taxes or subsidies on purchases or sales of foreign exchange.	No	Yes Limited exchange control measures	Over borrowing abroad, Prior approval required in some cases, see note a/				Industrial, tourist, agricultural, and mining enterprises are granted, under certain conditions, a reduction/exemption in duties and taxes. 3 categories of preferential treatment (requests for approval must be submitted to the Minister of Industry) .		Yes repatriation and surrender requirement for export proceeds	
Chad	CFA Franc***	Pegged to the French franc. No taxes or subsidies on purchases or sales of foreign exchange. Forward cover for imports is permitted only for specified commodities; requires authorization.	No	Yes Limited exchange control measures	Over borrowing abroad, Prior approval required in some cases, see note a/.	FDI must be declared. Inward FDI and all outward investments in foreign countries.		Full or partial liquidation of FDI must be declared to the Minister of Finance.	Under the Investment Code any foreign enterprises is granted, under certain conditions, reduced duties and taxes on specified imports and exemption from direct taxes on specified income.		Yes surrender requirement.	

Country	National currency	Exchange rate arrangement	Payments restrictions		Special controls applied on:			Restrictions on repatriation of capital and profits	Preferential status/incentives to foreign investments	Forex bureaus	Surrender and repatriation requirement for export proceeds	Access to local finance (local banking system)
			for current transactions	for capital transactions	Other capital movement	Foreign Direct Investments(FDI)	Foreign investments in some sectors					
Comoros	Comorian Franc	Pegged to the French franc. No taxes or subsidies on purchases or sales of foreign exchange. Forward cover against exchange rate risk is authorized by the Central Bank and provided by the commercial banks	Yes	Yes Limited exchange control measures	Over borrowing abroad, Prior approval required in some cases, see note a/	On inward FDI (that must be declared) and all outward investments in foreign countries.		Repatriation of dividends and other earnings from FDI is authorized and guaranteed under the Investment Code.			Repatriation and surrender requirement.	
Djibouti	Djibouti Franc	Pegged to the U.S. dollar. No taxes or subsidies on purchases or sales of foreign exchange. No arrangements for forward cover against exchange risk. Enterprises are free to negotiate forward exchange contracts through local banks or banks abroad.	No	No				No restrictions	Under the Investment Code, enterprises established or expanded to undertake specific economic activities are eligible for various tax exemptions. Export-oriented manufacturing and services are exempt from the profit tax during first 10 years.		Export proceeds may be retained.	
Equatorial Guinea	CFA Franc***	Pegged to the French franc. No taxes or subsidies on purchases or sales of foreign exchange. No arrangements for forward cover against exchange rate risk.	No	Yes Limited exchange control measures	Prior approval required in some cases. See note a/.			Free transfer abroad of debt payments and net profits.	A number of privileges may be granted to authorised foreign (Investment Code 1982). Current legislation aimed at stimulating foreign investment in the agricultural, forestry, construction, public works, mining, and industrial equipment soutenance sectors.		Repatriation and surrender requirement.	
Eritrea	The provisional legal tender is the Ethiopian Birr	Flexible arrangement: managed floating. No taxes or subsidies on purchases or sales of foreign exchange. No forward cover provided in foreign exchange.	Yes	Yes	Foreign exchange proceeds representing capital inflows must be registered at the National Bank to ensure the smooth transfer of dividends and interest, amortization of principal, and proceeds of the sale of shares or from the liquidation.	The Ministry of Trade and Industry has the authority to regulate foreign investments (Investment Proclamation); it vets and licenses investment projects (including joint ventures) that are eligible to take advantage of tax and foreign exchange facilities.	FDI is permitted in all sectors. Domestic retail and wholesale trade, and import and commission agencies are open to foreign investors only if Eritrea has signed a bilateral agreement of reciprocity with the country of the investor.		Approved investments and their subsequent expansion enjoy exemption from customs duties and sales tax for capital goods and spare parts associated with the investment		Repatriation requirement only.	

Country	National currency	Exchange rate arrangement	Payments restrictions — for current transactions	Payments restrictions — for capital transactions	Special controls applied on: Other capital movements	Special controls applied on: Foreign Direct Investment(FDI)	Special controls applied on: Foreign investments in some sectors	Restrictions on repatriation of capital and profits	Preferential status/incentives to foreign investments	Forex bureaus	Surrender and repatriation requirement for export proceeds	Access to local finance (local banking system)
Ethiopia	Ethiopian Birr	Flexible arrangement: independently floating. No taxes or subsidies on purchases or sales of foreign exchange. No arrangements for forward cover against exchange rate risk.	Yes	Yes	Borrowing abroad require approval from the Exchange Control Department and is restricted.		Foreign investors are permitted to hold a majority share through a joint venture, except in the following sectors: Precious metals, telecommunication, banking and insurance, transport, and trade in products deemed essential to the economy.	All recognized/registered FI may be terminated on presentation of documents (liquidation and payment of all taxes/liabilities). Proceeds from the liquidation of a joint venture (as dividends) may be remitted abroad without restrictions	Exemptions from income taxes are granted for up to 5 years for new projects and for up to 3 years for major extensions to existing projects. Exporters are allowed to retain 10% of their earnings in foreign currency accounts.	Yes. Foreign currency for business travel, tourism, education and medical is available at forex offices.	Exporters are required to surrender foreign exchange earnings. All receipts of capital in the form of foreign exchange must be surrendered.	All established businesses have access to local finance.. To encourage borrowing from banks, the cost of loanable funds (lending interest rates) is adjusted from time to time. Discriminatory lending interest rates policy have been abolished.
Gambia	Gambian Dalasi	Flexible arrangement : independently floating. No taxes or subsidies on purchases or sales of foreign exchange. No arrangements for forward cover against exchange rate risk.	No	No	Inward transfers for purposes of direct equity investment are not restricted but must be reported to the Central Bank for statistical purposes.			There are no restrictions on the transfer of capital and dividends abroad from The Gambia abroad. Non-resident investors registered in The Gambia can remit profits and dividends abroad at prevailing exchange rates without any control.	Projects in priority sectors are awarded incentives in the form of duty waiver on capital equipment, spareparts materials, and raw and/or semi finished material inputs. Other incentives for projects in the export sector.	Yes. Central Bank continues to set limits on foreign exchange working balances held by exchange bureaus.	No repatriation or surrender requirement.	Access to local finance for long-term projects has been controlled.Commercial banks in the Gambian banking systems used to favour borrowers in the shorter end of the market, especially for trade-related facilities, e.g. L/C
Guinea	Guinean Franc	Flexible arrangement: independently floating. No arrangements for forward cover against exchange rate risk. Payments and transfers fully liberalized since July 1994.	Yes	Yes	All capital transfers through the official exchange market require authorization from the Central Bank			The Investment Law provides preferential tax and custom treatment for the transfer of profits, interest, amortization, and liquidation proceeds	The Investment Law provides guarantees against the nationalization of FI in the industrial and mining sectors.	Yes. Exchange rates in the market determined by supply and demand conditions	Repatriation and surrender requirement.	
Guinea-Bissau	Guinea-Bissau Peso	Flexible arrangement: managed floating. No taxes or subsidies on purchases or sales of foreign exchange. No arrangements for forward cover against exchange rate risk.	Yes	Yes				The Investment Code recognizes the right of foreign investors to transfer foreign currency abroad in respect of profits (net of taxes), to sell or liquidate investments.	The Investment Code provides incentives to FDI, protection against nationalization/ expropriation, recognizes the right of foreign investors to service loans obtained to project financing and to make payments for imported supplies and technical assistance.	Exchange bureaus are in place	Surrender requirement on export proceeds. In July 1995 the portion of export proceeds that must be surrendered at the official exchange rate was reduced from 40% to 30 %. (There is no surrender requirement on proceeds from services received from abroad)	Foreign and domestic investments are subject to the same terms with respect to access to domestic credit.

Country	National currency	Exchange rate arrangement	Payments restrictions — for current transactions	Payments restrictions — for capital transactions	Special controls applied on: Other capital movements	Special controls applied on: Foreign Direct Investments (FDI)	Special controls applied on: Foreign investments in some sectors	Restrictions on repatriation of capital and profits	Preferential status/incentives to foreign investments	Forex bureaus	Surrender and repatriation requirement for export proceeds	Access to local finance (local banking system)
Haiti	Haitian Gourde	Flexible arrangement: independently floating. No arrangement for forward cover against exchange rate risk operating in the official or the commercial banking sector.	No. Penalty, equal to 20% on any commercial foreign exchange transaction not conducted through a bank established in Haiti.	Yes		FDI requires prior government approval.	Permission is normally not granted for non-residents to invest in Handicraft industries				Repatriation requirement. In March 1995, surrender requirement was eliminated	
Kiribati	Australian Dollar	Pegged to 15 currencies. No central monetary institution. No taxes or subsidies on purchases or sales of foreign exchange. No arrangements for cover against exchange risk	No. Purchases and sales of foreign currencies in exchange for Australian dollars must be undertaken with the Bank of Kiribati, the only authorized foreign exchange dealer.	No		Applications for FI must be made to the Foreign Investment Commission.		Repatriation of profits and capital is normally unrestricted.	Under the Foreign Investment Promotion Act, investors may be granted duty-free imports of capital goods and raw materials. Investments in pioneer industries are eligible for a tax holidays of up to 6 years.		No surrender or repatriation requirement	
Lao P.D.R.	Kip	Flexible arrangement: independently floating. No taxes or subsidies on purchases of foreign exchange. No arrangements for forward cover against exchange rate risk.	Yes	Yes				Under the Foreign Investment Law, profit remittances and the repatriation of foreign investment capital are not restricted.		Forex Bureaus are permitted to buy and sell foreign exchange rate at freely determined rates.	Repatriation requirement. Export earnings are subject to the surrender requirement, and they may be kept in foreign exchange deposits.	
Lesotho	Loti (plural Maloti)	Pegged to the South African Rand. No taxes or subsidies on purchases or sales of foreign exchange. Forward exchange cover is not common.	No	Yes	No person may borrow foreign currency, register shares in the name of a nonresident, or act as a nominee for a nonresident without prior approval.			Repatriation of interest, dividends, profits and other income facilitated. The transfer by nonresidents of dividends and profits is not restricted, provided these funds were not obtained through excessive use of local borrowing facilities.	Certain tax incentives are provided to manufacturers.		Repatriation and surrender requirement.	Local borrowing facilities.

239

Country	National currency	Exchange rate arrangement	Payments restrictions for current transactions	Payments restrictions for capital transactions	Special controls applied on: Other capital movements	Special controls applied on: Foreign Direct Investment(FDI)	Special controls applied on: Foreign investments in some sectors	Restrictions on repatriation of capital and profits	Preferential status/incentives to foreign investments	Forex bureaus	Surrender and repatriation requirement for export proceeds	Access to local finance (local banking system)
Liberia	Liberian Dollar	Pegged to the U.S. dollar. No taxes or subsidies on purchases or sales of foreign exchange. No arrangements for forward cover against exchange rate risk.	No	Yes					Under the Investment Incentive Code, enterprises undertaking new investment projects may be granted: a 5 year 90% duty exemption on imports of raw materials and machinery; total tax exemption on reinvested profits, a 50% exemption on distributable profits.		Repatriation and surrender requirement.	
Madagascar	Malagasy Franc	Flexible arrangement: independently floating. Limited arrangements for forward cover against exchange rate risk	Yes	Yes	On borrowing and lending abroad by residents, on all inward and outward investment.	FDI are subject to prior authorization from the Ministry of Finance.		Proceeds from the liquidation of foreign investment may be repatriated with the prior authorization of the Ministry of Finance.	Enterprises benefiting from preferential treatment under the Investment Code (1989) are exempted from import taxes exceeding 10% on materials used in the production process.		Repatriation and surrender requirement.	
Malawi	Malawi Kwacha	Flexible arrangement: independently floating. No taxes or subsidies on purchases or sales of foreign exchange. Authorized Dealer Banks (ADB) are free to make arrangements for forward cover against exchange risk.	No	Yes	Inward transfer of nondebt-creating capital are not restricted.			Free repatriation. Apart from the need to obtain the ADBs' approval, there are no restrictions on the transfer abroad of dividends and profits, provided that no recourse is being made to local borrowing to finance the transfer.		Authorized to conduct spot transactions with general public on the basis of exchange rates negotiated with their clients.	Repatriation and surrender requirement.	
Maldives	Maldivian Rufiyaa	Flexible arrangement: managed floating. Limits access to foreign exchange through the Government Exchange Counter. No arrangements for forward cover against exchange rate risk.	No	No		Inward direct investment requires prior approval. Foreign investors are required to provide at least 75% of their capital investment in the form of either cash or capital goods financed from outside Maldives.		Transfer of profits are permitted freely	Exemption from duties and taxes may be granted for a period as specified by the government.		Repatriation and surrender requirement.	
Mali	CFA Franc*	Pegged to the French franc. No taxes or subsidies on purchases or sales of foreign exchange. Foreign exchange transfers subject to a stamp tax.	No	Yes. Limited exchange control measures	Over borrowing abroad, Prior approval required in some cases. See note a/	On inward FDI (that must be declared) and all outward investmens in foreign countries.			Investment Code (1991) simplified procedures to obtain preferential treatment with respect to domestic taxes for investment that meet specific criteria on employment creation, domestic content of production, and value of investment.		Repatriation and surrender requirement.	

Country	National currency	Exchange rate arrangement	Payments restrictions for current transactions	Payments restrictions for capital transactions	Special controls applied on: Other capital movements	Special controls applied on: Foreign Direct Investment(FDI)	Special controls applied on: Foreign investments in some sectors	Restrictions on repatriation of capital and profits	Preferential status/incentives to foreign investments	Forex bureaus	Surrender and repatriation requirement for export proceeds	Access to local finance (local banking system)
Mauritania	Mauritanian Ougulya	Flexible arrangement: independently floating. No taxes or subsidies on purchases or sales of foreign exchange. No arrangements for forward cover against exchange rate risk.	Yes	Yes. Capital transfers to all countries require Central Bank approval and are restricted, but capital receipts are normally permitted freely.	Residents must have prior authorization from the Central Bank to invest abroad.	FDI must be declared to the Central bank before they are made.		The Investment Code stipulates that profits and dividends can be transferred freely.	The Investment Code provides for various benefits for private investments.	Free to set their commissions for foreign currency transactions.	Repatriation and surrender requirement. The rate of export proceeds required to be surrendered to the Central Bank was reduced from 40% to 30 %.	
Mozambique	Metical	Flexible arrangement: independently floating. No taxes or subsidies on purchases or sales of foreign exchange. No arrangements for forward cover against exchange rate risk.	Yes	Yes Foreign Exchange accounts may be open in all commercial banks in the country.	On public and private enterprise for borrowing abroad.Government and the Bank of Mozambique are allowed to borrow abroad.	Foreign investment proposals are processed by the Foreign Investment Promotion Office.		The FDI law (1994) guarantees investors the right to repatriate capital and transfer abroad a portion of profits.	The incentives for foreign investments include tax and customs exemptions for specified periods and for access to domestic credit.		Repatriation and surrender requirement. The surrender requirement was reduced to 35 % of the proceeds.	Incentives for access to domestic credit. All companies formed and registered with the participation of FDI are entitled to access to domestic credit borrowing on the same terms and conditions applicable to Mozambican companies.
Myanmar	Myanmar Kyat	Pegged to a basket of currencies. Foreign Exchanges Certificates -FECs (see note b/) issued by the Central Bank. No taxes or subsidies on purchases or sales of foreign exchange. No arrangements for forward cover against exchange risk.	Yes	Yes		Under the Union of Myanmar FI Law of 1988, the Investment Commission accept proposals for FI for full ownership and under joint venture, with the share of foreign capital representing at least 35%.	Types of economic activity and the sectors open to FI are specified in a detailed positive list.	Repatriation of profits is allowed trough banks after payment of taxes and prescribed funds. The Law also guarantees the repatriation in foreign currency after the termination of the business.	Exemption from customs duties and other internal taxes, exemptions from the income tax. Accelerated depreciation allowances may be granted. Guarantees to cover investors against nationalization.	10 agencies were authorized to trade FECs in exchange for local currency at a new exchange center and at a market-determined rate	Repatriation and surrender requirement. Export proceeds must be obtained in accordance with existing foreign exchange management regulations.	
Nepal	Nepalese Rupee	Pegged to a basket of currencies. Possibility to obtain forward exchange cover for trade transactions.	No	Yes	Nepalese citizens are prohibited from making any type of investment in foreign countries.	All FDI require prior approval in the form of a guarantee from the Industrial Promotion Board or the Department of Industry. Foreign investors can hold 100% equity in large- and medium-scale enterprises.	In cottage, small-scale, basic areas like poultry, tertiary industries including travel and trekking services or defense-related industries unless substantial transfers of technology are involved.	Foreign investors with an investment guarantee may make remittances abroad for all or part of the sales proceeds of investments, equity, dividends, interest, or principal repayment.	Generous and attractive income tax allowances with a minimum five year tax holiday for most of the industries. - No tax on dividends and exports		Proceeds from exports must be repatriated, but are not required to be surrendered	Local and foreign collaborations projects, have equal access to the financial institutions regarding the project financing.
Niger	CFA Franc*	Pegged to the French franc. No taxes or subsidies on purchases or sales of foreign exchange.	No	No	Over borrowing abroad. On inward and outward investments	FDI must be declared.		The full or partial liquidation requires prior declaration to the Minister.	Privileged treatment is reserved for enterprises deemed to be of special importance to national economic development. Indemnities in the event of expropriation. Nondiscrimination. Tax exemptions.		Proceeds from exports must be repatriated and surrendered within 15 days of the date of receipt.	

Country	National currency	Exchange rate arrangement	Payments restrictions — for current transactions	Payments restrictions — for capital transactions	Special controls applied on: Other capital movements	Special controls applied on: Foreign Direct Investment(FDI)	Special controls applied on: Foreign investments in some sectors	Restrictions on repatriation of capital and profits	Preferential status/incentives to foreign investments	Forex bureaus	Surrender and repatriation requirement for export proceeds	Access to local finance (local banking system)
Rwanda	Rwanda Franc	Flexible arrangement: independently floating. No taxes or subsidies on purchases or sales of foreign exchange. No arrangements for forward cover against exchange rate risk.	No	Yes	All outward transfers of capital require the prior approval of the National Bank. Portfolio investments by residents abroad require prior approval from the National Bank	Direct investments are allowed after approval from the National Bank.		Repatriation are pursuant to the investment code and must be registered by authorized banks.		Operate in the exchange market.	Repatriation and surrender requirement.	Local and foreign investors have equal access to financial institutions.
Samoa	Western Samoa Tala	Pegged to a composite of currencies. No arrangements for forward cover against exchange rate risk.	No	Yes	Inward capital does not normally require approval.			Both the repatriation of capital and profit remittances on foreign capital must be approved by the Central Bank; such approval is granted when the appropriate documentation is supplied.	In specified activities. Under the Enterprises Incentive Act, persons engaged in approved enterprises are granted some relief from income tax and business license fees.			
Sao Tome and Principe	Sao Tome and Principe Dobra	Flexible arrangement: independently floating. No arrangements for forward cover against exchange rate risk.	Yes	Yes		Inward foreign investments governed by the Investment Code (1992).	The extraction of hydrocarbons and other mining industries	Repatriation of profits is permitted up to 15% a year of the value of the investment. Transfers are permitted for repayment of financing under agreements with the government and for the amortization of private sector investments.	Foreign capital investments are permitted on the same basis as domestic investment.		Repatriation and surrender requirement.	
Sierra Leone	Sierra Leonean Leone	Flexible arrangement: independently floating. No taxes or subsidies on purchases or sales of foreign exchange. No arrangements for forward cover against exchange rate risk.	No	Yes	Capital payments to nonresidents are subject to exchange control. Issuance and transfers of securities are subject to exchange control.	To be eligible for FI Protection Act guarantee, a certificate of approval from the Ministry of Finance is required	Noncitizens are prohibited from owning or controlling certain types of business.	Investments, including profits, may be repatriated at any time, provided that exchange control approval is obtained at the outset. The FI Protection Act guarantees capital repatriation and remittance of dividend and interest.	Income tax and customs duty concessions are granted to foreign companies undertaking industrial or agricultural activities that are needed for the development of the country.	Limited to spot transactions.	Repatriation and surrender requirement.	Registered Foreign Businesses are allowed to borrow funds from the local banking system subject to the existing rules.
Solomon Islands	Solomon Islands Dollar	Pegged to a composite of currencies. Forward cover facility was discontinued in 1995.	No	Yes. All outward transfers of capital require exchange control approval.	Control on new investment abroad and on portfolio investments by residents or companies operating in the Solomon Islands. Approval is difficult to obtain for the acquisition of overseas portfolio investments	Require approval from the Foreign Investment Board.					Repatriation and surrender requirement.	
Somalia	n.a.	n.a.	n.a.	n.a.	n.a.	n.a.	n.a.	n.a.	n.a.	n.a.	n.a.	n.a.

Country	National currency	Exchange rate arrangement	Payments restrictions — for current transactions	Payments restrictions — for capital transactions	Special controls applied on: Other capital movements	Special controls applied on: Foreign Direct Investments(FDI)	Special controls applied on: Foreign investments in some sectors	Restrictions on repatriation of capital and profits	Preferential status/incentives to foreign investments	Forex bureaus	Surrender and repatriation requirement for export proceeds	Access to local finance (local banking system)
Sudan	Sudanese Dinar	Flexible arrangement: independently floating. No arrangements for forward cover against exchange rate risk.	Yes	Yes		FDI are permitted in accordance with existing laws and regulations				Began to operate in September 1995.	Most export proceeds must be repatriated and sold to the domestic banking system within 45 days of the date of the bill of lading	
Togo	CFA Franc*	Pegged to the French franc. No taxes or subsidies on purchases or sales of foreign exchange.	Yes	Yes	Over borrowing abroad. On inward direct investment and all outward investment.	FDI in Togo must be reported to the Ministry of Economy and Finance before they are made.		The investment Code guarantees the right of free transfer abroad of capital invested in Togo and of all investment income therefrom			Repatriation and surrender requirement	
Tuvalu	n.a.	n.a.	n.a.	n.a.	n.a.	n.a.	n.a.	n.a.	n.a.	n.a.	n.a.	n.a.
Uganda	Uganda Shilling	Flexible arrangement: independently floating. No taxes or subsidies on purchases or sales of foreign exchange. No arrangements for forward cover against exchange rate risk.	No	Yes	Capital transfers to all countries require individual exchange control approval	Foreign investment in Uganda is permitted wiht or without government participation		To secure a guarantee of repatriation, it is necessary to obtain "approved status" for the investment in line with the Investment Code of 1991.		yes	Repatriation requirement. Exporters may retain proceeds from exports and sell them in the interbank foreign exchange market	It is possible for foreign investors to secure local financing.
U. R. of Tanzania	Tanzanian Shilling	Flexible arrangement: independently floating. No taxes or subsidies on purchases or sales of foreign exchange. Authorized dealers may enter into forward contracts.	Yes	Yes	Capital transfers to all countries are subject to approval by the Bank of Tanzania. Investments of foreign funds are not restricted.		Yes. Some investment areas are reserved exclusively for Tanzanian citizens.	Repatriation may be authorized if investments are recognized by the Investment Promotion Center.		Yes	Yes, export proceeds subject to repatriation requirements	
Vanuatu	Vatu	Pegged to a composite of currencies. No taxes or subsidies on purchases or sales of foreign exchange. No arrangements for forward cover facilities operating in the official sector.	No	No							No surrender requirement for exports proceeds	No distinction is made between the accounts of residents and nonresidents. Debits and credits to all accounts may be made freely.
Yemen	Yemeni Rial	Pegged to the U.S. dollar. No arrangements for forward cover against exchange rate risk.	Yes	Yes		FDI is subject to the provisions of the Investment Law administered by the Public Investment Authority.	Foreign investments are authorized by the Public Investment Authority for projects deemed to be economically viable and socially acceptable.	The Investment Law guarantees the transfer abroad of net profits after taxes attributable to foreign capital, and the repatriation of registered capital on liquidation in the currency of investment	Certain tax and import duty exemptions and concessions are granted for five years to approved projects that meet specific economic criteria		No surrender or repatriation requirements for exports proceeds	Commercial banks are permitted to open freely transferable foreign-currency-denominated accounts for residents and nonresidents.

Country	National currency	Exchange rate arrangement	Payments restrictions		Special controls applied on:			Restrictions on repatriation of capital and profits	Preferential status/incentives to foreign investments	Forex bureaus	Surrender and repatriation requirement for export proceeds	Access to local finance (local banking system)
			for current transactions	for capital transactions	Other capital movements	Foreign Direct Investment(FDI)	Foreign investments in some sectors					
Zaire	New Zaire	Flexible arrangement: independently floating. Forward transactions may be conducted in the foreign exchange market	Yes	Yes				The repatriation of foreign capital brought in under the provisions of the investment code is permitted only at the time of liquidation, nationalization, or partial or total transfers of shares.			Surrender and repatriation requirement for export proceeds	
Zambia	Zambian Kwacha	Flexible arrangement: independently floating. No arrangements for forward cover against exchange rate risk.	Yes	Yes	All borrowing outside Zambia must be registered with the bank of Zambia. Outward transfers of capital are free of control					yes	Surrender and repatriation requirements. Zambia's Investment Act 1991 allows exporters to retain up to 70% of export earnings in the initial years of investment and 50% thereafter.	Nonresidents may participate in the treasury bill and government bond market without restrictions

Sources: Exchange Arrangements and Exchange Restrictions, 1996, IMF, responses to the questionnaires received from countries

* The CFA franc is issued by the Central Bank of West African States (BCEAO) and is the common currency in Benin, Burkina Faso, Côte d'Ivoire, Mali, Niger, Senegal and Togo

** The CFA franc circulating in these countries (Central African Republic, Chad, Equatorial Guinea) is issuing by the Bank of Central African States (BEAC) and is also legal tender in Cameroun, Congo and Gabon

a/ Capital movements to other countries than France (including overseas depart and territ), Monaco and countries linked to the French Treasury through an Operation Account require prior approval, but capital receipts from such countries are free permitted

b/ FECs are widely used and serve the needs of both visitors and investors in Myanmar. Holders of FECs may convert them into foreign exchange at a licensed foreign exchange bank.

FI: Foreign Investment

FPEI: Foreign Portfolio Equity Investment

FDI: Foreign Direct Investment

File: Progress.xlw.   16.06.97

كيفية الحصول على منشورات الامم المتحدة

يمكن الحصول على منشورات الامم المتحدة من المكتبات ودور التوزيع في جميع انحاء العالم · استعلم عنها من المكتبة التي تتعامل معها
أو اكتب الى : الامم المتحدة ،قسم البيع في نيويورك او في جنيف ·

如何购取联合国出版物

联合国出版物在全世界各地的书店和经售处均有发售。请向书店询问或写信到纽约或日内瓦的联合国销售组。

HOW TO OBTAIN UNITED NATIONS PUBLICATIONS

United Nations publications may be obtained from bookstores and distributors
throughout the world. Consult your bookstore or write to: United Nations, Sales
Section, New York or Geneva.

COMMENT SE PROCURER LES PUBLICATIONS DES NATIONS UNIES

Les publications des Nations Unies sont en vente dans les librairies et les agences
dépositaires du monde entier. Informez-vous auprès de votre libraire ou adressez-vous
à : Nations Unies, Section des ventes, New York ou Genève.

КАК ПОЛУЧИТЬ ИЗДАНИЯ ОРГАНИЗАЦИИ ОБЪЕДИНЕННЫХ НАЦИИ

Издания Организации Объединенных Наций можно купить в книжных мага-
зинах и агентствах во всех районах мира. Наводите справки об изданиях в
вашем книжном магазине или пишите по адресу: Организация Объединенных
Наций, Секция по продаже изданий, Нью-Йорк или Женева.

COMO CONSEGUIR PUBLICACIONES DE LAS NACIONES UNIDAS

Las publicaciones de las Naciones Unidas están en venta en librerías y casas distri-
buidoras en todas partes del mundo. Consulte a su librero o diríjase a: Naciones
Unidas, Sección de Ventas, Nueva York o Ginebra.

Printed at United Nations, Geneva
GE.98-50094–March 1998–3,580

UNCTAD/GDS/GFSB/3

United Nations publication
Sales No. E.98.II.D.2

ISBN 92-1-112423-9